China
and Her Shadow

China
and Her Shadow

TIBOR MENDE

COWARD-McCANN, INC.
NEW YORK

PUBLISHER'S NOTE

In an effort to maintain consistency in their editions of this volume, the British and American publishers have agreed to retain certain European usages, notably the following: milliard, *which for practical purposes is the same as the American* billion; *occasional references to wage scales in terms of pounds sterling; and the customarily English* hoardings *for the American* billboards.

CONTENTS

PART ONE

New China in the Making

THE RESTAURANT of the *Great Concentrated Morality* is one of the remaining shrines of Peking's art of gastronomy. Quite near the Imperial Palace, it is the famed specialist of the *Canard Lacqué*. Its otherwise inconspicuous entry is marked by the two freshly lacquered red columns and, above them, the establishment's poetic name, engraved in gilded characters. Once inside, one proceeds through ill-lit and cosily untidy corridors before being ushered into one of the special rooms where private parties are held. There, already enveloped in delicious vapours, a number of people were waiting.

It was the day after I had arrived from Hong Kong by train. The invitation was to one of those unforgettable dinners, which the hospitable Chinese extend even to visitors of such modest distinction as myself. Those present included representatives of cultural associations and of the official news agency, as well as an American-educated, charming woman from the Foreign Ministry. Ten in all, we were sitting around a circular table and once the toasts were over, the procession of the waiters began. All present spoke either English or French and very soon the atmosphere was set for a friendly and relaxed conversation.

Sheer hospitality and kindness apart, such dinners have a definite aim. They are intended to provide a frame to assess the visitor, to sound his views and, more precisely, to find out his purpose in coming to China. The continuous poking of chopsticks into the ever-changing mosaic of plates, rice-wine, however, and Chinese politeness, tended to postpone the major question. The well-mannered and indirect probing continued, as well as the inexorable march of new dishes. Then, the lacquered duck was shown to us in its exquisite entirety before it was rushed off to a side-table to be sliced into small mouthfuls. After that, with due ceremony, the pieces of duck were placed between thin pancakes; they were smeared with a sweet, hot condiment; and were folded into small packages ready to be popped into the mouth. Yet once that ritual and its accompanying jokes were over, obliterating the effect of food and rice-wine, suddenly, a matter of fact sobriety descended on all the participants. Casually, the official presiding over the gathering, posed the much-postponed question.

'Well, then, what would you like to see in China? what are your interests in our country?'

I realized that the moment had arrived. All those present were listening, probably thinking of the report they were to write to their organizations. If my answer was satisfactory, doors would open, interviews would be arranged and my time in China would be profitable. A slip, and all my preparations and all the time reserved for the trip would have been in vain. As a matter of fact, I had no very clear ideas about what I wanted to see. I did not want to ask for a string of institutions, for a crowded programme of factory inspections or for interviews where long lists of statistics would be recited. Confronted by nine pairs of scrutinizing eyes I was painfully aware that I did not really know what exactly to say. I was bound to disappoint my companions. They were used to precise demands. But I had to answer and, still under the impact of the lavish meal, my reply was both unmeditated and somewhat vague.

'There are really two things I would like to see during my stay', I said. 'First of all I would like to know whether your Government is more cruel than is necessary to achieve the aims which you have set yourself. Secondly, I would be interested to find out what proportion of the Chinese people does still offer its energy and exertions merely under the influence of persuasion?'

The people around me looked at each other. Quite clearly, there was a moment of consternation. Evidently, this was disturbingly different from what they expected. Then, for the first time, I had a sample of what conversation with educated officials was like in present-day China. In a disciplined fashion, each took it in turn to prove that my very attitude was mistaken. Official A's Marxist arguments were polite but self-confident. B resorted to even more refined shades of Marxian dialectics. C quoted from Mao Tse-tung. D, E and F gently continued the detailed, Marxist-Leninist-Maoist over-solicitation, each attempting to be still closer to the purest official line than the one who had spoken before him. But the patient monologues barely concealed unmistakable yet controlled irritation. More and more clearly it was implied that my basic assumptions were wrong, that cruelty did not exist in China, that even persuasion was unnecessary as all Chinese acted out of enthusiasm and that, in any case, Westerners seemed unable to comprehend the mood and the motives of the Chinese.

Then, to end the round of politely formal indignation, one of the officials remarked with barely concealed reprobation: 'Your questions are those of a typical Western intellectual.'

Being my second day in China, I listened with genuine curiosity even when I felt tempted to interrupt and to argue. What really irritated me was that my companions had evidently missed what I considered to be the basic goodwill in my questions. I decided to argue out my case. After listening for so long, I had the moral right to make a little speech.

I began by saying that I was not one of those for whom events in China appeared in black and white only. I did not expect to see in everything I would be shown mere milestones on the road to perfection. Nor did I believe, as some Westerners did, that whatever was happening in China was merely a frightening symptom of a wholly sinister process. I wanted to steer clear of these sterile extremes and to do so I had come with a certain number of premises in my luggage.

First of all, I accepted that a people numbering nearly 700 millions, occupying a huge and potentially rich area, and recognized by all impartial observers as being both intelligent and industrious, had the right to do all in their power to become as prosperous, as advanced, as powerful and, therefore, as respected as any of the other materially advanced nations. Secondly, my observations in quite a number of other, economically backward countries had convinced me that in order to realize these justified aspirations, a very poor and overpopulated country had no great choice of methods. To be effective, those methods must be harsh even if the country could count on massive foreign aid. And China, I added, had to rely mainly on her own efforts.

I knew from how low a rung of the ladder they had to start their climb. Moreover, China's population was expanding very fast. I went even further. I had accepted that after her experiences during the past hundred years China had every reason to believe that only the possession of heavy industries could put an end to her dependence and its resulting humiliation. Those industries were needed not merely to supply all the turbines, the machine-tools, the tractors and the locomotives or the modern weapons needed to ward off the danger of foreign aggression, but also to repair a proud nation's historically damaged self-respect.

Then, I continued, in the absence of very large scale foreign aid, someone has to foot the bill. Three-quarters of China's population being peasants, it was inevitable that they should carry the main burden. It was from their labour that most of the savings had to be extracted to pay for equipment and modernization.

I knew from what I have seen elsewhere that as soon as a poor country's investments in its productive equipment approaches a fifth of its national income, there appear symptoms comparable to the human body's reaction when its temperature mounts over 98°. Such an effort caused strains and tension was the inevitable result. And I knew that China's investments were already well over a quarter of her national income.

For all these reasons, I added, I accepted that to lift such a mass of largely illiterate, disease-ridden and superstitious people into the industrial age; to educate them and to shake them out of their inertia; or to transform them into the highly productive and skilled workers of a modern society, tremendous efforts and very harsh methods were needed. These inevitably implied techniques of mass-indoctrination, of subordination to a simple, central mystique, and they, in turn, rendered it difficult to resist the temptation to make use even of the age-old incentive of xenophobic nationalism. All this, I admitted, we have seen, in their corresponding phase of development, both in Japan and in the Soviet Union. Most of it we had to apply to ourselves even in the West, during our own period of industrialization, though we had so much more time to accomplish our aims.

All this, then, I accepted in advance. These were my premises. All this I more or less expected to see. What I wanted to know in addition was whether all this was being applied with only as much cruelty as was inevitable or with more? Whether the need to command did or did not breed the habit of ordering people around merely for the pleasure of exercising authority? Behind my questions, I readily admitted, there was the basic issue of speed. The process was admittedly severe. By accelerating it, it had to be made even more so. China's security, unlike that of the U.S.S.R.'s during its modernization, was guaranteed by a powerful ally. One may argue, then, about the speed with which resources were being diverted to the edification of heavy industries. But for a variety of reasons China wanted to go fast, even faster than the Soviet Union. So, with their enthusiasm and their efforts stretched to their utmost limit, what proportion of the Chinese people could still be induced by mere argument to follow the rhythm prescribed by their leaders?

This was what I meant by my premises, I said in conclusion.

They went quite a long way to meet Chinese reality. Still, they left open some questions.

My long monologue was listened to with the usual courtesy. The plates had gone and only the tea-pot and the stains on the table-cloth remained. My companions were sipping tea from tiny cups.

I could not expect my tiresome speech to pass without objections. Indeed, long observations followed. I had the impression, however, that I had redeemed myself of at least some of the incomprehension and condescension that Chinese officials so understandably attribute to all Westerners. Once again, and in a variety of forms, I was assured that all what I had described was being done with the greatest tolerance and with the enthusiastic collaboration of all. And to conclude a long argument on an amiable tone, the senior official present wound up by assuring me: 'You will be allowed to go wherever you wish, so that you can see it for yourself.'

In fact, I have travelled over 15,000 miles inside China but I did not come much nearer to answering my own questions. Excesses are not displayed for inspection by foreigners. One hears more about them outside than inside the country. Neither is the speed imposed a subject which the Chinese would discuss with visitors. As for the proportion of persuasion and force applied by the authorities, one's impressions cannot be but fragmentary. Next to measurable material progress there are imponderables like hope in a better future or pride in growing power, which no outsider could accurately assess. Moreover, between a foreign visitor and the Chinese people there still exists an invisible screen. It is not alone due to the presence of officials or to the organized nature of most encounters. After all, one can walk around alone in any city wherever and whenever one chooses to do so. The screen is woven of the fine fabric of fear. The ordinary citizen's prudence warns him to avoid unwitnessed contact with foreigners. It does not necessarily lead to complications with the authorities but it may and, quite understandably, people wish to avoid them. The phenomenon is not unfamiliar to anyone who has lived under contemporary dictatorships even in the West. During their corresponding periods, the atmosphere was similar in Japan as well as in the Soviet Union. With time, one hopes, it will mellow. In the meantime, instead of answers to my questions, I could merely confirm my premises. In fact, given a backward and overpopulated agrarian society as a starting point, any emotionless practitioner of economics might have prescribed most of what is being done in China today even if he had never heard the word Communism.

The emphasis, of course, is on emotionlessness. Because logical as the whole process is, it must be terrifyingly difficult to prescribe, to direct and then to enforce all that logic dictates. Yet, perhaps, it is even more painful to be logically obedient in the execution of orders which, though in conformity with reason, both physically and mentally strain the endurance of even the most enthusiastic.

It is in that sense that I too experienced the feeling of suffocation so many visitors to Communist China had known before me. It was not the sensation arising from wholesale condemnation. It was rather the consciousness of tragedy behind most of what one had seen. One moves around in a country where everything is being done that one imagines has to be done in a land with such problems. Yet most of what is being done, even when evidently necessary and useful, and even when demonstrably leading to a distant but unquestionably better future, causes untold suffering at present.

Constantly, then, one is in the presence of the eternal conflict between good and evil. This almost visible co-existence of the noblest idealism with unavoidable and large-scale suffering remorselessly keeps on reminding us of the inescapable weight of the human condition. And it is in that sense that, for anyone capable of sympathy, China's monumental and extraordinary experiment is doubled by a profoundly moving drama of no lesser dimensions.

I Modernizing a Traditional Society

WITNESSING THE amazing spectacle of China's rapid material progress one may forget that during their first few years in power, China's new masters have been occupied by a different task. Between 1949 and 1952 their major efforts were dedicated to the transformation of the basic ingredient of their future plans: of the individual Chinese.

There have, of course, been important changes and material achievements even during those early years. But they now seem relatively unimportant next to the unprecedented attempt to remould the thinking of 600 million people within a few years.

The temptation is strong to explain most of what is happening in China today as part of the fast and all-embracing process of economic modernization. Events indeed seem to fit into such a simplified historical perspective. Nothing was more natural than that, after Japan and the Soviet Union, China too should wish to catch up with the materially advanced West. But both in Japan and in the U.S.S.R.—as to a lesser extent even in Western countries—the totalitarian consolidation of minds developed parallel with the great, regimented material effort. In a sense, it was its by-product. But in China the time-table was reversed. There, the generalization of *Correct Thinking* preceded the physical exertion.

The model for China's new course had been the Soviet Union. But, naturally, imported ideological impulses have merged with indigenous, historical ones. The first stood for the reconciliation of theoretical prescriptions with China's own material reality. The second, the indigenous impulses, for China's own, subjective ambitions.

To reconcile the Stalinist strategy of industrialization with China's own material reality already implied important modifications of the original model. In 1949 China's industrial base was much more modest than Russia's in 1928. Trained personnel was much more scarce. Then, the Soviet Union's natural resources were much more considerable than what was known to be at China's disposal in 1949. Finally, the Soviet Union had no population problem. In China it was of decisive importance. If, as a consequence, the Soviet aim was rapid mechanization in factory and on the land, conditions in China called for the maximum utilization of over-abundant manpower as a substitute for limited capital.

The compromise resulting from these differences would already have given Chinese Communism its own distinct personality. But it underwent further and significant modification under the impact of China's own, subjective ambitions.

China's present leaders had become fanatical Communists long before Stalin's model of industrialization took shape. When that new component entered their consciousness they already had a

well-defined concept of their own of China's future. A year
before Stalin launched his first Five-Year Plan, Mao Tse-tung—
following on an abortive peasant revolt—was already organizing
his first model community in Chinkanshan. Between 1931 and
1934, in the Chinese Soviet Republic that grew out of the experiment, that concept of the future was tested in action. It matured
in virtual isolation from the outside world. In the Kiangsi Soviet
first, and in the loess caves of Yenan after, without outside help,
without even first-hand knowledge of events beyond China's
borders, relying on an odd selection of books and decisively
conditioned by lessons derived from the guerrilla activities of an
isolated peasant community, the strategy and the aims of Chinese
Communism were given their main outlines. Students of the
agrarian policies of the early Chinese Soviet Republic, or readers
of Edgar Snow's celebrated report from Yenan may measure how
little those ideas or the Chinese leaders' views of the world have
changed up to this day.

Together they added up to the Chinese incarnation of the
orthodox Marxists' faith. They were held with the puritanic and
sectarian rigidity of an isolated and persecuted minority. In
Communist doctrine the millennial Chinese craving for ordered
and imposed uniformity appeared to have found its infallible
guide. Once again circumstances appeared ripe for another of
those attempts to establish a socialistic order which have been
punctuating Chinese history since the first century B.C. After
chaos, rigidity, decadence and humiliation, the need was once again
felt for an orthodox philosophy able to harmonize thought and
action in the service of contemporary ambitions. The traditional,
messianic urge towards Universal Order was offered satisfaction
in the broad unity of a philosophy applicable to all mankind. And
in that universality, restored to her role of the Celestial Empire,
China could once again see her mission as one of converting the
'barbarians' of Asia first; those in the rest of the world after; to
emerge, finally, as the new Middle Kingdom of a converted globe
ready to welcome its peace and its classless, ideal society.

It was against this instinctive, messianic background that, in the
isolation of Yenan, the discovery was made that the peasantry,

instead of being a conservative force, could be turned into a revolutionary vanguard. To do so, they merely had to be enlightened and persuaded, and made conscious of their new role. From there it was only one step further to imagine that the psychological therapy of thought-reform could make the whole people display the idealized qualities which Marx, in less privileged lands, reserved for the proletariat only. By these means, in embryo, the distinct message of Chinese Communism was already there long before Stalin's model of forced industrialization entered the stage. Rather than to modify the whole, it merely became part of it. It became just one strand among others, leading to China's ideal society.

The basic raw material of those pilot experiments was the peasant. He had been oppressed by a decadent and corrupt society. Yet as soon as his mind was remoulded, he became a willing collaborator of the new order. The aim, of course, was not to turn him into an individualist with his own ideas but rather to replace his old set of ideas with a new one imposed, as always in the past, from above.

The external danger in which the pilot experiments developed both in Chinkanshan and in Yenan, greatly helped the creation of collective attitudes. Later on, the demands of the guerilla war against the Japanese invader merely accentuated the need for such mental solidarity. Then, after 1949, the Korean war and American threats rendered the same psychological service. All these experiences have left behind them a predisposition to associate external danger with ideal unanimity inside the country. What is more, they also bequeathed the trained personnel and the tested methods to bring about that unanimity. And as soon as all China was under control, the habit, the method and the cadres were there to repeat the performance on a gigantic scale.

Thus the aim was generalized *Correct Thinking*. The need for complete change merged into the wider stream of the messianic vision of a perfect society. Progress towards both depended on a herculean effort. It could not rely on intuition, on imagination or on individual energy but only on a broad-willed, total devotion. It needed the mystique of the *Great Collective*.

While still utilizing and manipulating tradition, China's new rulers had to change the national point of view. They had to involve the masses in their organizational network and to enmesh in it every aspect of their daily lives. This implied a frontal attack, led by disciplined cadres, upon the contemplative, individualistic and humanistic elements in traditional Chinese civilization. The classical emphasis upon the past had to be exposed as a sterile concept of spiritual superiority masking material inertia. And if tradition was upheld, it was only to serve the new contemporary purpose.

The task was no less than to change a whole nation's assumptions and aspirations. To do so, the Chinese were thrown into the whirlwind of meetings and debates, of mass-trials and public executions and into orgies of self-analyses and self-accusations. They were to undergo an uninterrupted bombardment by written and broadcast slogans. They were to participate in marches, meetings and demonstrations, in frenetical campaigns aimed at real or imaginary enemies or directed against habits, customs or ways of thinking. They were to do all these things simultaneously and ceaselessly until the combined effect of cajolery, of persuasion and of coercion by professional associations, by party-cells and street committees or by neighbours and relatives, had achieved such a degree of physical and mental malleability that both body and brain surrendered to the dictated stimuli of the ubiquitous, irresistible remoulding authority.

During those decisive initial years it was as if an impersonal virtuoso had been playing on a quarter of humanity's psychological key-board. Following the tune, one after the other, waves of hypnotized masses were hurled into the fantastic enterprise to raise and to turn around the colossal Sphynx-like mass representing a whole nation's petrified mentality. Once accomplished, China's mind was facing in a new direction. Instead of contemplating the past, it was turned towards the present and the future.

Was this amazing performance merely a psychological preparation for the material tasks to come? were its dimensions so unprecedented because the physical effort to follow was also to be without example? or was there some less obvious, deeper purpose? was not, perhaps, the whole extraordinary phenomenon a foretaste of the dynamic qualities and of the messianic content of China's resurrected, utopian nationalism?

Admittedly, a traditional society which embarks on moderniza-tion needs an intellectual and social revolution that reaches down to the smallest cells of its social fabric. To consider this as an indispensable preliminary, rather than to let it develop gradually, prodded on by material change, might be well-calculated tactics destined to yield rich results. In China, the preliminary effort to remould minds, has certainly helped to accomplish the peasantry's advance towards total collectivization with much less violence or resistance than in the Soviet Union. It helped to maintain at the régime's disposal most of the people with entrepreneurial and managing experience who, otherwise, might have chosen passive resistance or exile. It is probable that it also permitted the formation of the personnel an industrial society needs, with far greater speed than in other countries in their comparable phase. In a larger perspective, that preliminary effort, and the advantages it procured, may even have been calculated to impress other, economically under-developed countries by the comparison of their own difficulties with China's rapid industrial take-off.

But could considerations be so logically utilitarian? is it not equally possible that the messianic motivation of China's new élite was as important as were their economic and political aims?

Travelling around in China ten years after the great change, inevitably, one poses these questions. In almost every conversa-tion I could find traces of this utopian conviction. From the highest leaders down to local cadres, from officials, professors or students, I heard expressed this apparently sincere and occasion-ally fanatical faith in their role as builders of an unprecedented, ideal society. One is soon forced to wonder whether this egal-itarian and perfect society defined in Communist terms is not, in fact, a more attractive and a more urgent objective for them than is even the improvement of their compatriots' standard of living and the question seems the more justified if one considers that already more than once, when faced by a difficult choice, the solution more satisfying to the messianic vision of the future was the one that triumphed.

Even when reinforced by personal impressions, the examples could hardly justify sweeping generalizations. Yet they do signal a powerful undercurrent in the thinking of China's new leaders. They emphasize the fact that predictions based on the assumption that economic considerations are uppermost in Chinese decisions, have often been wrong and are likely to remain so in the future. The warning is there that whenever alternatives have to be considered, this messianic craving will be likely to tilt the balance. Moreover, this powerful ingredient might turn Chinese Communism after its 'forced march' into something very different from what Soviet Communism has become once its own Stalinian phase was over.

What the real proportion of the essentially economic and of the messianic motives in the thinking of the new China is, no one can tell. All that is certain is that this particular amalgam conditions all those who have been affected by China's preliminary effort to remould her citizens' minds.

Even if the enterprise was only partially successful, a new road has been cut through the debris of old and discredited mental scenery. Henceforth it leads towards the land of Reason where all are expected to agree on the fundamental ideological tenets of 'socialist construction' and, for the time being at least, are left with little more mental liberty than to contribute ideas likely to aid higher production.

2 Faith in the Future

I WAS TRAVELLING one day with an official in a jeep in Central China. The road was narrow and winding deep between high earth-banks. Each time we encountered a vehicle our jeep had to manœuvre carefully neither to touch the passing car nor to drive into the wall of earth on the other side. Then, suddenly, we came to a halt behind a long line of stranded vehicles. We got out and walked up to the lorry at the head of the waiting queue and realized that it was caught up with a bulky country bus which it had tried to by-pass. Both had their noses deep in the earth-banks.

Altogether some thirty men were standing around discussing what to do. Soon they dispersed and came back with odd pieces of wood and metal as substitutes for spades. They threw off their jackets and with extraordinary speed they began to shovel away at the earth on both sides of the road. In barely half an hour it was broadened along a stretch of some fifteen yards. The bus and the lorry backed out of their forced embrace and normal traffic was re-established.

Clambering back into our jeep I remarked to my companion how efficiently and fast the men had worked and with how little discussion they had reached the decision to do so. His answer was interesting. 'Our production of lorries is fast growing but we still have only very few,' he said. 'Those which move along the roads are on some important job and they cannot afford to lose time. All the men you have seen know that. . . .'

In Peking itself, the boulevard on which I lived was being broadened. In the open ditches along it youthful volunteers were shovelling the sand with the rhythm, the precision and the speed of a newly-wound clock. A little further away new sewers were being laid and, in place of pneumatic asphalt cutters, successive teams of some eighty youngsters had been operating an impro-vised contraption reminiscent of Leonardo da Vinci's war-machines. Over a pulley they were pulling a rope which, in its turn, lifted a huge block of stone. At their team-leader's signal they freed the rope and the block of stone, high in the air, crashed to the ground. It cracked the asphalt and revealed another chunk of the street's belly. Pulling and dropping it again, they sang a gay tune and successive teams, with identical movements and with the same song, went on for several days and nights until the whole street was broken up. Their song was not that of the Volga boatmen. It was cheerful and it was punctuated by laughter.

They even appeared exalted by their collective effort. And I was told that they were all volunteers.

A few days later the newspapers announced that the tramcars would be replaced by trolley-buses along the same boulevard. The old trams were to rattle along it for the last time at midnight on that day. At eleven next morning when I looked out of my window, the rails had already been lifted. Pieces of it were on the move like strange caterpillars, with dozens of blue shoulders and legs beneath them.

All over the city millions of gay posters and coloured paper streamers were proclaiming aims, time limits and the required spirit to achieve them. On enormous billboards the enemy of all that febrile activity was identified in the form of humiliated little figures bearing anglo-saxon emblems. Running after them were giant, threatening Chinese, or the molten lava of Chinese steel. Other hoardings were dominated by burning red production curves. In the wake of space rockets they were soaring towards target figures to be reached or already surpassed. Everyone seemed to be active and in a hurry. One day in Peking, I remember seeing two men, each pushing a wheelbarrow loaded with vegetables and with coloured paper flags floating on each squeaking vehicle. 'We Fulfill the Norms of the Plan'—was written on one. 'We Stay Within the Lines of Socialist Edification'—said the characters on the other. As they were advancing along the wide avenue the ceaseless clutter of hammers echoed from the new buildings going up on both sides. They were followed by a small procession of workers, complete with drums, cymbals and models of their products, marching behind posters announcing the over-fulfillment of their production norms. And as the drumming group overtook the two men pushing their wheel-barrows they were all passing under a tremendous, red streamer stretched across the street with huge, golden ideographs along it proclaiming that 'Twenty Years Are Concentrated In One Day'.

Yet all these people were impersonal. Like the fine dust in the air, they were everywhere, anonymous particles of the Chinese quarter of mankind made to hurry history with their naked hands. One could learn little about their minds. One could observe a multitude of details, but the omnipresent living background, the people of China, remained elusively reduced to prototypes.

The new manager, for instance, I met in a steel plant near Peking. A son of peasants, Mao's soldier since his youth, now at forty-three he was director of a huge plant employing some twenty thousand men. His story was familiar: low production under the capitalists; a sharp increase after Liberation; continuous expansion ever since thanks to machines made in China. He was massive, commanding and when he tried to smile one felt the muscular effort. Like a party pamphlet on legs, he spoke in questions and answers which he promptly provided. 'Why is our production growing so fast?' he asked himself. 'It is because here there is planning. We have no strikes, no profit motive, and here people work for more than mere wages. . . .' Then again: 'Why have we stepped up our targets?' he asked. 'We did so because our Five-Year Plan was too slow. We had to brush it aside. Our workers wanted to go faster. In a few years we shall surpass Britain. . . .'

A few days later I came across the Levellers in an engineering workshop of Peking University. They were surrounding a machine-tool in a hall plastered with slogans. The technologically most advanced country was the U.S.S.R.—the students said. 'The Sputniks have shown that,' one explained. But China would soon be third, behind the Soviet Union and the United States. But would China progress so much faster than even the U.S.S.R.? I asked. 'We can rely on Russia's experience; on the disinterested help of the Socialist countries; and we have a very big population,' another student summed up. That France or Britain will be left behind in steel, was taken for granted. In general output or in per head production? I insisted. A student assured me that in ten years or so China's steel output would be higher than France's even per head of population. I remarked that China's population being at least fifteen times that of France, that would mean over 200 million tons of steel within a decade. If it took forty years for the Soviet Union to reach 60 million tons, how would, then, China progress ten times faster? 'I told you what our advantages were . . .' the same student replied somewhat irritated. But before we could continue, their professor intervened, reminding us that the students had to go on with their work.

The Perfect Cog was encountered in a train between Sian and Chengchow. Each coach had its attendant and, for hours, the train's loudspeakers were giving details of the competition between them. Volunteer inspection teams were examining each car and every hour the Red Flag of Cleanliness went to the attendant whose waggon in that hour was the most immaculate. The man in our coach worked indefatigably; washing the toilette, the windows, the floors, catching flies or dusting whatever he could reach. The loudspeakers were blaring the findings and the results. Everyone was involved. When our attendant won, he beamed with joy and held his trophy with triumph. Then, he went on cleaning and dusting in the hope of winning another round. And in the China about whose dirt so much has been said, I travelled in the cleanest railway coach I have ever seen.

One meets other prototypes, more or less near the final perfection of the Nirvana of Reason. There was, for instance the director of the Institute of Nationalities not far from the capital. There were really no problems, only progress, he told me. 'Press reports all over the world speak of difficulties in Tibet. Do you think that they are exaggerations or pure inventions,' I asked him. They were pure inventions, he assured me. Then, to prove his point he enumerated the reforms and the improvements Tibet's liberation brought to her people. I expressed some surprise at the lack of problems affecting China's nationalities. 'If we have no problems that is because they whole-heartedly applaud the enlightened leadership of our Government,' he recited. 'There is constant elevation of the People's cultural level and there is rapid material progress. The nationalities are all happy.' Then we visited the Mosque and the temple for Tibetans and we saw in the garden Uighur, Mongol and Korean students frolicking and throwing snow-balls.

On another occasion, on the Trans-Siberian, I shared a sleeping-car compartment with a young woman. She was pretty and intelligent. Daughter of a teacher near Canton, she was trained to become a Russian interpreter. Her husband and her baby were in their home in Manchuria but she was often absent accompanying Soviet technicians on their trips. She looked tired, wore heavy boots and the padded blue uniform. When I noticed her admiration over the tiny soap tablets which the Russian train stewardess had distributed, she defensively remarked: 'A few years and we shall surpass the living standards of both Russia and America.' Later on I asked her if she ever thought of using a lipstick or or wearing a smart silk dress? 'We have to forget those things for a while,' she said seriously. 'I rather think of the future of my child. A few years of sacrifice and, then, poverty and humiliation will be things of the past. We owe that much to our country. . . .' Later we talked about other peoples; of how long it takes to modernize a country. I gave examples. 'But here it will go much faster,' she insisted. 'Our results are already without precedent.' When I remarked that there is even the incalculable possibility of a war throwing back progress, as it happened even to the Soviet Union, she looked at me as if I had physically hurt her: 'They would not dare to do that . . .' she said with sudden vivacity. 'The Socialist countries are now stronger; and we stand for peace.' Then, wistfully, she added: 'Nobody can stop us on our way. . . .'

In Urumchi, the capital of Sinkiang, we were standing in a workshop with the thirty-year-old director of what was to become Chinese Turkestan's first tractor plant. All around us new buildings were going up and there, in front of us, mechanicians were dismantling a Czechoslovak light tractor. 'We are changing parts to adapt it to Sinkiang's conditions,' he explained. 'We are building a new model. It will unite the advantages of all the tractors we have imported. In two years we shall build five thousand. And they will be better than any we have received. By the time you come back here again, Urumchi will be a centre of heavy industry. We have our plans and they will be realized in record time.' After that, he gave me the inevitable list of statistics. When I remarked on his youth and on his great responsibilities, he answered with what appeared to be genuine modesty: 'The authorities must have been convinced that I would give my utmost to build up this province. It is an inspiring task. . . .' And as I was looking at his smiling, bright face, he seemed the exact antithesis of what, in the West, we define as *angoisse*.

In Canton, a University Professor of Literature, just back from six months labour in a village, said over a lunch table: 'Through physical labour and contact with the masses I feel reborn.' And with convincingly genuine enthusiasm, he added: 'Now, at last, I fully appreciate the generous wisdom of our Government.'

In other surroundings, I asked someone how the reasonable limit of human endurance could be decided. 'We reach decisions after long discussion,' he answered. 'Opposition? We rely on persuasion only. There can be no question of someone resisting a decision for opponents would be persuaded about the right course until there was unanimity.' But how was unanimity reached on what was the right course? I interjected. My question caused some irritation: 'Black is not white. Truth is known,' the answer came. 'There is one truth only and with patience that can be explained.' And that conversation did not take place in a Buddhist monastery but with the administrative director of the giant Anshan steel-combine.

One may slip involuntarily into irony in such recollections. It would be unjust. The enthusiasm and the sincerity of most of these people has a background which we Westerners could hardly be expected to appreciate and even less to be able to share.

While in the West our forefathers had been attempting to harmonize freedom and power, for hundreds of years the Chinese disagreed only over systems of authoritarian rule. All through those centuries the elements shaped their harsh society and they voluntarily submitted to men who could maintain order, conquer floods or render famines less murderous. Rather than the reconciliation of freedom with authority, the ever-recurring motive of Chinese civilized life has been the integration of the individual in the Chinese totality. For brief periods the writ of the Emperor ran from border to border. More often, he merely presided over a confederation of warlords whose only uniting force was formal obedience, custom, and Confucian prescriptions. But whenever the central authority weakened, distance and mass have disintegrated the fragile union. The edicts of the Emperor ceased to be acted upon and chaos, violent death on a monumental scale, and national humiliation followed in their wake.

Periods of history have no exact birthdays. Yet the new orientation might be traced to China's defeat in 1895 at Japan's hand. Mighty China was suddenly revealed helpless against the arms of, what had been considered, an inferior neighbour. The shock was both unexpected and profound and ever since China has been living in revolutionary ferment. Suddenly China had been threatened with India's fate. Her gates were already forced by the West. The need for change was urgent. Only its aims and content were open to debate. But the need to adopt Western ways and means had become as evident as was the rejection of all that the humiliating presence of the West stood for. And intellectuals as well as politicans were groping for a new purpose and for a political doctrine for twentieth-century China.

Dr. Sun Yat-sen bequeathed the lesson that the reformer could get nowhere with only a doctrine but without a solid instrument of executive authority. Not even an authoritarian régime could solve China's problems without an ideology to provide the required enthusiam. And so, the logic of history has almost invited China to westernize with the aid of an anti-Western creed. She was driven to wish to possess all the West's instruments of progress, yet also to acquire them in the élan of a gigantic protest against the West's dominant civilization.

'We have become a tray of loose sand,' Dr. Sun Yat-sen once said. 'We must break down individual liberty and become pressed together into an unyielding body like the firm rock which is formed by the addition of cement. . . .' His advice was listened to. The result was almost calculable. It grew out of chaos, confusion and humiliation and followed on the breakdown of traditional Chinese society. The quest for a new and expedient faith to replace the decaying Confucian order, the yearning for a total solution, was fulfilled. The loose sand was

pressed together under the weight of an all-embracing simplification. The particles united in a new sense of purpose. And the
cement was provided by the fanatical orthodoxy of a minority
holding it with the fervour of men revolted by the past.

For the first time after a century of agony and disintegration,
China was effectively governed. She had a government that
functioned from the summit of the pyramid down to its gigantic
base of innumerable villages. For the first time she had the
effective organization indispensable to the creation of a modern
state. She had an army which was powerful, which was united
and which obeyed. And the unprecedented concentration of
power was in the hands of men who had the determination
to mobilize all of China's resources. This was the essence and
the fulfillment of half a century of fermentation and of revolution.

What at the end replaced the individual liberty which Dr.
Sun Yat-sen had judged so excessive was the common denominator of pre-fabricated reason and the prototype mass-produced
by the Communist Party. Together they represented the propelling force behind the new purpose and they replaced the
categories which Confucian scholars had imposed in the past.

And by so changing the national point of view, and by so
reducing to near uniformity the vision of the future of the
Chinese, the stage was set for the largest enterprise in the history
of mankind.

3 Atlas with a Milliard Shoulders

IN JUNE 1949 Mao Tse-tung promised that as soon as the destiny
of China should be 'in the hands of the people' she would 'swiftly
dash away the dirt left behind by the reactionary government'
and would 'heal the war wounds'. That promise was fulfilled
during the same three years which were needed to accomplish
the psychological preparation of the Chinese masses.

When all China came under Communist rule both industrial and agricultural production were far below pre-war levels. During the twelve years which preceded the change of régime prices increased more than eight thousand million times in what had been history's most spectacular inflation. Transport was disorganized as a result of long years of international and civil war. A substantial proportion of the industries of Manchuria the country's major industrial base, was either dismantled by the Russians or was looted by the retreating Kuomintang troops.

By 1952, despite the stresses of the Korean war, the disruption caused by rapid land-reform, and the series of mass campaigns leading to the beginnings of the socialization of private trade and industry, the country's economy was restored. Once again China had a stable currency. It was claimed that, in most sectors, industrial production surpassed by about a quarter the highest pre-war peaks. The output of grain and cotton too were reported above the highest levels known before 1936.

It was against this background that systematic economic planning began.

China's first Five-Year Plan was launched at the beginning of 1953. More precisely, the first Plan remained a succession of yearly improvizations up to July, 1955, when, for the first time, its details were published. There were, however, important economic and political reasons to explain this curious time lag.[1]

During 1950 and 1951, while fighting in Korea was continuing, over 40 per cent. of the state budget was devoted to defence. As a result the newly established stability of the currency was under serious strain. To avert the danger a quick remedy was needed and, as usual, the emergency measures envisaged were also to serve the régime's ideological aims. If the still considerable private sector of the national economy had been encouraged to play its full part in reconstruction, the time had now arrived to bring it under greater control as well as to make it contribute more heavily to the restoration of financial stability. It is in this context that the feverish 'five anti' and 'three anti' campaigns of 1952 have to be considered. Economically interpreted, they served to impose a capital levy on private enterprise and thus acted as an anti-inflationary device. Incidentally, it also made it possible to reduce the remaining economic influence of the private sector.

When these violent campaigns were over, towards the end of 1952, only a third of wholesale trade, a little more than half of retail trade, and barely over a third of factory production remained in the hands of private entrepreneurs. Before the campaigns the private sector was nearly twice as important in all three fields.[2] Yet the inevitable price was disorganization and so the need for co-ordinated and nation-wide efforts to revive the economy have become urgent. This, then, was the moment early in 1953 when the programme of industrialization, implying massive state investment, was put into operation.

A truce in Korea was negotiated. True, Stalin had just died and Sino-Soviet relations were becoming warmer, but it was not yet known for certain what form Russia's aid to the Plan would take. Then, in May, 1953, two months after Stalin's death, the Soviet Union committed itself to supply ninety-one large industrial plants. In July of the same year the war in Korea came to an end. But well before the consequences of these two decisive events could be fully measured and integrated into the Plan, the stresses of the war effort combined with dislocations caused by the rapid socialization of much of trade and industry, made it impossible to postpone the launching of the Plan.

China's first Five-Year Plan was a very ambitious project. It revealed priorities and, in particular, an overwhelming emphasis on the rapid creation of a heavy industrial base. Above all, it provided quantitative proof of the willingness of China's new rulers to impose sacrifices surpassing those which the Japanese and Russians had endured in pursuit of comparable aims. It was clearly implied between its lines that the growing volume of steel would not be turned either into motor-cars or into washing-machines, but into the building of further blast furnaces; that the ever growing quantities of coal to be mined would not heat houses against winter cold, but feed plants and power-stations; and that the new materials produced, instead of providing homes for an expanding population, would rather be used to erect new factories to house yet more and still bigger machines.

In more concrete terms, China's first Plan foresaw the investment in capital construction, between 1953 and 1957, of the equivalent of eighteen milliard dollars.[3] During each year of the Plan, the investments were to reach the impressive sum of about three milliard dollars.[4] But the staggering effort to come was further underlined by the distribution of these large investments. Those which could have paid quick dividends in the form of improved standards of living were extremely modest. In fact, the bulk of the investments foreseen were to be devoted to projects unlikely to contribute to better living for many years to come.

Between 1880 and 1912, while the United States was becoming a world power, only nineteen out of every hundred dollars investment went into the building of industries. Even during the Soviet Union's first Five-Year Plan the share of industry did not surpass forty dollars. Not so in China. Actually, nearly sixty out of every hundred dollars investment were to go into the building of industries. What is more, over fifty dollars out of every hundred were to establish *heavy industries*. Contrasting with the astonishing tempo prescribed for industrial growth, agriculture, forestry and water conservation were to obtain no more than seventy-six cents out of each ten dollars of investment foreseen.

Clearly, the aim was to turn China rapidly into an industrial giant. The die was cast. Already pressed into line during the preceding three years, the Chinese had been given the signal to embark on their arduous and long forced march. Henceforth they were tied to the wheel of the inescapable and tyrannical Plan. Starting gently at the beginning, it was to turn faster and faster. An ever growing proportion of the national income was to go into the construction of the future. Sixteen per cent. in 1952; eighteen the next year; nearly twenty-two the year after; it was to grow to a quarter of the national income by 1956.[5] Then, after 1957, with the Great Leap Forward, the acceleration became breathtaking until, today, the proportion set aside for investment is believed to have surpassed a third of the total.

Of every hundred yuans[6] earned by the Chinese a steadily growing proportion was to be given up to finance the construction of factories, laboratories, machine-tools or jet aircraft. An ever expanding volume of the goods produced had to be offered to the State to enable it to export them in payment for imported equipment. The pace was set by the unchallengeable authority of the state and the rhythm was guaranteed by the volume of investments diverted from consumption.

But what kind of effort did all this imply?

Figures being abstract notions, comparison may best provide the answer. The volume of products a nation abstains from consuming in order to pay for the expansion of its productive capacity, is a fairly reliable index of its effort.

In the West that effort never surpassed a fifth of the national income and even so caused much privation and suffering. In Great Britain—the first to carry out her industrial revolution and, therefore, unhurried and without rivals—investments in the 1860's reached nearly 17 per cent. before they steadily declined in the following decades. During the United States' great period of industrial growth, investments never surpassed 15 per cent. France's effort oscillated between 9 and 13 per cent. during the first fourteen years of this century. As for Germany, a latecomer on the Western industrial scene, her investments reached nearly a fifth of her national income during the years before the first World War.

In the East, the efforts to catch up with the industrialized West inevitably involved even greater sacrifices. After about 10 per cent. in Japan between 1890 and 1914, her rate of gross investments grew to an average of 18 per cent. between 1914 and 1936. Still higher rates were achieved in the Soviet Union. According to official figures nearly a quarter of the national income went to investment in the first year of its first Five-Year Plan. Then, from 1929 to 1932, it grew to a quarter. Later on, with the shadow of war approaching, the Stalinist forced march led beyond 27 per cent. Yet none of these rates surpassed those which were to be extracted from the Chinese during and, especially, after their own first Plan.[7]

Nothing perhaps could better bring out the dimensions of China's exertions than comparison with a parallel experience, with that of India. Embarking on her own first Five-Year Plan almost simultaneously, between 1951 and 1956 India's domestic investments were two and a half times less than China's, during her first Plan, for a population only 40 per cent. smaller. Though the average income of the Indians was higher than that of the Chinese, and though India's industrial base and system of communications were far more developed, India's rate of investment during her first Plan barely surpassed 7 per cent. of her national income. In China it reached a level three times higher. Moreover, an important proportion of India's investments were provided either by foreign aid or by her own foreign assets accumulated during the last war. In China, in contrast, virtually all had to be accumulated by the country's own, unaided efforts.[8]

It would seem, then, that the demands made on the Chinese masses have been without precedent. Their sacrifices and their sufferings too must have been on a hitherto unknown scale. But who really was paying the price?

China had to start her climb from a lower economic rung than any Western country, the Soviet Union of 1919, or even the India of 1948. The backwardness of her agriculture, her industry and her transport system all combined to produce an extremely modest national income. According to some estimates the pre-war average income of the Chinese was no more than a quarter of what the average Japanese earned. Even the legendary poverty of the Indian allowed for an average income a third higher than what the average Chinese earned.[9] The yield of his land was low. Under-employment in the villages was widespread. Draft animals being scarce, even their labour was better remunerated than that of the over-numerous Chinese labourers.[10] As late as 1949 China had no more than three million workers in factories and her industrial base was very narrow.[11] When the Communists took over, in most sectors the output of China's industry represented only a half or a quarter of industrial production in the Russia of 1913. Per head of population the comparison was even less flattering. As for transport, a decisive factor in a country's modernization, China's rail and road network lagged far behind even that of India.

Thus, as the majestic sweep of a Greek tragedy unrolls, so began China's new, heroic age with her first Five-Year Plan. Fired by hope and passion, the actors appeared to be blind to the effect of their words and deeds. Yet the outcome was preordained by cruel and inflexible facts.

For industry's share in the national income was very modest. Four out of five Chinese being agriculturists, their activity had to provide the bulk of the capital needed to finance rapid industrialization. It had to be in the form of raw materials either to feed industry or to provide exports to pay for foreign equipment. To dispose of such surpluses the Chinese peasant had to produce more or eat less, if not both. To purchase his surpluses, the state should have been in a position to offer consumer goods in exchange. But to turn out consumer goods on such a scale, light industry ought to have had priority over heavy industries. That, again, would have implied a much slower rate of economic transformation as well as the postponement of the rapid creation of modern, industrial power.

To break out of this vicious circle, China—like any other predominantly agrarian country that wishes to modernize fast and virtually unaided—scarcely had any other choice left but to extract the required surpluses *without* offering consumer goods in exchange. That, in its turn meant the placing of the peasantry under economic and political controls able to enforce both austere living and greater production efforts against nothing more than the mere hope of better days to come.

The central figure, the man singled out by history to be the hero of the tragedy, was the Chinese peasant. Like Atlas, inevitably, he was condemned to carry on his shoulders the burden of China's fast changing world. And that, in the words of Hesiod, the Greek who put the sufferings of Atlas in verse, 'was a load not easy to be borne'.

In fact, it was to become so heavy to bear that even the sturdy figure of the Chinese peasant had to be prepared gradually for it.

4 Phases in Economic Control

WHAT NORMALLY renders travel such an exciting and stimu-
lating experience is the occasional encounter with the unexpected.
This is almost impossible in China today. Logic rules and nothing
is left to chance. Activities are ordered and there is no room for
surprise. As for a foreign visitor's impressions, his movements
are so organized that neither chance nor surprise should affect their
predetermined course.

Every encounter and conversation serves to confirm that the
Chinese have all been thoroughly schooled in *Correct Thinking*.
Ideas are exchanged in the form of slogans. Arguments are replaced by statistics. People appear to live only to serve targets.
Men and women wear the same uniforms because they are more
economical to manufacture. Enthusiasm and effort are orchestrated with scientific precision. They are formulated in the shape
of collective reflexes conceived by some impersonal, remote
brain. The delivery system maintains their intensity down to the
million terminal points in villages. Persuasion, perfected into
psycho-therapy, is employed before recourse to coercion. The
electric current feeding the network is supplied through mass-
campaigns. They are set off with a vehemence bordering on
terror, then relaxed to leave time for adaptation, and are intensi-
fied again to consolidate the final triumph. Should there remain
any reluctance or insubordination, they are short-circuited by
all-pervading fear.

Evidently, the levers are in the hands of men with iron will and
with precise ideas about their aims. Their knowledge of their raw
material comes from long years of experience and direct contact.
Obviously, they are masters in taking calculated risks.

Against such a background, it is irresistibly tempting to
imagine that on the eve of her first Five-Year Plan, China was
under the control of an electronic computer dictating its orders
to a gigantic control-board. Logical, inflexible and precise as
machines are, how would it have faced China's problems from
that momentuous departure onwards?

To begin with, like all electronic computers, it would have been 'fed' with its basic data.

The country's thinking, its habits and its mode of action were to be changed. Within about fifteen years a complex of heavy industry was to be built able to produce practically all the equipment needed by industry and national defence. Simultaneously, there was the objective to create a classless society, as original, as envied and as powerful as the China of the most brilliant periods of her great prestige in the past had been. Moreover, progress towards all these aims was to be gradual and to avoid the use of force whenever persuasion could achieve the required results.

Digesting this basic data, the electronic computer would have quickly defined five decisive sectors where to act on the control-board.

The first would concern psychological problems. By 1953 already the control-board was fully equipped in that sector. Its levers and switches were in full working order. There, the computer had to consider only the occasional danger signals and to manipulate levers able to deal with them.

The second sector would concern export markets. There, the computer's task would be to search out buyers for the goods China could export; to find purchasers who could either offer the required equipment in exchange, or who would pay with convertible currencies. Here, again, the machine's work would be relatively easy. Long-term trade agreements with Communist countries assured markets for much of China's exports and, in most cases, supplied the goods China needed. There may be moments when the computer would have to act to change established routine. China may need imports which the Communist countries cannot supply in the required quantities. Or she may wish to export things which her allies do not need. Different levers may then have to be pulled to find new markets; to establish trade contacts with Afro-Asian lands; with South-east Asia; with Western neutrals; or with countries in the Western world where no discrimination bars such trade. Later on, perhaps, even some large scale reorientation may become desirable in order to lessen China's overwhelming dependence on trade with the Communist bloc. Yet complicated as the computer's task in this field may become, it would remain a lesser problem for it to find the markets than to procure the needed volume of exports able to pay for all that has to be bought abroad.

Thus, the third and much more complicated task of the computer would be to circumscribe domestic consumption so as to leave adequate surpluses for indispensable exports. Here the task becomes a little more complex. Slight concessions may be needed. But with its usual logic the machine would have to curb appetites. Some segments of the population, like the dwellers of fast growing industrial cities, would obtain indispensable services which go with urban living. Elementary social services and greater educational opportunities may be provided for many more. Yet consumer goods and even food would remain scarce. Only the greater equality in individual shares would remain as main compensation for continuing austerity. And there, inevitably, the computer would begin to trespass on another sector: on the one concerned with the number among whom the shares have to be distributed.

The fourth task of the electronic computer, then, would be a delicate one. It would have to face the problem of population growth. Driven by its mechanical reasoning, again and again, it would try to set the levers of birth-control in motion. The speedometer would continue to call for a slow-down. But each time the mechanical arms would reach out for the appropriate lever, their action would be hindered, if not arrested, by the force of doctrine. The anti-Malthusian creed of Marxism would intervene. Thus, the computer would be driven to exert all its power over the fifth sector; over the one where alone both the forces limiting consumption and those which call for population control could be overcome. That fifth and really decisive sector would be the one concerned with the general increase of agricultural output.

Even after several years of feverish industrialization, agriculture remains the bed-rock of China's economic structure. Throughout the first Plan two-thirds of the consumer goods available to the

Chinese consisted of food; one-fifth of articles for daily use; and 13 per cent. only of clothing. Yet, directly or indirectly, agriculture provided 85 per cent. of all these.[12] But that isn't all. Rural China furnishes 90 per cent. of all raw materials for consumer goods' industries, and buys over two-thirds of their output. What is more, three-quarters of China's exports are farming products, or manufactured goods made of agricultural raw materials.[13] By supplying the bulk of both consumer goods and exports, then, China's agriculture conditions the nation's entire economy. A good harvest provides the textile mills with cotton, hemp and jute; it fills bellies and state granaries; it increases the surplus available for export to pay for equipment; and so it determines the very pace of economic progress.

Clearly, then, the land and its products, the men who grow them, and the methods they use, would claim much of the computer's attention. Neither the export markets nor the control of population growth, or the level of domestic consumption would call for such carefully calculated interventions as the problems affecting China's agricultural production. In fact, it is in that sector that every action would be accompanied by the incessant flashing of red danger signals. Doctrine would continually have to be harmonized there with economic necessity. Even the imperative of speed would have to yield to the limitations of human endurance. And even so, however careful the handling, uncertainty would persist concerning the results.

5 Agricultural Collectivization of 1956

LIKE MORE THAN one dynasty before them, the Chinese Communists had come to power on the wave of peasant revolt. The under-privileged of the countryside formed their armies. The hope of land reform sustained their fidelity and enthusiasm. They personified the popular will in whose name the new régime took power. And they succeeded in doing so because they could prove that they would take the land from the landlords and give it to those who tilled it.

The heretical originality of the power strategy of Chinese Communism was, indeed, in its reliance on peasant, rather than on urban proletarian support. Moreover, much of its strength has been derived from the fact that this strategy followed the Chinese tradition of revolution rather than that prescribed by Karl Marx.

In actual practice China's Communists rehearsed their tactics in two separate laboratories. The first was in Kiangsi, between 1931-34, during the Chinese Soviet Republic. There, they classified the status of various rural classes and their determination to break the landlords culminated in veritable massacres. On the waves of the rural class-struggle a radical land reform was carried out and only the forcible end of that early experiment prevented the execution of the proclaimed next stage, that of collectivization. The Long March intervened. From Kiangsi the Communist experiment was transferred to its second laboratory, in Yenan.

By then the political situation was changed. The war against the Japanese invaders called for changed tactics and that was to modify agrarian policies as well. Reluctant to let the Kuomintang monopolize the championship of national resistance, the Communists needed the support of all classes and the memory of the Kiangsi excesses obstructed this aim. Thus, instead of rekindling the remorseless war against landlords and other class-enemies— during the Yenan period (1935-45)—Chinese Communist agrarian policies became markedly more tolerant. A new, reformist line was adopted. As long as they collaborated with the Communists and helped the anti-Japanese struggle, landlords were spared. Officially, the land reform programme hardly went beyond the reduction of rent and interest rates. Besides enhancing the prestige of Communists as potential leaders of a wide coalition, this was also very successful in economic terms. It led to great increases in productivity and to a general improvement in the region's standard of living. What is more, it helped to convince public opinion that Chinese Communism was a mere reform movement whose triumph was to inspire no excessive fears.

Looking back at the Yenan experiment, it may appear as an alternative which, had all China been under their control, the Chinese Communists would have rejected. It may be argued that applied to all China, the Yenan model might have produced more satisfactory economic results than the course later adopted. Bigger crops, growing prosperity and relative tolerance between classes had permitted the accumulation of adequate funds to support a large military force even in a poor, mountainous region. The same methods generalized over all China, so the argument runs, might have yielded adequate surpluses to finance even an ambitious programme of industrialization.

In reality, as soon as their power was consolidated over the whole country, the Communists' policy changed. The Yenan experiment emerged as a mere deviation from the preferred line of development. Soon it became clear that ideological considerations triumphed and agrarian policy was to revert to the original, Kiangsi model.

Continuous shifts in tactics failed for some time to make this quite clear. Yet from the time of Japan's surrender onwards the pendulum of land policy continued to swing to the left. At the end of 1947 the Central Committee re-issued the two decisive documents of the Kiangsi Soviet days on the classification of the status of rural classes.[14] In the meantime the experiments with rural revolution had been going on in the area already freed of Kuomintang control. Their aims were clear. The power of the landlords, petty officials, merchants and usurers had to be broken. Above all, the rural gentry who provided the backbone of the old Confucian order, was to disappear. To achieve these aims, the villages were engulfed in campaign after campaign each bringing a more perfected technique in the harrying, the pillorying and, quite often, in the brutal liquidation of the proscribed categories. With each new wave of orchestrated hate another group was hurled against the next one above it until chaos and economic disorganization threatened. The steam-roller for the smashing of China's old rural order was well run in. A pause was needed to prepare for systematic action.

After the Communists' final triumph, the pattern became uniform all over the country. Only a year after the change of régime the cadres went into action. The general rule was to crush the landlords. Except for a small patch left to cultivate themselves, their land was distributed among the tenants in occupation of it. Following that, holdings were equalized and the tenants who emerged with too big a slice were deprived of some of it in favour of poorer farmers. Landless labourers too obtained a share of what was confiscated and, quite often, rich peasants cultivating their land with little hired labour, were untouched. Rack rents were abolished and, in their place, all peasants were to pay a tax varying from 12 to 15 per cent. of their produce. The detailed rules were fixed by village meetings under the guidance of the local activists.

By 1952, except for Tibet and a few other areas inhabited by minorities, the programme was completed. Though in some regions, at least, the middle peasants were the principal beneficiaries of redistribution, undoubtedly a very substantial proportion of China's arable land changed owners.

Inevitably, a change of such dimensions and within so short a time involved a great deal of violence.[15] But whatever the number of victims or the cost in sufferings, this was the new régime's first major achievement. Rural statistics in China being rudimentary, the exact results were never really seriously tabulated. In the words of Liao Lu-yen, the Minister of Agriculture, '. . . about three hundred million peasants, including those in the old Liberated Areas, or between 60 and 70 per cent. of the nation's agricultural population have received economic benefits from the land reform. Some 700 million *mu* of land have been distributed. . . .'[16]

That the land reform came to most as a tremendous and welcome revolutionary change, there is no doubt. By becoming an owner the peasant's dream was fulfilled. Even if his possession was too small and even if he lacked draft animals or equipment, his gratitude went to the new régime. By 1952, according to official figures, the output of grain as well as cotton was higher than ever before. For the Chinese peasant this was evidently the beginning of a new era. .

But not so for the Government. For the Communist leadership land reform was merely the end of a preliminary phase. The country needed time to digest the change but the Government never left any doubt about its final aims.

'The grave problem is that of educating the peasants. The peasant's economy is scattered. According to the experiences of the Soviet Union, it requires a long time and careful work to attain the socialization of agriculture', wrote Mao Tse-tung a few months before the new State was proclaimed in Peking. And though he foresaw a long period of transition, he clearly stated his intentions: 'Without the socialization of agriculture, there will be no complete and consolidated Socialism. And to carry out the socialization of agriculture, a powerful industry with state-owned enterprises as the main component must be developed. The State of the people's democratic dictatorship must step by step solve this problem of the industrialization of the country. . . .'[17]

That in the minds of China's rulers the collectivization of agriculture was an indispensable preliminary to the financing of industrialization, was once again made plain by their leading theoretician. 'After the completion of the land reform and after two or three reasonably good harvests,' said Liu Shao-chi in his 1950 May Day address, 'the present shrunken purchasing power in the rural districts will be swiftly revived and will gradually increase so that industry and commerce in the urban areas will flourish.'

But to feel their dream really fulfilled the peasants wanted the actual physical possession of the land. Also, it was in the traditions of Chinese Communism to move by stages, each prepared by education and persuasion. Though the Government certainly had the power to move on directly to the system of collective farming, in Mao's own words 'a long time' and 'careful work' were needed to attain that aim.

Indeed, when the first Five-Year Plan was launched in 1953 it contained merely the hope that by 1957 one-fifth of the peasants would be in co-operatives. Even as late as February, 1955, when the Plan's finalized version was beginning to emerge, only one-third of farming households were expected to belong to producers' co-operatives by the end of 1957. Yet the same Plan fixed ambitious industrial targets as well as crop increases which were to pay for them. And these prescriptions, as it turned out, were bound to upset the time-table proclaimed. In fact, land reform was barely completed when, already, the drive began for the reorganization of agriculture to give the state absolute control over the peasant, his land and his produce.

The plots of the new owners were too small. Implements were inadequate and draft animals were scarce. To overcome the most obvious difficulties, loose mutual aid associations were encouraged to begin with. This meant co-operative work with, at first three or four families pooling their resources. As the advantages of group work became apparent, mutual aid teams expanded to embrace twenty to thirty households. Working members were earning a fixed amount for their labour and each ox or plough was compensated by a share from the harvest. But the units were still too small and the application of improved methods called for their extension. The next stage was the introduction of co-operative farms. Within these a hundred or more peasants pooled their land as share capital. They removed the boundary stones and considered their implements and animals as the property of the community. This way, units up to a thousand acres were worked in co-operation.

The changeover of course needed intensive propaganda. Model co-operatives were set up in each district and next to the cadres, officials too were sent to the countryside to help with the administrative reorganization. The more rational use of scarce resources, tax relief for the docile and heavier charges for the reluctant, all contributed to induce the peasant to risk the new experiment.

In the meantime, as in the towns, the state was tightening its grip. In the autmn of 1953 a state monopoly of the grain trade and rationing of cereals down to the village level were instituted.

Even so, progress was rather slow. As late as the summer of 1955 only 14 per cent. of peasant households had joined the new 'primary producers' co-operatives'.[18] Though there had been waves of persistent propaganda campaigns, co-operatives were spreading at a leisurely pace only. Early in 1955 the process even seemed to be halting. Instead of the 'two or three reasonably good harvests' contemplated by Liu Shao-chi, the Plan started off with years of poor crop. According to all evidence agriculture was failing to offer what was expected of it.

The conviction and the fear that, unless squeezed out in time, private property would spread and swallow the rest, called for action. In any case the fast growing urban and industrial population had to be fed. Then, the census revealed that population was expanding at an alarming rate. Industrialization was obtaining the lion's share of state investments and Soviet credits provided barely 3 per cent. of them. As the slowing down of the tempo of industrialization was out of question, bigger crops and the stepping up of exports became the more urgent. Inevitably, then, agriculture had to be made more responsive to central direction so that prescribed areas could be put down to cotton, others concentrated on grain or oil seeds, or on whatever industrial crops were needed by the factories or by the export market.

It is true that millions of voluntary or conscripted labourers had been working on irrigation canals, on reservoirs and on other improvements beneficial to agriculture. But the land was still the step-child of the state. Even when taken together with what the co-operatives and the few collectives did set aside, agriculture's share of state investments was far less than half of what industrialization devoured. And this neglect in the investment programme, added to all the other difficulties, was bound to be reflected in output. Official statistics claimed that the average, yearly growth of food crops was 3·7 per cent. But there was little evidence that the peasants were eating better or more. In the towns the food queues did not grow shorter. In fact, independent estimates came to the conclusion that between 1952 and 1955 the growth of food-grain production was not much faster than population expansion. Industrialization was to cost more rather than less. The state needed even bigger funds. And that implied even more stringent control.

So, brushing aside risks, in July, 1955, Mao Tse-tung decided to act. Foreshadowing the thunder, a virulent campaign against 'rightists' and for the 'liquidation of counter-revolutionaries' had been unleashed. Even within the Party '. . . during the past three years . . .', Vice-Premier Chen Yi accused, '. . . they dragged the masses away from the road of Socialism'.[19] The softening-up period was evidently over. Then, on July 31, speaking to a gathering of provincial activists, Mao lashed out at cadres and Party members who were '. . . tottering along like a woman with bound feet, always complaining that others are going too fast'. Collectivization, he ordered, was to be speeded up in a dramatic fashion. Over half of China's peasants were to work in collectives by 1957 and all of them by 1960.

Probably in order to avoid disruption of the bumper autumn harvest, Mao's decision was not immediately made public. But once the new crop had been gathered, the army of inhumanly devoted activists descended on the villages. In an unprecedented organizing drive, hundreds of millions of peasants experienced the assault of argument, discussion, sleepless self-examination and public self-criticism. Some were convinced. Some recalcitrants succumbed through sheer physical and mental exhaustion. Others again were changed by the usual mixture of promise, persuasion and coercion. Inevitably and wearily, the countryside yielded to the superhuman persuasiveness of the blue-uniformed messengers of reason. At the end, all the aims and targets were realized and even surpassed well before the time limit set. To the amazement of the whole world, within about a year over 96 per cent. of China's peasants were brought under the control of roughly a million co-operatives. And nearly nine out of every ten of them, without going through the stage of 'primary producers' co-operatives' first, became directly 'developed types' or full collectives. There was no time for the traditional 'gradualism'. By the end of 1956, for all practical purposes, China's agriculture was fully collectivized. At last the state was in complete control of the broad agricultural base of China's economy. And according to all evidence Mao Tse-tung succeeded in advancing bloodlessly where Stalin's path was strewn with corpses.

If the proof was needed, this rapid and drastic transformation without any violence provided eloquent testimony of the political power of China's new régime. Moreover, following on the exceptional harvest of 1955 a long period of consolidation was to follow that the peasant should feel himself better off in the collective than he had been before being induced to enter it. In 1956 the state poured three times as much agricultural credit into the countryside as during the previous year. Even more important, at last, state investments in agriculture too were stepped up and were almost double as much in 1956 as in the year before.

Optimism soared and a comprehensive twelve-year plan for agriculture was being worked out. Between 1956 and 1967 it was to bring huge increases in yields as well as in total production. Everything was prepared to give a sound basis to the coming second Five-Year Plan.

Ultimate success, however, depended on the attitude of the individual peasant. Did his performance confirm official optimism? has collectivization really helped to raise output? The picture emerging from official statements was one of unqualified success. Yet scattered symptoms slowly revealed that results were somewhat less satisfying than the world was given to believe.

Though peasant resistance was evidently mild compared to what the Soviet Union had experienced after Stalin's forced collectivization, nevertheless, it gradually transpired that not all was well in the countryside. Even Party journals kept on reporting fairly widespread slaughter of farm animals and, in some cases, even destruction of farm implements. It was revealed that in some regions collectives existed in name only and their members were occasionally tempted to work for clandestine free markets. Concentration on basic crops such as grain and cotton, tended to diminish the output of industrial crops. Regimented labour left no time for subsidiary activities and that caused additional hardship. It seriously affected the peasants' revenue which '. . . from sideline production'—like handicrafts or fishing—'generally makes up about one-third of their total income'. In fact, from the winter of 1955 to the spring of 1956 'in many areas sideline production registered a great decline. In some areas income from sideline production dropped by between one-third and half of original figures.'[20] The shortage of draft animals, too, was causing official concern. A Tientsin paper revealed that '. . . cattle slaughtered this year has shown an increase of more than 70 per cent. compared with the same period last year, and calves have constituted a very large portion of the animals slaughtered'.[21] As for pigs, their numbers declined from 100 million in June, 1954 to 80 million in June, 1956.[22] And consumers were particularly hard hit by the severe shortage of pigs and vegetable oil, both basic to the Chinese diet.

Nor was the weather on the side of the planners. In 1956 nearly 15 million hectares of the cultivated areas—the highest proportion for several years—were affected by natural calamities. Notwithstanding the herculean labours in water conservancy, food production showed no important increases. It may be that in the collectives the hitherto poorest peasants could eat more rice than before and there is indeed evidence of higher rural consumption of food grains. But in contrast, and according to official figures, the consumption of cereals actually declined in the urban areas.[23] It is not surprising, then, that once again there were audible voices even within the Party saying that the decision of sweeping collectivization was too hastily taken.

Yet in the meantime heavy industry continued to absorb an ever growing share of the state's funds. Capital investment in 1953 as in 1954 increased by 8 per cent. After that came the exceptional harvest of 1955. Also by that time the state's means to extract from the countryside whatever it needed had become much more effective. As a result, capital investment in 1956 made an unprecedented jump. It was 63 per cent. higher than in the year before and, as usual, most of the increase went to speed the creation of heavy industries. Then, when in 1956 the weather was once again indifferent, it became clear that the pace could not be kept up. Even after collectivization, agriculture continued to lag and kept on creating basic pressures and strains. It remained the critical sector of China's economy. The number of mouths to be fed was rapidly growing. The need to export was becoming still more pressing. Yet not even the régime's extraordinary political and organizational apparatus could afford to press on any further.

There was growing strain and more and more frequent references to 'internal contradictions' between savings and investment. Evidently, collectivization did not provide the magic formula for the rapid expansion of production. Exports, on the other hand, could not be much increased without further depressing consumption to a politically dangerous level.

The control-board's little red lights were ominously flashing their warning signals. So, guided by its inflexible logic, the electronic computer turned to the one sector not yet interfered with and attempted to use the levers of birth-control.

And that decision produced perhaps the most unexpected interlude in China's search for a solution, that could save the rapid fulfilment of her basic ambitions.

6 The Birth Control Experiment of 1957

TOWARDS THE END of 1954 demographers had the unprecedented experience of their findings making sensational headlines all over the world. More exactly, it was the announcement, on November 1, of China's first scientific census results, which startled all mankind. A disquieting, new intruder in our fast changing world, China's presence had become even more formidable with the revelation that her population was approaching 600 million.[24]

The first reaction was surprise tinged with incredulity. Statistics in Asia are not a highly developed art and the only two countries on the continent with a long record of more or less reliable census techniques were India and Japan. Moreover, previous attempts at estimating China's population had given widely varying conclusions. When the Manchu government attempted a rudimentary census in 1911, the estimate was 374 million. An effort in 1918-19, relying on the experience of missionaries, reached the figure of 453 million. In March 1945, a not much more scientific exercise under the Kuomintang yielded 455 million. As late as 1948 the United Nations' official figure for China's population was 463 million.

Though not necessarily absolutely accurate, this latest census—with June 30, 1953, as its critical date—was certainly by far the most serious yet carried out in the country. Over two million census workers had been specially trained and Soviet demographers had provided technical help. Only remote and inaccessible areas were surveyed by indirect methods while for the rest of the country modern, scientific practices were applied.

The most unexpected of the findings was the unsuspected rapidity of the growth of China's population. Before 1949 it was generally believed that expansion was no faster than about 1 per cent. per year. Now it was revealed that mortality rates were in rapid decline and that the yearly growth already surpassed 2 per cent. and may, in fact, be heading towards 3 per cent.[25] War, civil strife and famines were no longer taking their toll. Moreover, as in most other economically under-developed countries, the spread of hygiene and the large scale application of modern medicine were setting off the demographic explosion. So, next to the already superhuman effort to improve the living standards and to modernize the existence of 600 million Chinese, each year an additional Czechoslovakia was to be fed and provided with at least a minimum amount of shelter, clothing, services and education.

Incidentally, the census also revealed how youthful China's population was. In fact, there were twice as many Chinese under fourteen years as the total population of the Soviet Union. Or they alone numbered more than the total population of the United States, of Canada and of Great Britain combined.

All of a sudden mankind was to take cognizance that the number of the Chinese with whom it was sharing the planet, was growing each year by about 14 million, and was to reach 700 million by 1961; about 850 million ten years later; and, in all probability, over a milliard by 1980.

Though at first somewhat proud of this additional, quantitative proof of their country's importance, it is hardly surprising if the Chinese themselves were amazed by their own revelations. The original text of the first Five-Year Plan made no reference to the subject of population. Yet its rate of growth, even more than its actual size, was of decisive importance to the planners.[26] While agricultural output grew no faster than 3 or 4 per cent. a year, it could not be a matter of indifference to see how closely it was followed by population expansion. The difference between the two was bound to affect the tempo of capital accumulation. Clearly, then, the success of China's industrial revolution was being menaced by the counter-revolution of babies crying for food.

The new revelations were inevitably followed by discussion and suggestions how to confront the newly discovered menace. But progress was slow and hesitating. It was inhibited by the conflict between the Communists' anti-Malthusian faith in technology and applied science as the solvent of all human problems, and the pressure arising from their preoccupation with the speedy edification of a heavy industrial base.

Long before the census results became known, a provision of the Marriage Law—promulgated in April 1950—raised the age of consent from 18 to 20 years for men, and from 16 to 18 for women. Then, from 1953 onwards abortion and sterilization were legalized under certain conditions and, later on, this measure was further liberalized so as to make it virtually free.

But the opening shot for the real campaign of birth-control was fired at the first session of the People's Congress held in Peking in September, 1954. The task was allotted to a venerable old man, Shao Li-tzu, spokesman for the independent parties which have been existing in the shadow of the Communists. As there are few precedents in Communist China for a spontaneous beginning to a movement of such importance, it is not unreasonable to presume that the government itself had its own good reasons to draw attention to the problem. The most important among them may have been the very unsatisfactory food situation throughout 1954 as well as the growing pressure for better housing. Having made it clear that, of course, there was no population problem in China in the conventional, 'bourgeois' sense and that his plea had nothing to do with reactionary Malthusian doctrines, Deputy Shao still asked for birth-control measures. He repeatedly underlined, however, that these were needed merely to protect mothers and to improve their health. 'A big population is a good thing,' he pointed out, 'but there should be a certain limit to it when there are many difficulties.' His opening was followed by several other speakers intervening in the same sense. As a result, the State Council instructed the Ministry of Public Health to look into the matter and to educate the masses on the need for practising birth-control.

There matters rested for the time being. A year later, on December 27, 1954, however, a personality of no lesser importance than Liu Shao-chi himself convened a special conference to discuss the problem. This resulted in an organ of the State Council designating 'the responsible officials of the competent departments to organize research groups for the discussion of contraception problems'.

But even by that date China's leaders seemed to be less than unanimous on the issue and there was no sense of urgency in the preparations. In fact, early in 1955 when Mr. Nehru visited Peking, in a private conversation Mr. Chou En-lai scoffed at the idea of birth-control. China's vast territory, he argued, could absorb millions of new settlers. A few months later, however, speaking on behalf of the Central Committee, Mr. Chou En-lai himself provided the highest official seal for 'appropriate control in respect of births'.[27] In the meantime China's land was collectivized and agriculture remained the central problem. When, in November 1956, the Chinese Premier visited India one of his first requests was for information on that country's experience in 'family planning'.

Finally, the incubation period apparently completed, in March, 1957 Madame Li Teh-chuan, China's Minister of Health, raised the curtain on the first, full birth-control campaign in a Communist state. 'Our country is a big and over-populated one and in the course of our Socialistic construction, various undertakings are being developed in a planned manner,' she said before the National People's Congress. 'If our population growth is not in accordance with planned child-birth, it will prevent our country from quickly ridding itself of poverty and from becoming prosperous and powerful.' Then, she was referring to a yearly population growth of 15 million. 'With such a huge rate of growth, the increases of our agricultural and industrial production, however rapid, will fail to satisfy adequately the basic requirements of the increased population.' And her plea for a nationwide birth-control campaign was given substance in the March 5, 1957, issue of the *People's Daily* which announced that the organization was ready and that the required contraceptives were already being manufactured on a large scale. '. . . if the speed of our population slows down, improvement in the livelihood of our people will quicken correspondingly,' the article argued. 'Therefore, we advocate, except for the sparsely populated Minorities zones, all areas in our country must promote appropriate birth-control.'

Thus the green light was given. Tens of thousands of activists all over the country knew the meaning of the word *must* in a directive. The formidable mechanism for the moulding of minds moved rapidly into highest gear. During the following months propaganda for birth-control reached the intensity and the thoroughness which the Party apparatus reserves only for subjects with the highest priority. A wave of lectures, meetings, pamphlets, slides and films swept the country. Posters and slogans were pasted on millions of walls. Exhibitions were organized in towns and travelling exhibitions visited smaller localities and villages. They displayed pictures showing harassed parents surrounded by a numerous and screaming offspring preventing them getting on with their work. In contrast, other pictures depicted small families with two or three children only and with parents enjoying their leisure and doing their work unharassed by their progeny. If for thousands of years the Chinese have been taught to venerate the large family, now talkative woman guides were explaining to amazed throngs on animated diagrams the complete and intimate details of methods for the prevention of conception. The stark realism of pictures, models and posters left nothing to imagination and they were clearly designed with the aim not to leave even the dumbest peasant woman in doubt about how to proceed.[28] In the meantime a flow of newspaper and magazine articles were spreading the knowledge of birth-control. Comic-strip booklets, talks on the radio and exhortations on the factory notice-boards served the same purpose. From Manchuria to the borders of Tibet, few men or women could have remained ignorant of how and what they were expected to do.

Then, as suddenly as the storm came, it was over. By the end of the year there were no more lectures, no more films, no meetings; the posters and the slogans were allowed to pale, and the exhibitions were closed down. Just when at its height the campaign was abruptly turned off. If it was patriotic to limit the size of one's family, it became a bourgeois aberration a little later.

The contraceptives remained available in the shops and the birth-control clinics were left open. But they were no longer popularized. Of the four contraceptive factories opened during the campaign, two were closed down. Gradually the virtues of a large population were again extolled.

When, in March, 1959, in Peking, I visited Madame Shu Fu-ching, head of the Health Ministry's department for mother-and-child welfare, and wanted to find out what was achieved by birth-control, she valiantly tried to convince me that the campaign had never really existed. When I recalled that in 1957 her own Minister made an impassioned plea for it, and that shortly afterwards millions of square yards of wall were covered by posters and pictures describing how it should be practised, I had to regret making her feel uncomfortable. 'The aim was merely to improve the health of mothers; to teach them how to space pregnancies. . . . In any case, why shouldn't we be happy if our population grows faster?' she asked with engaging innocence. 'We need more people to spread our development.'

Madame Shu, of course, was not the only one who wanted to forget. That staggering uniformity born of fear led to my getting about the same answer from everyone to whom I put the same question. Clearly, sometime in the autumn of 1957, the important decision must have been taken to halt the feverish birth-control campaign and to rekindle the flames of the anti-Malthusian war. The more babies the better, so it seemed to have been ordered from somewhere near the top. Birth-control suddenly became an unpronounceable word. And to make it sure that the new decision was duly appreciated, as usual, scapegoats had to be found.

In view of the dimensions of the campaign, they were not difficult to find. Yet even in the pinning down of responsibility, mass campaigns need simplification. The uncomfortable role, finally, was given to Dr. Ma Yin-chu, a scholar of repute and President of Peking University.

His contribution to the problem and his subsequent denunciation constitute not merely an intriguing episode in China's treatment of her population problem, but may even throw some light on why the birth-control campaign was so suddenly given up.

On July 3, 1957, with the campaign approaching its peak, Dr. Ma read out a paper before the first National People's Congress, entitled *A New Theory of Population*. Explaining why, in his view, China's population growth would become even faster with all the care showered on the masses, and that already it was expanding much faster than the assumed 2 per cent., Dr. Ma continued: 'Though production has increased, national consumption has also grown. The way to increase capital formation is not to cut down consumption but to cut down the number of people. . . . My Principle of Population is different from that of Malthus. I believe that the more developed the Socialist enterprises are, the more expanded will mechanization and automation become. A thing which formerly required a thousand persons to accomplish will require only fifty. Then, may I ask, what are we going to do with the 950 persons? For this reason I am worried that with more people we cannot become mechanized and automatized at a high speed. . . .' After this, referring to low productivity in the countryside, he described that in some provinces 'there appeared recently the phenomenon of using manpower to pull the plough because many draft animals died and many of the living ones were lean and weak, thus still more adversely affecting agricultural production . . .' Then, insisting once again that rapid population growth lessens the chances of capital accumulation and, therefore, of speedy industrialization, Dr. Ma summarized his thesis: '. . . For this reason, if we do not try to solve the population problem at an early date, sooner or later the peasants will change all the favours and kindness they have received into feelings of despair and discontent; and though the result may not be the same as what happened in Poland and Hungary, it inevitably will bring a lot of headaches for the Government. Hence, I advocate the elevation of peasants' labour productivity, accumulating capital on the one hand, and controlling population on the other. Otherwise we would simply make efforts in vain.'[29]

There is evidently nothing particularly original in Dr. Ma's thesis to justify the virulent attacks which were to come later on. Where he may have overstepped prudent limits was in his unconcealed pessimism concerning the peasants' lot and, in particular, in his implied suggestion that rural discontent might lead to an explosion of the Eastern European kind. His principal fault, however, was simply that he failed to foresee that official policy may change. Yet the change was there and it relegated population control to a vague and distant future.

'It is the people who create social wealth', summed up the new line in an official commentary later on. 'Rapid development of socialist production is the essential way to solve the population and employment questions. But this does not mean that China intends to let her population grow in a blind, uncontrolled way. On the contrary, the socialist system, which has changed the context and nature of the population question, also makes it possible gradually to plan population increase. But the planned birth we advocate is different in principle from the views of the old and new Malthusians. China's aim is to adjust her population growth in such a way as to benefit the whole socialist planned economy and the welfare of the people. With culture and scientific knowledge spreading on a mass scale, the prospect is that planned birth will be progressively understood and accepted by the people.'[30]

Thus, after all, birth-control was not for tomorrow. But what caused this sudden and complete reversal of the earlier attitude?

That birth-control, at best, was a slow remedy must have been known right from the beginning. A more convincing interpretation claims that the hectic campaign made the peasants wonder whether it was not an implied admission that the new régime was unable to fulfill its promises; that, in a sense, it was inviting a vote of no confidence. This may have played a certain role. But subsequent developments have revealed that the real reason had been very different.

If the moment for the beginning of the campaign was determined by the economic difficulties of 1956, paradoxically, its calling off was prompted mainly by their further aggravation throughout 1957. When the decision was taken, China's leaders were already leaning over the alarming economic and political balance sheet of the decisive year of 1957. By then, at least some among them must have been thinking of a totally new approach.

In the meantime the scattered warning lights which had twinkled before them on the control-board by the end of 1956, have become a year later a thousand red lights urgently calling for some new and sweeping remedy.

7 1957: The Year of 1000 Red Lights

AS RINGS IN a tree stump give away its age, so the layers which have to be cleared away to get at the origin of a decision, give away its importance.

The decision in question is the sudden ending of the birth-control campaign in the autumn of 1957; a decision which, as it later became known, was merely the prelude to much more important revolutionary developments.

The chain leads back to the bumper harvest in the closing months of 1955. The year after was dedicated to the rapid extension of the state's grip on all economic activities. Handicrafts were taken over by co-operatives. Whatever private industry or commerce still remained came under joint state control by entire trades. Soon, not a single ambulant street-vendor remained outside some state-controlled association. Above all, private property was being eliminated from the lives of the biggest peasant mass in the world.

Admittedly the Chinese peasant was more amenable to persuasion and pressure than his Russian counterpart. His past had been very different. But the question still remained open whether an enterprise so speedy and of such dimensions could be accomplished without the very methods which were by then openly denounced in the Soviet Union?

For in Russia the liquidation of Stalinism was gathering momentum. Khrushchev's 'secret' revelations about Stalin's methods were already known all over the world. Still, not till April, 1956, did the *People's Daily* of Peking join the rising chorus of condemnation. Stalin's errors were analysed with studied detachment, without a hint that they may have been part of the price a backward country had to pay for too rapid industrialization. Given the fact that mass collectivization of the Russian countryside brought with it the large scale application of Stalinist terror, with the same process just getting under way in China this was the least opportune moment to push analysis too far.

If the Soviet Union could afford to relax, China was still obliged to cut off increasing slices from the small incomes of her citizens. Nor, for all the virtuosity of Chinese leadership, could this be done entirely free of tension. The exclusion from the Party, in the spring of 1955, of nine important dignitaries revealed dissension in the highest spheres. Then, the mysterious suicide in jail of Kao Kang, a former chief planner and the master of Manchuria's economy, only further underlined the malaise. Clearly, behind the monolithic façade of uninterrupted success, China's revolution, too, could devour its children.

Traditionally, power in China rested on two pillars: on the intellectuals and on the peasants. Succumbing to successive waves of indoctrination campaigns, the intellectuals appeared disciplined. The rare recalcitrants had to pay dearly for their individualism. They were humiliated and heavy punishments were inflicted on them if they dared to defy the Party's directives. The branding and incarceration, with all the attendant publicity and incitement, in 1955, of Hu Feng and his literary friends, was to convince all the potential heretics that they were not yet to have the freedoms which their Soviet colleagues were slowly being accorded. And the crushing weight of mental conformity was producing its results. A few rebels apart, methods of indoctrination seemed to work so well that by 1956 China had become intellectually as stagnant as she was when Confucianism moulded the minds of the educated élite. Indeed there was the danger that the hundred thousand or so 'superior intellectuals'—to whom Chou En-lai was to address himself later on—were growing dangerously sterile. Rigid ideological controls were stifling the creative initiative of this tiny but precious minority and, to that extent, hampering even the nation's development programme.

As for the peasants, the cadres were at work in their villages. The diagrams depicting the number of collectives were rising vertiginously. The ways of living of enormous masses were being changed with brutal rapidity. There were inevitable difficulties and even some evidence of resistance. In the countryside the real test was yet to come. And no one could be certain whether, in the end, the peasants might not turn against the very government they have helped to power.

The time had come to open the safety valves. And to begin with, it was tried on the side of the intellectuals.

The careful loosening started with a conference of scientists and intellectuals, convened in January, 1956. Addressing them, Chou En-lai noted that of the hundred thousand 'superior intellectuals' of the country, 40 per cent. only had a 'positive attitude' and implored the rest to become active workers of Socialism and, if possible, to join the Party.[31] He also invited them to put forward non-conformist views and promised them more liberal treatment. Early in May, writing on the occasion of *Youth Day*, the *People's Daily* encouraged students to rely on 'independent thinking' and not 'just to say what others have said, and do what others have done'. Other publications took up the same line, extolling the merits of more controversy and freer discussion. Declaring that intellectuals were too valuable to be ostracized simply because they had been trained in the West, the Prime Minister himself asked a gathering of scientists to study techniques employed in Western countries. Finally, on May 26, Lu Ting-yi, chief of the Propaganda Department, speaking to artists, writers and scientists, launched the celebrated phrase of 'Let a hundred flowers blossom and diverse schools of thoughts contend'.

So far the new campaign had been directed chiefly towards professors and scientists and no one was left in any doubt that the new liberties were to remain within the framework of general support for the régime, and for its Marxist-Leninist creed. Though only too ready to give vent to their revolt against political dragooning, China's non-Communist intellectuals were measuring the assurances and the risks. The memories of the fate of Hu Feng and the other victims of premature liberalism were still fresh in their memories. Yet the post-Stalinian ferment was spreading. Moreover, in the autumn of 1956 the news arrived of the Hungarian insurrection. That even a long-established and well-organized Communist régime might be shaken by the popular forces of discontent, could not have failed to impress many among China's 'superior intellectuals' whom Chou En-lai had admonished for their 'non-positive' attitude. That much Mao Tse-tung himself admitted in February next year. 'Certain people in our country were delighted when the Hungarian events took place,' he went on to say. 'They hoped that something similar would happen in China.' Undoubtedly, the news from Eastern Europe spread doubt even among the highest leaders. The voices of the rigid and of the doctrinaire became audible, calling for an end to further liberalisation. For a few weeks it seemed that, barely opened, the safety valve would soon be closed again.

But on February 27, 1957, Mao Tse-tung delivered a four-hour discourse to the Supreme State Council which was a spectacular opening to that exceptionally important year. Though his speech, entitled *On the Correct Resolution of Contradictions among the People* was not published before June, and by then only in a revised form, its essential points transpired in subsequent articles in the *People's Daily*.

First of all it soon became plain that Mao came down on the side of the liberals. He re-launched the phrase about the 'Hundred Flowers'. The doctrinaries were told that Marxism can only benefit from reasoned argument, 'free from one-sided arbitrary sectarianism'. Also gradually revealed was what Mao had to say about 'contradictions' between the people and their leaders. These 'contradictions'—by implication, the people's discontent with prolonged austerity, the lack of consumer goods and harsh methods—may indeed arise from the bureaucratic attitude of some leaders who, having attained power 'are unwilling to listen to the views of the masses and even rudely suppress their opinions and demands. . . . Leaders must study the suggestions of the masses, earnestly carry out those that are practical and explain publicly why some are not. . . .'

Mao's strictures clearly foreshadowed the decision of the Central Committee, revealed on April 27, to launch immediately a 'campaign of rectification of its working methods'. Members were urged to free themselves with the aid of 'criticism and self-criticism' of the triple shortcoming of 'sectarianism, bureaucratism and subjectivism'. Next month the rectification campaign was extended to the small, auxiliary parties within the government coalition and, soon after, to those belonging to no party.[32]

All these categories were only too ready to oblige. Articles, speeches, declarations and public accusations soon mounted to a violent crescendo. All the hidden irritation and resentment piled up during the previous years burst out in a veritable explosion of discontent. The agitation spread like the plague and was beginning to gain the Universities. Despite continuous indoctrination the critical faculty of important groups of Chinese intellectuals survived evidently unimpaired. Their bitter criticism first aimed mainly at the methods of the Party and its activists but soon began to question even the primacy of the Communists itself. Clearly, the campaign was getting out of hand. It had to be checked.

On June 8, 1957, down dropped the guillotine. A severe editorial in the *People's Daily* set the tone of the counter-offensive. Critics were branded 'rightists', a terrible label that has been casting its shadow over Chinese politics ever since. Indignation was further reinforced by implied accusations of counter-revolutionary activities. The 'rightists' who, in the words of the paper, were 'not just talkers, but doers' would be punished 'only in cases where, despite repeated warnings, they refuse to mend their ways and continue their sabotage and violation of the law. . . .' Then, a few days later, revised to suit the changed atmosphere, Mao Tse-tung's February speech was published.[33] And according to the modified text some 'internal contradictions' were to be dealt with severely.

The rectification campaign was reversed within a few days. It became a violent hunt to expose bourgeois tendencies and anti-Socialist elements, and to spot and to expose 'rightists'. Politicians, professors, artists and writers, all who had responded to the original invitation to express their griefs, were to make grovelling public confessions of guilt prefaced and wound up by fulsome tributes to 'the inspired leadership of the glorious Communist Party'. They were to go through the ritual of humiliating self-accusations, the denunciation of colleagues and relatives, and were to compose abject dissertations analysing their base motives which had prompted their treacherous attitudes. 'Poisonous weeds have freedom of growth, but we have the responsibility of eradicating them,' said Kuo Mo-jo, President of the Academy of Sciences. 'Serpents,' argued the *People's Daily*, 'can only be exterminated if they are brought out into the open. . . .' And the hurricane was soon to sweep through every locality and through every organization all across the country.

That after only a month of relatively free criticism the Communists retaliated with a deadly 'anti-rightist' campaign directed at the régime's political opponents, has been interpreted in various ways. Sceptics maintain that it was merely a cynical trap to induce critics to commit themselves. Others, referring to Mao's February speech, see in the events a genuine tentative of liberalization. If for no other reason but for the steady worsening of the economic situation and for the events in Eastern Europe, the bridging of the gap between the régime and the intelligentsia had been urgent. Moreover, the healing of 'internal contradictions' with all the medicaments of persuasion and re-education was a deeply rooted idea in Chinese thinking even before Mao redefined it in his February speech. According to this interpretation, then, the amount of bitterness and disaffection brought to light must have caused pained surprise and real distress to the leadership and, even if reluctantly, obliged it to counter-attack. Yet, whatever the real motives had been, the campaign against the 'rightists' served a supplementary purpose. It enabled the Communists to purge the small, auxiliary parties in the coalition and thus to deprive them of any pretentions of ever becoming a potential opposition.

These small parties represented groups who had gone over to the Communists during the civil war and, though shorn of all real power or influence, were permitted to exist as distinct political units in coalition with the Communist Party. This arrangement enabled the Communists to dispose of the managerial and technical experience of their members. In exchange for their political subordination some of them were given high posts, even ministerial portfolios in some of the technical departments.[34] The coalition worked smoothly during the preceding years. But as long as organized parties other than the Communist remained in existence, they provided at least a potential nucleus for an alternative government in case Communist control weakened. The exceptional political and economic strains of 1957 provided the first occasion since the change of régime when the more sanguine among the auxiliary parties' leaders may have entertained such hopes. This may provide at least a partial explanation why, when the liberalization attempt was abandoned, its aftermath was utilized for the decapitation and—through the abject confessions of their leaders—for the self-degradation of these surviving, distinct political formations.

Rather than strengthening the bonds between the government and the non-Communist intellectuals, then, the net result of the hectic political spring was instead the intensification of the frictions which divided them. The discontent of the Chinese intelligentsia was driven even deeper underground. True, the government's control of the country came out of the storm reinforced. The more rigid among the leaders triumphed and their influence seems to be in the ascendant. But the initial purpose has misfired.

Failure with the intellectuals, however, rendered it all the more urgent to relieve pressure on the population as a whole. Concessions to the peasants and to consumers in general, seemed to be the logical counterpart to render the situation less explosive. And while the rings of the anti-rightist campaigns were spreading wider and wider, the other safety-valve, this time on the side of the peasantry, was cautiously loosened.

The official version of Mao Tse-tung's February speech—as published in June, after revision by its author—insisted that forced savings should not be 'overdone' and hinted even that higher priority should be accorded to light industries and to investments in agriculture. It would not matter greatly, the text implied, how many years it would take to 'consolidate' the new collectives.

The need for a pause was felt. News from the economic front could leave no doubt.

In the seventh year of the Communist régime it was abundantly clear that economic growth depended closely on the output of the land. The amount of savings from which investments could be made mirrored the volume of the previous year's harvest.[35] If 1955 brought a record crop, the year after was mediocre. Then, in 1957, though collectivization was still making phenomenal progress, there were signs that a good many of the new units were not yet functioning in a satisfactory way. Many were still in a confused state and some were reported even to withhold grain and other commodities from the authorities. Also there were natural calamities again. Though they affected a smaller area than the year before, still, the cropping surface in 1957 was reduced by two million hectares. The irrigated area, too, expanded slower than during the preceding year.[36]

With the enormous stepping up of investments in 1956 the state appeared to have overstepped the consumers' tolerance. Both urban wages and the labour force expanded beyond expectation and the new collectives needed more loans for their consolidation than was foreseen. There was more money going around without any corresponding increase in goods on which to spend it. The dreaded symptoms of inflation reappeared and the government was compelled to raise retail prices and to make rationing more severe. For the average person in China 1957 was a year of rigid belt-tightening. Not only the major investment projects had to be curtailed but there occurred the first general reduction in the budget since the start of the Five-Year Plan.

Unemployment, too, was a problem claiming urgent attention. Driven by worsening living conditions in the villages, there was a 'blind flow of peasants to the cities'. Yet employment opportunities in the towns had already been lagging behind the number of the new entrants into the labour force.[37] Urgent remedy was needed and a nation-wide campaign was initiated to reverse the movement, and to send peasants back to the villages. The age-old scholastic Chinese contempt for manual labour had already been broken by several years of intense propaganda. Now, in any case, the anti-rightists campaign yielded large numbers of intellectuals, government employees, students and other urban workers for more or less prolonged periods of forced intimacy with the 'everyday realities' of the countryside. The Chinese Communists' faith in re-education through labour was here conveniently married to economic and political aims. In fact, from the middle of 1957 onwards, an ever-growing number of redundant or politically unreliable city dwellers were being sent to the countryside to aid field work or to be enrolled in labour gangs executing various public works projects.

To complete the sombre picture, by 1957 China reached the bottom of the barrel of Soviet aid. The official budget figures for that year revealed that while only $10 million of Soviet credits remained, in contrast, repayment of past loans and interest payments amounted to $271 million in 1957. More plainly, in 1957 over a tenth of all China's exports went simply to repay and to service already exhausted Soviet loans.[38]

The impact of all these circumstances seemed to force the State to retreat. Cuts were to be made in practically every sector of the nation's economy. Capital construction was deprived of a fifth of its initial allocation. National defence lost a tenth of its original share. When speaking to the National People's Congress in June, Chou En-lai revealed that instead of the projected 18 per cent. increase in production as a whole, only 4·5 per cent. would be accomplished. It became known that the economy drive was reaching down even to the quality of fodder fed to army horses. But the most alarming news of all emerged only after the summer and winter harvests were gathered in. They fell far short of what the enthusiasts of sweeping collectivization had expected. In fact, food output during 1957 increased by 1·3 per cent. only (from 182·5 to less than 185 million tons). It was the first year since the Communists came into power when population grew faster than the amount of food at their disposal.

Whether these difficulties were foreseen and were at the origin of the 'rectification campaign' of the spring or, inversely, whether they were unexpected and have merely helped to accentuate the repression once liberalization had misfired, is anybody's guess. Be as it may, the problem of assuring a tolerable standard of living to the population came to dominate all others. Yet the basic tenets of the régime were at stake. Should investments in agriculture be sharply increased during the second Plan? and could this be done without endangering the basic aim of the rapid creation of a heavy industrial base? Like the successful and self-confident mountaineer who suddenly finds himself losing his balance and slipping back on a steep slope, for the first time, the Chinese Communist régime appeared to be hesitating about the decisions to take.

That for years back there had been serious misgivings about too hasty collectivization was no secret. Already in 1955 Vice-

Premier Chen Yi spoke of 'rightists' who argued 'on the question of the co-operativization of agriculture within the Party during the past three years'. With the tremendous speeding up of collectivization both the numbers and the anxiety of the critics must have grown. Their objections even appeared to have been listened to when, in September, the Central Committee issued new directives: '. . . experiences in different localities during the last few years have proved that large collectives and large teams are generally not adaptable to the present production conditions . . .', read the most important among them.[39] '. . . Therefore, except the few that have been well managed, all those that are too big and not well managed should be divided into smaller units in accordance with the wishes of members. Henceforth, a collective should generally be of the size of a village with over 100 households. . . . As to the size of production teams, twenty neighbouring households is the proper number. . . .' Moreover, '. . . After the size of the collectives and production teams has been decided upon, it should be publicly announced that this organization will remain unchanged in the next ten years. . . .'

Thus, far from any further advance towards even larger units, reduction first and consolidation after. If the radicals gained the upper hand after the 'rectification campaign' on the political scene, by the autumn the moderates appeared to be winning on the economic front.

Their victory, however, was very short-lived.

Only ten days later another directive already revealed some hesitation. Then, an editorial in the October issue of the Planning Commission's official publication foreshadowed in its very title the change to come: 'Industrial Development Requires Simultaneous Development of Agriculture.'[40] That this simultaneous development was not to be to the detriment of speedy industrialization became clear on October 25, when the revised draft of the twelve-year agricultural development programme (1956-67) was published. For the first time, it revealed that below the surface waves of boldness and hesitation, the Communist leadership had been re-thinking its economic policies and was feeling its way towards decisive and revolutionary modifications. A totally new approach, a kind of economic short-cut was needed. And very soon it became clear that China's leaders have not lost their capacity to innovate and, if need be, even to gamble when faced with overpowering problems.

An inconspicuous passage in Mao Tse-tung's speech published in June, suddenly supplied the key to the ideas germinating in the secret councils. 'We have a population of six hundred million . . .', he said '. . . this is an objective fact and . . . this is our asset. We have this large population. It is a good thing. . . .' And in preparation for the forthcoming demonstration that China's fast expanding population was a 'good thing' or, at any rate, that it could be turned into an 'asset', the feverish birth-control campaign was unceremoniously buried in November, only seven months after it had been launched.

Twenty-three years earlier, in Kiangsi, too, China's Communist leaders felt that the ring was closing around them. After much deliberation, they had taken then the heroic decision to break through the blockade and to undertake an arduous, long trek towards a new base where their experiment would be beyond the enemy's strangling hand.

That was the *Long March*. This time, it was to be another arduous break-through. And it became known as the *Great Leap Forward*.

8 The Mass Mobilization of 1958

FOLLOWING THE autumn harvest of 1957 travellers in China have witnessed an extraordinary film racing past the windows of their trains. The countryside was in convulsion. Marching in columns and working in dense crowds, immense peasant masses were spending their over-spilling energy. As in some fabulous pantomime, innumerable men, women and adolescents were on the move, perpetually purposeful and with apparently precise

missions. Enormous crowds were carrying sand to swell embank-
ments along rivers. Innumerable little figures were swinging their
shovels to dig new canals. Marchers in formation were following
coloured flags on bamboo poles, on their way to replace teams
laying railway tracks. Monumental ant-heaps were busy on the
sites of future reservoirs. Endless lines of blue-clad men and
women were filing up mountain-sides like some unnatural
stream changing its course. In the background, scattered all over
the fields, multitudes of people were moving around with two
buckets hanging from their shoulder poles. All together, they
recalled the rhythmic breathing of some mythological colossus,
suddenly awakened and flexing its milliard muscles in a supreme
effort to change the face of the earth.

By the beginning of 1958 the phenomenal mobilization of the
masses was general all over China. Hundreds of millions of people
were bending their backs to lift their country to a new level. An
emotional fervour such as arises in the critical periods of a great
war was moving the innumerable, nameless individuals. Twenty
or thirty million people were gathering natural fertilizers. Thirty,
or perhaps forty million were digging canals. Fifty or seventy
million, probably no one knew the exact number, were working
on afforestation. Ceaselessly, without a rest, new and even bigger
masses were hurled into the battle of production like armies
thrown in to reinforce the critical sectors of a fighting front. As
in the engines of an aircraft preparing for the supreme effort of
the take-off, every particle of the huge and complicated mechanism was working at top speed, each driven to the limit of its
physical endurance.

Visibly, China was entering upon her climacteric years.

The gigantic organizational effort, however, was merely the
translation into reality of what had been foreshadowed in the
twelve-year plan for agriculture. It had prescribed enormous
increases in output and in yields. It had called for an end to
erosion and for liberation from the hazards of droughts and
floods. It had envisaged giant belts of forests to protect fertile land
from the deserts. Above all, it had demanded a totally new
experiment in social engineering.

The underlying idea of this new approach was implied in a speech by Chou En-lai, in January, 1956. At the time it sounded like an inoffensive arithmetical exercise rather than the blue-print destined to revolutionize China's life.

China has 120 million peasant families, each representing the labour capacity of one and a half persons, the Premier said. These 180 million workers were often without work for up to a hundred or more days a year. When the new, twelve-year plan was put into practice, each able-bodied man would have to furnish 250 days of work a year; and each woman 120. Every family, then, would offer a yearly 370 work-days, or 44·4 milliard days of labour for the whole country. But as work devoted to the fields represents no more than about two-thirds of the normal daily activities of the peasant, the remaining third—or another 14·8 milliard work-days—would become available for other tasks. They could be devoted, the Premier continued, to the increase of production; to political work, or to other economic, cultural, educational or sanitary activities.[41]

Throughout 1957 the major problem facing the government was to dispose of more capital for investment in agriculture without, at the same time, being forced to reduce the share of the privileged sector of heavy industries. Thus, the solution was to be found in the hitherto untapped 15 milliard labour days.

In the north of China work used to be over in October and, normally, the peasant had little useful work to do until the spring when the ground had thawed out. But in China as a whole, as in practically all the economically backward agrarian countries, peasants are idle during the slack season. According to circumstances they work from 100 to 200 days a year and hardly ever all the year round. So, especially in densely populated agrarian countries, the villages store large quantities of unutilized, surplus manpower. Moreover, next to this total unemployment, there is also the large-scale concealed unemployment of those who do merely occasional jobs or whose labour is really needed during the ploughing, sowing and harvesting periods only.

The task, then, would be to employ fully those who are really indispensable on the land; to direct to other tasks the surplus labour; and, finally, to organize into mobile teams and to render 'interchangeable' those whose presence in their villages is needed for brief periods only. The project is certainly logical and the task sounds relatively simple. Yet if China was the first country with the imagination and the drive to try its execution on a large scale, that was mainly because none of the under-developed countries have ever commanded the organizational apparatus to attempt such a mobilization of its idle hands.

Collectivization of the countryside was practically completed. Criticism and discontent, whether in the towns or in the villages, were stamped out by the steam-roller of the anti-rightist campaigns. The doctrinal extremists and the partisans of swift and bold action seemed to triumph within the highest councils of the Party. Thus, the moment must have appeared propitious to them to exploit their victory and to drive on towards even bolder improvizations, promising still more spectacular results.

What the traveller could see from the window of his train was the awe-inspiring process of turning those 15 milliard wasted labour days into capital. It was a tremendous and original experiment and, like a magic carpet, it promised at last to accomplish China's take-off and to leave behind the difficulties of the past. What is more, thanks to the inexhaustible energy and endurance of the Chinese masses, the gamble soon appeared to be turning into a success. Less than half a year after the experiment was launched, the country was invited to examine the first, victorious balance-sheet.

'The spring of 1958 witnessed the beginning of a leap forward on every front. . . . Industry, agriculture and all other fields of activity are registering greater and more rapid growth,' Liu Shao-chi reported by the spring.[42] 'The upsurge in agriculture last winter and this spring gave a vigorous push to the new industrial upsurge of this year. . . . In agriculture, the most striking leap took place . . . (in the building of) . . . irrigation works. From last October to April this year, the irrigated acreage through out the country increased by 350 million *mu* . . . (that is) . . . 110 million *mu* more than the total acreage brought under irrigation in the thousands of years before liberation. . . .'[43]

The victory bulletin continued to list equally extraordinary results in other fields. During the first four months of 1958 production in general was 26 per cent. higher than in the same period of the previous year. Comparable progress was registered in soil improvement, in the accumulation of natural fertilizers, in afforestation, as well as in the mass movement to improve farm tools.

But the triumphant statistics were accompanied by meaningful political salvoes. Those who regarded the great achievements of 1956—or, in plainer language, the inordinate stepping up of investments in heavy industry—as a 'reckless advance' have, with their pessimism, 'dampened the initiative of the masses and hampered progress . . . in 1957, and particularly on the agricultural front'. Having thus fixed the blame for the disappointments of 1957, and with the unshakable assurance which seemed to imply pride in the paternity of this latest 'reckless advance', Liu Shao-chi continued: '. . . (with the revised twelve-year agricultural plan) . . . the Central Committee . . . issued a militant call to overtake and surpass Britain . . . in fifteen years. Such correct guidance . . . combined with the initiative of the masses evoked by the rectification campaign and the anti-rightist struggle, gave rise to the all-round forward leap which is currently developing on an even larger scale. . . . In putting forward revolutionary tasks in good time, so that there is no half-way halt in the revolutionary advance of the people, the revolutionary fervour of the masses will not subside. . . .'

That this revolutionary fervour was accompanied also by some reluctance, he readily admitted. '. . . As a result of the anti-rightist struggle, the anti-communist, anti-popular and anti-socialist bourgeois rightists have been thoroughly isolated by the masses and their ranks have begun to disintegrate. . . . The anti-rightist struggle has also been of profound significance within our Party. We expelled a number of rightists. . . . They were alien class elements who sneaked into the Party. . . . They developed individualism, sectarianism, localism and nationalism to an extreme degree. . . . In league with the rightists outside the Party, they attacked the Party and the socialist system. . . .' The stern warning was then followed by a review of the critics' points:

'. . . Some people wonder whether the implementation of the (new) policy . . . won't lead to waste. . . . Others are worried that (it) . . . will throw the various branches of production off balance. . . . Some people doubted whether agricultural production could expand very rapidly. . . . Some scholars even asserted that the rate of agricultural growth could not keep pace with the growth of population. . . .' As for the decisive issue '. . . Some comrades are worried that, though the development of agriculture can accumulate funds for industrialization, it will for the present at least divert some funds which could be used by the state for industrialization. . . .'

Leaning over the text of his speech, the taut figure of China's most uncompromising ideologist stiffened as he proceeded to demolish one by one the arguments of his more prudent colleagues and opponents. As for the last and major objection, Liu Shao-chi's rebuttal was outspoken: '. . . The upsurge in agriculture in 1956 and 1958 have proved such worries unnecessary. So long as we know how to rely on this great force of our 500 million peasants, we can greatly expand the scope of agricultural construction even if there is no increase in state investments in agriculture. . . .'

This was clear enough. The immense mobilization of the masses was not to bring better living for them. Anyway, not yet. Moreover, it was only natural that Liu Shao-chi personally should explain 'how to rely' on the great force of the masses. Since Yenan days it has been he, more even than Mao Tse-tung, who occupied himself with the theory and practice of organization. Prior to 1949 almost all of his known speeches and writings dealt with methods of organization, with discipline, and with the techniques of mass-movements. Unrivalled master of the psychological keyboard, his role was bound to grow even more decisive each time the activities of the Chinese masses were to undergo a further acceleration. Thus, to forestall eventual opposition to the continuous leap decreed, Liu Shao-chi himself announced that new campaigns of indoctrination were on the way. In the '. . . enterprises, offices, organizations, schools and army units where reforms have been carried out, the rectification campaign will soon enter the fourth stage when each individual studies documents, and undertakes self-criticism and self-examination so as to raise his own ideological level. . . '. All categories of people '. . . must be given help in educating and remoulding themselves'. Thus, '. . . from now on the method of the rectification campaign, the method of criticism and self-criticism through full and frank airing of views, great debates and posting *tatsepao* must be made the regular method of reforming ideology and improving work. All-round rectification campaigns should be launched at set intervals. . . .'[44]

For the time being there was little more to offer in exchange than the promise that '. . . within a very short historical period' China will 'certainly leave every capitalist country in the world far behind . . .'. Until then '. . . we have a population of more than 600 million and our Party has ties of flesh and blood with this vast population. By relying on this great force we can, or soon can do anything within the realm of human possibility. . . .'

That was in May, 1958.

As promised, the rectification campaigns continued to come in regular waves. The number of those in labour-camps, who were re-educating themselves through hard labour, must have been on the increase. Again and again millions were to tell and then to recount their life-stories, to analyse their past failings, to make public confessions and, finally, to promise to mend their ways. The peculiar bloodless form of terrorism that is China's special contribution to dictatorial techniques, produced refined new gadgets. Millions of men, women and children all over the country were painting *tatsepao*. Pupils were scribbling denunciations of their teachers on them and the teachers were criticizing each other or themselves. The ubiquitous street committees were driving all to stigmatize everyone else until even the *People's Daily* printed a letter by hapless clerks complaining that after all the *tatsepao* painting and all the anti-waste and rectification meetings they had no time left to carry out the suggestions they had received. Then, in conformity with the new policy of industrial decentralization, villagers began to build simple machines and improvise 'industries'. The first, tiny blast furnaces made of mud bricks were making their appearance in the countryside. Millions of office employees, civil servants and intellectuals were joining the ranks of the rural workers. In the meantime the dense peasant columns continued to move across the fields. Backs were bending even lower under the weight of even heavier buckets hanging from the shoulder poles. The new canals were growing longer and the new railways were crawling deeper into deserts. The Chinese continued to live in an intoxicating forest of steeply rising production curves. New record-breaking figures were being announced with the exultation of military victories. The muscles continued to stretch and then to contract again, and China was building faster and producing more.

The break-through, at last, was within sight. The first of the three years of extraordinary effort asked for in place of the second Plan, was beginning to yield its results. And, as the authorities never tired to repeat, the revolution was to continue 'uninterrupted'.

While a mid-year report triumphantly announced that industrial output was one-third higher than during the first half of the preceding year, and that food crops in 1958 would increase by more than during the whole Five-Year Plan, the world learned with amazement that shortage of labour was developing China. The mobilization of the masses was total. The exploitation of idle manpower had reached its limits. Yet the new canals were there and even more people were needed to divert the water to the crops. The simple village industries were built but there were not enough hands to mine and to carry the coal, the iron-ore and the other raw materials needed to feed them. Tremendous quantities of fertilizers had been collected but the shoulders were lacking to carry the buckets in which to distribute them over the fields. To accomplish all these tasks in order to take full advantage of the labour already invested, at whatever cost, even more labour had to be found.

Here and there common mess halls were put up to save the time spent in walking long distances for meals at home. The newcomers disgorged by the cities were soon absorbed in the work brigades. But all this was inadequate and more and more women were inducted in the labour force. Before their numbers could seriously increase, however, a solution was needed to replace their work in their homes. Even more mess halls were organized. Sewing teams and nurseries were improvised and someone had to be left behind in charge of the babies and the aged. Yet, with multiplying improvisations and with large masses of peasants and their womenfolk working on different jobs far away from their homes, the need was felt for more effective, comprehensive solutions. Inevitably, thinking went in the direction of even larger units able to co-ordinate all the tasks under execution, to enforce labour discipline, to allot daily tasks to the veritable armies of labourers, as well as to plan the activities of all the canteens, the nurseries, the sewing teams or the centres for the aged.

The Great Leap was imposed simultaneously on agriculture, on industry and on various other activities. Within and outside the collectives, the new strains compelled various interests to compete for more capital, for more land, as well as for more labour. For many of the enterprises undertaken the size of the collective had become restrictive. Instead of darting around breathlessly stopping leaks in the dam and then declaring it impermeable, a new total solution was needed. It was against this background, and in order to avoid chaos, that yet another reorganization of the Chinese countryside was decided.

A few, scattered hints apart, the public was not prepared for the new upheaval either by the press, the radio or by the meetings which usually herald such decisions. Beyond the feverish bustle of the Great Leap, the pounding of Quemoy by Chinese coastal batteries was diverting people's attention. Then, in its ceaseless effort to reshape Chinese society, on August 29, unexpectedly, the Communist hammer delivered its decisive blow.

On that day, meeting at Peitaiho, the Central Committee formally adopted a Resolution on the establishment of People's Communes all over the rural areas. 'The People's Communes are the logical result of the march of events', the text began. 'Large, comprehensive People's Communes have made their appearance. . . . They have developed very rapidly in some areas. It is highly probable that there will soon be an upsurge in setting up People's Communes throughout the country and the development is irresistible. . . . Large-scale agricultural capital construction and the application of more advanced agricultural techniques are making demands on labour power. The growth of rural industry also demands the transfer of some manpower from agriculture. The demand for mechanization and electrification has become increasingly urgent in China's rural areas. Capital construction in agriculture and the struggle for bumper harvests involve large-scale co-operation which cuts across the boundaries between co-operatives, townships and counties. The people have taken to organizing themselves along military lines, to work with militancy, and to lead a collective life, and this has raised the political consciousness of the 500 million peasants still further. Community dining-rooms, kindergartens, nurseries, tailoring groups, barber shops, public baths, "happy homes" for the aged, agricultural middle schools, "red and expert" schools, are leading the peasants towards a happier collective life. . . .'[45]

Before concluding on an optimistic note, saying that '. . . It seems that the attainment of communism in China is no longer a remote future event . . .', the Resolution also referred to the speed of the coming transformation. It would depend on local conditions but '. . . no matter when the merger (of the collectives) takes place, whether before or after autumn, in the coming winter or next spring . . .' plans should be worked out jointly and in advance for an even bigger harvest next year.[46]

Only three days later, the Central Committee's theoretical fortnightly, the bible of all activists, was emphasizing the practical considerations which have led to the establishment of People's Communes. They would provide a suitable frame for the development of small and medium industrial enterprises. They were needed as the collectives '. . . can no longer meet the requirements of the development of the productive forces'. Then, '. . . to make full use of labour power, to enable women to play their full part in field work and to ensure that there is no waste of the labour time of men and women' the People's Communes were the answer.[47] The article devoted particular attention to evident fears caused by the original Resolution's reference to military discipline. 'Although the organization of agricultural labour along military lines at present is for waging battles against nature and not human enemies, it is none the less not difficult to transform one kind of struggle into another. . . .' That the formation of a militia in the Communes was giving rise to widespread anxiety, was acknowledged by the even more detailed refutation of the dangers of 'commandism': 'In our opinion,' the journal argued, 'for the People's Communes to be organized along military lines and to arm the entire population is a completely different matter from commandism. Without the People's Communes, without the organization along military lines and without citizen soldiers, commandism can occur all the same. . . . To organize along military lines, to do things the way battle duties are carried out and to live collective lives certainly does not mean that the intensity of labour should be infinitely stretched. . . .' And in case the prospect of working under armed surveillance still alarmed the peasants, the journal ended on a liberal note: '. . . Only through a full airing of views and debates, only when the people in a locality are willing to go in for it entirely out of their own accord, should the agricultural (collectives) be transformed into People's Communes. . . .'[48]

Barely were the Resolution and this article printed when it was given to understand that the government expected that the movement would be completed within a few weeks. With frenetic concentration the propaganda machine began to popularize the new idea. The press and the radio were pouring out reports of peasants celebrating their entry into People's Communes all over the country with music and gay festivities. Entire provinces were 'spontaneously' organizing themselves into Communes and in some places people were even seen to tear down their family huts before moving into communal quarters. Newspapers were inundated with enthusiastic letters from men and women telling in dithyrambic terms of their joy over this latest advance towards the fraternity of this bigger and wider family. And once again the tremendous transformation appeared to be accomplished without any visible sign of serious resistance.

But how to explain the sudden eruption of the idea of People's Communes on the Chinese scene?

Mao Tse-tung, like other Chinese leaders, has more than once expressed his preference for large productive units on the ground that they were more rational. But the Central Committee's directives after the 1957 collectivization drive implied a long period of stabilization and promised no further changes. There was no trace of any ideas resembling the Communes in Mao Tse-tung's celebrated discourse in February, 1957. As late as May, 1958, Liu Shao-chi's speech contained no hint of their coming. It was only in August, and quite unexpectedly for most Chinese, that the newspapers began to speak of 'new socialist relations' appearing between men and pointing to 'a profound change in the spiritual as well as material life of the Chinese people'.[49] It was only by then, that it became known that in Shansi province a new labour organization had been experimented with, complete with mobile labour brigades and with local militia,[50] or that a veritable model People's Commune had been in existence in Hunan province for more than four months.[51] In fact the impression of improvisation seemed to be supported by the wording of the August 29 Resolution itself. In contrast with other directives of such importance, it was loosely formulated. It did not contain the usual minute details and, by implication, almost invited the local cadres to take the initiative and to adapt the general instructions to local conditions.

Recalling the ideas of nineteenth-century utopists or of Russia's abortive experiment with 'agro-towns', some Western commentators promptly suggested that China's new policy was due to the pressure of doctrinaire enthusiasts or even that the desire to outpace the Soviet Union in its advance towards Communism had played a decisive role. The same writers attempted to trace back the origins of the movement right to the launching of the 'Hundred Flowers' experiment. In their view, to expose and then to crush opposition was merely a prelude to the premeditated chain of events bound to culminate in the People's Communes. Though, as usual, ideological predilections have undoubtedly influenced the final shape, such commentaries have discounted all the available evidence that most of the major policy changes in previous years had been determined by essentially practical and empirical considerations. Though impossible to be certain, it seems probable that the decision to resort to People's Communes was taken only shortly before its official announcement.

In the very nature of the rural organization of the Chinese Communist Party, a very large number of totally devoted activists are in constant and intimate contact with the everyday problems of the peasantry. Witnessing the growing shortage of labour, as well as the mounting difficulties and the disruption caused by the Great Leap, it is probable that the village cadres were calling for new directives. It is equally plausible that, simultaneously, at least the devoted and indoctrinated minority of young peasants began to be convinced of the desirability and of the rational advantages of larger organizational units and of mobile labour forces within them. The symptoms and the observations must have been communicated to higher political echelons and, in all probability, new ideas emerged from the dialogue. Throughout the summer the activists were sounding the views of the peasants and, at the same time, they were putting forward suggestions received from above. As it had happened before, with their customary and ruthless efficiency, the cadres went on explaining and popularizing the new ideas until, in Mao Tse-tung's own terms, the masses embraced them as their own, stood up for them and translated them into action.

It is only this way that the official claim of the spontaneity of the movement can at all be taken seriously. It provides at least a partial explanation how a transformation of such magnitude could be accomplished at such speed and with so little violent resistance.[52]

But whatever share pressure from below or the need for emergency solutions have played in the decision, as several times before, rather than determining the rhythm of change, circumstances seemed to be driving the Communist leaders to adopt urgent and desperate remedies. With difficulties mounting on all sides, they were once again forced to seek a new, overall and rational solution to the baffling agricultural problem. Moreover, as always when sudden and bold decisions have to be taken, the extremists and the most impatient were to ride highest on the tidal wave. They were the readiest to take the risks involved. And their growing role inevitably broadened the movement with auxiliary, doctrinaire aims.

Thus the People's Communes promised simultaneous progress on three fronts. They immeasurably strengthened the régime's political grip on the whole population. They also provided a still more perfect instrument to control consumption and to extract the maximum amount of labour and thereby the capital required to maintain the tempo of industrialization. Finally, they offered satisfaction even to those who wished to see in them an imposing, new step forward towards the régime's messianic aims.

In any case, in the exuberant revolutionary gallop towards a fully Communist society, within a few months half a milliard Chinese peasants had been transformed into the salaried workers of a state that, henceforth, was controlling their existence right down to such details as the size and the taste of their meals.

One significant consequence of this historical change became known soon. Investments allotted to agriculture—10 per cent. in 1958—were to diminish still further—to only 7 per cent.—the next year.[53]

Other consequences, not less significant, were to emerge only a few months later.

9 Communes and the Village Steel Industry, 1958-59

THE QE PU People's Commune was one of the 26,000 which were set up during the weeks following the Party's call at the end of August. It was about 50 miles south-west of the great industrial city of Wuhan, in Central China, and together with some local officials, we travelled for about three hours in a jeep to reach it. At regular intervals we passed brightly coloured triumphal arches marking the entrances to newly formed Communes. Finally, we passed through one of them soon after we had left the main road. Gay paint and coloured paper gave it a festive air. Across it a huge red banner announced that in that particular Commune, henceforth, 40,000 people were pooling their energies 'for Socialist construction'.

Mr. Liu, the director of the Commune, was waiting with his staff to greet us in front of the committee building. It was a simple, one-storey wooden edifice facing a large square which seemed to be the centre of a small township. It was flanked by a stone building, now the assembly-hall; by an equally modest house which served as the savings bank; as well as by the grain store and a retail shop displaying daily necessities. With their two buckets hanging from their shoulder poles men and women were moving across the square flooded by the March sunshine. Rather surprisingly, there was a long queue in front of the savings bank. On the white-washed wall opposite the committee building, there was a large drawing in colour, depicting a Chinese volunteer in Korea busy piercing a decrepit tiger whose features recalled those of President Eisenhower. 'In Korea we have shown that they are paper-tigers,' said the string of large characters painted under the caricature.

We climbed the stairs and sat down in a curious, large room where the Commune's management committee usually met. Its walls were completely pasted over by pages of Peking's *People's Daily*. A long table and two benches along it were its only furniture. Facing the entry a large window framed a pleasing view of endless fields dotted with blue figures working and moving along in geometrical formations. We sat down. The director and his collaborators on one side of the table, we on the other. Behind us, a series of coloured prints were nailed on the wall: Mao Tse-tung, Liu Shao-chi and the other leaders. Facing them, above the heads of the Commune officials, were symmetrical prints of Communism's Western prophets: Marx, Engels and Lenin next to Stalin. Mr. Khrushchev's print was not among them.

A mug of green tea was placed in front of us and piles of peanuts were poured along the table which we went on cracking all through the conversation. Mr. Liu was facing me. His colleagues sat next to him, silent and intervening only when the director asked them for some detail.

A stocky man of thirty-three, Mr. Liu appeared to be the personification of the new, rural China. There were the inevitable two fountain pens stuck in the breast pocket of his blue uniform. The latest issue of *Red Flag* was rearing its head from his side pocket while the one on the other side bulged with two, much-fingered copy-books. Time to time he consulted their pages though, as a rule, he relied on his memory. Mr. Liu's face was hard but friendly, capable to respond to a smile. His quick and piercing eyes emphasized that he was a dynamic person though he tended to become tense each time he tried to reconcile strict Party line with an answer to a question he disliked. As so often in conversation with Chinese officials, insistence on details usually provoked his irritated condescension, for any probing beyond the facts he had given he evidently equated with a foreigner's suspicion. But these passing strains apart, the conversation went smoothly and underlying it there was his obvious pride in being the man through whom the almighty state fashioned the lives of 40,000 Chinese.

Mr. Liu, of course, had good reasons to be content or even proud. His father had been a rickshaw-puller in Hankow and he could not afford to offer his son more than three years in school. He became a village labourer. 'I used to pull the plough myself, there were no animals to do the job,' he said. 'I had worked on the land since I was a lad and, before Liberation, I hadn't the slightest idea what Marxism or Communism meant. Never heard of the words, as a matter of fact. . . .' By 1952, however, Mr. Liu was already Party Secretary of his co-operative, not far from there. And, in 1958, when the thirty-nine co-operatives of his region were joined together to form the *Qe Pu* Commune, he had already sufficiently proved his worth to be entrusted with the direction of this new mammoth unit. Overnight he found himself at the head of 8,850 families.

Having, somewhat reluctantly, satisfied my curiosity about his person, Mr. Liu began his exposé. To start with he expressed his indignation with all the 'rumours' spread about the Communes abroad. 'Our managing committee is elected by the assembly which, in its turn, is composed of representatives of every activity and interest within the Commune. The assembly meets twice a year but it may be called together more often. Every member can air his grievances or can offer his suggestions.' Exceptions? Ten people, altogether. They are 'former landlords' or 'reactionaries'. They had been deprived of their political rights and until they regain them they cannot vote. But, Mr. Liu hastened to assure me, they get the same food as the others as 'they too are Chinese'. However, they had to be supervised otherwise they might 'commit sabotage', 'spread rumours' or 'incite people to work less hard'.

As for work, eight hours a day was the rule. But longer hours may be necessary whenever there is urgent work and that is decided by 'common consent'. Two days a month were free and every member had to devote each day two hours to 'cultural activities'. This, it emerged, may mean 'politcal education' or 'technical discussions' both aimed at 'raising the cultural level and the political consciousness of the members'. The number of full-time officials was around thirty and the rest were only part-time functionaries and worked in the fields like the others. The Commune's militia consisted of 3,000 men with only one professional soldier there to train them.

Wages, for the time being, were rather modest. There were seven grades, ranging from 1.50 yuans to 6 yuans in exceptional cases. When Mr. Liu noticed my hesitation whether these were weekly or monthly wages, he broke off with hurt pride: 'They are for a month. But it is more if people surpass the norms. Besides, people get free meals in the canteens, you know . . .', he said with sudden earnestness. 'Three meals each day. There are tens of millions of people in this country who have known what it is to go hungry. It is something unprecedented in history for people not to have to pay for their food . . . to be fed free. . . .'

After that Mr. Liu's statistics continued to patter on my head like hailstones. The Commune was established in September and comprised 280 villages. Of its 40,000 members about a sixth were children under fifteen and 2,000 were over working age. Eighty per cent. of the total area was cultivated and, in order of importance, cotton, rice, wheat, corn, peanuts and other oil-seeds as well as vegetables were the main products. Besides, there were pigs, poultry and eggs. The river and the ponds yielded fish. Qe Pu had nearly 300 canteens; 18 schools (one among them secondary); and 30 children were already in town for higher education at the Commune's expense. Nurseries were being put up, over 30 were already in operation, but homes for the aged were not yet established. 'We hadn't enough time to do everything,' he remarked with an excusing smile.

I asked about tombs as I haven't seen any over the fields and was told that they had been regrouped into cemeteries on ground not needed for cultivation. To my question whether this could be done without difficulty, Mr. Liu assured me that his 'members have a very high degree of political consciousness' and that they would not put obstacles in the way of higher production.[54] Finally, we came to the problem of transport. Qe Pu had no lorry yet and it had to rely on 'simpler methods of transportation'.

Later on, as we descended the steps, Mr. Liu came back to the subject which especially appeared to worry him: 'We know what newspapers abroad are publishing about the Communes. It is all sheer invention. People are contented here. They can even raise their own poultry and sell it at good profit. . . .'

For the rest of the day we were driving around in our jeep along the lanes of the Commune. All around us there spread flat and fertile country. His arm sweeping over the endless carpets of vegetation which have replaced the old, individual plots, Mr. Liu remarked with evident satisfaction: 'Here we have finished with dispersed effort. From now on we work in organized teams like in industry. . . .' But his pride was even more noticeable when we came upon newly-built village industries. By then all Party publications were giving top priority to the creation of these simple, rural enterprises destined to supply local needs.

The cement 'factory' was a modest affair though it had a petrol engine which was pointed out with due respect. Farther away, quite a number of people were handling robust instruments pressing oil-cakes. Then, I was shown the fertilizer 'works' where, on the basis of the latest, detailed directives in the press, chemical fertilizers were being 'manufactured' of local raw materials. The workshop of the Commune was crowded with people hammering away on spades and other implements and old ploughs were lined up to be fitted with metal blades made of steel produced by the 'indigenous' blast furnaces. *Qe Pu* itself no longer had them. 'They were abandoned and bigger types are under study,' Mr. Liu said. 'They will be set up only where coal and iron-ore are nearby.' As for the implements themselves they were good enough as indispensable tools where none existed before. And the workers employed in these simple 'factories' all appeared to be proud to be training for the day when they will have real machines to handle.

But the most astonishing of *Qe Pu*'s 'industries' was the cotton ginning 'plant'. I was led into a big shed and to my amazement it was filled with large and complicated machines entirely made of wood. They were perfect copies of originals yet, with the exception of the ball-bearings, they contained not a piece of metal. 'They were all built by members and the ball-bearings too were made here of local metal,' Mr. Liu volunteered to explain, sensing my surprise. 'They used local wood and old boxes as their raw material. As far as possible we have to rely on our own means. . . .' Then, somewhat apologetically, he added: 'Perhaps they won't last as long as real machines, but they help to speed production. . . .'

Seeing these 'plants' and 'factories', I could understand better than from any article by economists that while, somewhere far away in the town, the 'big machine' worked for the future, the naked hands of the Commune members were to provide nearly all that was needed for the present. Mr. Liu and his colleagues at the head of other Communes were there to permit that division of labour; to see to it that the villages made next to no demand on the products of modern industry and put up with an austerity relieved by little more than what the peasants themselves could create.

In the meantime we travelled fairly large distances between sights and here and there we stopped to exchange a few words with people in the fields. Visiting a nursery or a mess-hall, inspecting small and widely scattered details, or talking to a handful of people in the presence of their superiors, I could have no illusions of being able to form an accurate picture of the functioning of so large an organization. At one point I noticed a group of militiamen training with guns across their shoulders. In two of the Commune canteens I had seen members eating from bowls generously filled with rice and vegetables though, on that day at least, without meat. The children in the courtyards of the nurseries had been gay and obviously well-fed. Several times, however, when we approached labour brigades in the fields, one of the officials went ahead and distributed, what seemed to me, rather harsh orders. By the time our group arrived, all were clearly on their guard and work went on with rhythmic movements and in hushed silence.

Finally, as the evening was approaching, our jeep stopped at the triumphal arch where we had entered. Ready for the parting, Mr. Liu's eyes were caressing the soft, green carpet of vegetation all around us. 'Last year we doubled our harvest. This year it will be a bumper crop again,' he said. 'The fields are ready to receive the tractors. They will come one day. . . . And things will get even better.' Then, with a broad smile and in the style of the official literature on which he lived, he wanted to end on clear-cut conclusions: 'Now you know what to think of the calumnies they spread about us abroad. You have seen that people continue to live in their houses, that they are not separated from their children, that they get a wage, that they can vote and get free meals. We have shown you everything, haven't we?'

I ought to have obliged him with an affirmative answer which he could have put down at the end of his report which he was bound to write about the visit of foreigners. I thanked him for his hospitality and remarked that, indeed, I had seen nothing to justify the sombre stories which appeared in the foreign press. Of course, I said, it was difficult to see everything in one day.

'Your Commune is rather big and there are many Communes in China . . .', I added.

'How couldn't you be sure,' Mr. Liu insisted. 'Haven't we shown you everything?'

'Supposing I had come on December 16 last year,' I riposted jokingly, 'wouldn't I have left with the same impression that everything went well?'

Ideal Party member, familiar with important figures and dates, as he was, Mr. Liu immediately understood what I wanted to say. He laughed, with his healthy peasant temperament suddenly triumphant over his official manners. 'We have learnt much since and we have carried out the instructions . . .', he added quickly. 'Things are improving and they are getting better every day. . . .' And with that we shook hands and the jeep took off towards the main road.

The date I had been referring to was the day before the Central Committee shook the country with a triple communiqué. It was exactly three months before my visit to *Qe Pu* Commune. The three sensational communications came at the end of the first Great Leap year, in a moment when, exhausted by their gargantuan labours, and in the midst of the latest reorganization of the countryside, the rumbles of discontent of China's half milliard peasants was becoming distinctly audible.

The first of the communiqués dealt with production.[55] It jubilantly confirmed the estimate that, in 1958 alone, China had doubled her output of cereals. As for industrial and agricultural production combined, it increased by more than during the whole of the first Five-Year Plan. It was also made clear that pressure would not slacken next year. Production targets for 1959 were not less fantastic. During 1959 steel would jump from 11 to 18 million tons. Coal from 270 to 380; and cotton from just over 3 to 5 million tons. As for grain, it would have to make yet another unprecedented advance from 375 to 525 million tons. Clearly, 1959 was to be another year of monumental effort.

But if these figures and what they implied more or less confirmed what had already transpired, the Chinese were totally unprepared for what the second communiqué had revealed. The

Central Committee, they were told, 'has decided to approve (the) proposal of Comrade Mao Tse-tung . . . not to nominate him again as candidate for Chairman of the People's Republic of China'. The Central Committee, it was explained, '. . . deems this to be a completely positive proposal, because, relinquishing his duties as Chairman of the state and working solely as Chairman of the Central Committee of the Party, (Mao) will be enabled all the better to concentrate his energies on dealing with questions of the direction, policy and line of the Party and the state; he may also be enabled to set aside more time for Marxist-Leninist theoretical work. . . . He will remain the leader of the entire people of various nationalities . . . (and) . . . If some special situation arises in the future which should require him to take up his work again, he can still be nominated again. . . .'

Sensing that inevitably the news would set off rumours and speculation, the brief text ended with instructions to Party workers on all levels 'to give full explanations' to the cadres and to the masses '. . . so that the reason for this may be understood by all and that there may be no misunderstanding'. But given the fact that no further explanation was ever offered, this could only mean that the cadres were to see to it that no dangerous rumours or hypotheses were spread and that all dutifully accepted that the Chairman's resignation had really no other reason than his desire to devote more time to theoretical and Party work.

If, inevitably, there was much speculation about the genuine causes of Mao's decision to share his powers, the third part of the triple communiqué perhaps contained a fragment of the answer. It dealt with the shortcomings of the Communes and was clearly intended to be comprehensible to the simplest of cadres. The main message was to all the 26,000 Mr. Lius at the head of China's hastily formed Communes. It told them to go more slowly. It was not quite clear whether the Resolution called for just one of those orderly strategic retreats which prepare even bolder moves at a more opportune moment, or whether it was the product of a compromise between rival views within the leadership. There were, however, admissions scattered in the text which appeared to confirm the criticism of those who wanted to go more slowly while, at the same time, it substantiated persistent reports of widespread discontent in the countryside.

Ever since the Commune movement was launched news had been seeping through the propaganda wall about both excesses in execution and even about scattered passive resistance. As usual, over-enthusiastic cadres were going too fast and too far. Taking the August Resolution to the letter they set about with their customary, harsh efficiency to build utopia. During the first few weeks the descriptions appearing even in the Chinese press had a distinctly nightmarish flavour. A magazine relating the new rural life at Chao Ying Commune in Honan province, for instance, spoke of bells ringing and whistles blowing in the morning, calling the members to assemble. 'In about a quarter of an hour the peasants line up,' the report continued. 'At the command of company and squad commanders, the teams move to the fields, holding flags. Here one no longer sees peasants in groups of two or three, smoking or going leisurely to the fields. What one hears are the sounds of measured steps and marching songs. The desultory living habits which have been with the peasants for hundreds of years are gone for ever. . . .'

But with the autumn harvest under way, working hours became still longer. Harvesters went on working late into the night in the light of oil lamps and in some districts twelve- and fourteen-hour work-days became the rule. There were reports of people collapsing of fatigue due to overwork. Later on, with labour progressively released from harvesting, another nation-wide mobilization followed, this time to build 'native style' blast furnaces. Tens of millions of peasants were to produce pig iron and steel with the methods of the Chinese artisans of the Middle Ages. Masses of them were marched off into the mountains, with picks and shovels, to mine the iron-ore and the coal while, following on a long working day in the fields, many other millions were to stand several hours more in the night in the heat of the furnaces. The production quotas fixed by the cadres had to be fulfilled and when ores were insufficient iron railings or even kitchen utensils were melted down. The press and the radio triumphantly reported the multiplication of the primitive furnaces. In Honan province half a million were built within a few weeks. In Kiangsi province alone, *Peking Review* said, the number of 'steel workers stemming from the peasantry shot up from 190,000 to 760,000 in a few days and the number of blast furnaces put into operation jumped from 1,224 to 2,239'.[56] But these were just examples to inspire others. Literally, millions of them were built around villages, along railway lines or even in the gardens of schools and houses in the towns. Like innumerable glow-worms they shone in China's night. Seeing them all over the country one had the haunting impression of fanatical alchemists feeding the flames in desperation to turn into gold the rocks they had carted from the mountains. The official forecast was that the village blast furnaces would provide nearly a third of the steel China was to produce in 1958. Then, gradually, it became known that the steel turned out was inferior in quality, barely suitable even for simple agricultural implements. By the spring of 1959 the movement was left to peter out. The millions of abandoned mud structures stood like silent witnesses of yet another demoniac expenditure of human energy. Their building and their supply with ore and coal not merely diverted labour from urgent agricultural work but also overstrained and further disorganized the country's already grossly inadequate system of communications.[57]

In the meantime, tension in the Taiwan Straits was worked up into hysterical demonstrations to stimulate still further the country's herculean effort. 'As the U.S. armed provocations and war threats continue unabated . . . the nation closes ranks and stands united . . .', reported *Peking Review*.[58] 'By September 16 more than 302 million people, almost half of China's population, had demonstrated against U.S. armed provocations.' Significantly, the article drew attention to the interdependence of external danger and internal exertions: 'This colossal figure completely bears out the saying (of Mao) that the tense situation created by the United States only serves to mobilize the people to oppose the U.S. aggressors. . . .' That this resistance was to take forms less directly connected with the exposed coastal areas than with higher production and with the creation of the Commune's militia, was made even clearer: 'When the news came through that the U.S.

imperialists were again engaged in armed provocation against China (the people) threw themselves into the movement to form militia units and to increase production with a spirit reminiscent of their earlier revolutionary struggles. . . .'

Yet if the resulting effort was beginning to reach the limits of 'human possibility', promises had to be proportionate: 'Can this tremendous rate of agricultural growth be maintained? The answer is yes,' said *Peking Review*.[59] 'In fact, even higher rates of growth can be expected. The good harvests this year are only the first step in China's agricultural leap forward. . . . Next year, the output of food crops will be 500 million tons or more which means 1,500 to 2,000 *jin* per capita.'[60] And if the promise of rice bowls piled high were not enough, there were even brighter, almost idyllic prospects: '. . . The vast areas that used to be farm-land in the past will be rearranged. One part may be used to plant crops, one part to plant trees and another part may be allocated to factories and plants, modern communications, living quarters, theatres, gardens and lakes.'[61]

While external tension was to stimulate physical exertions at home and that, in its turn, was to be compensated by more or less fantastic promises for the future, the assault on the labour-drugged Chinese masses was acquiring a further, sinister aspect. It was aiming at the last remaining focus of the individual's loyalty: at the institutions of the Chinese family. The newspapers were printing readers' letters expressing their pleasure over their passage from the traditional type of family to the larger one, embracing the entire Commune. The narrow 'biological family' was referred to as outmoded and 'reactionary'. Ominously, Engels was quoted in support of the demand to abolish the individual family as an economic unit, for this was a pre-condition of women's emanci-pation. Private housekeeping, it was demanded, should be 'trans-formed into a social industry'; and 'the care and education of the children (ought to become) a social matter'.

'If someone says that we are going to "destroy" the traditional family, it must be made clear that this "destruction" differs basically in nature from the destruction of the family by the capitalist system. What we want to destroy . . . (are) family relations built on (the) system of class exploitation and on undisputed patriarchal authority,' said *Peking Review*. '. . . people are not going back to the family life typical of individual production, class exploitation and the servitude of women and children to the male head of the family. They are going to build a new family life. . . .'[62]

Following all the physical and psychological trials of the year there was, thus, a macabre stepping up of even more violent expedients during the last few months of 1958. Both nerves and muscles were ready to snap. Neither statistical fireworks nor the Pavlovian frenzy could lessen internal tension any more. That was the moment when the triple communiqué was released.

By far the longest of the three was entitled *Resolutions on some Questions Concerning the People's Communes*. Written in the elephantine dialectics characteristic of most of Party literature, it was significant on two counts. It revealed with what blind devotion cadres can push ahead when left with only loose definitions of Party intentions. Secondly, and though indirectly only, it brought to light for the first time the issues on which, in all probability, differences existed between the moderates and the 'reckless' impatients within the Central Committee itself.

Much care was taken to clear up two 'misunderstandings': about the militia and about the nearness of complete Communism.

'What we describe as getting organized along military lines means getting organized on the pattern of a factory. . . . The leading bodies of the militia and production organizations should be separate and, in principle, the commanding officers of the various levels of the militia . . . should not be concurrently directors of communes. . . .' But to allay peasant fears even further, the text became more explicit: '. . . It is absolutely impermissible to use "getting organized along military lines" as a prextext or to make use of the militia system—which is directed against the enemy—to impair, in the least, democratic life in the communes. . . .'

As for the misunderstanding about the nearness of complete Communism, clarification was desirable for internal as well as external opinion. Before the creation of the Communes, China proclaimed that she was merely copying the Soviet model. After the Communes had been launched, and with the introduction of the subsistence principle—in the form of free meals and services next to wages—it began to be claimed that China had overtaken the U.S.S.R. in her advance towards a fully Communist society. The Commune, it was repeated, was the most advanced Communist institution. This was a serious pretension and after only mild publicity, the Soviet press had become openly discouraging. Considering some of the declarations of Mr. Khrushchev and of other Soviet leaders, the innovation was by no means acclaimed by Moscow. With an eye on Sino-Soviet relations, some Chinese leaders may have thought it advisable to clear up the matter. '. . . the elements of communism are bound to increase gradually (in the Communes) and these will lay the foundation of material and spiritual conditions for the transition from socialism to communism . . .'. But, 'though the pace at which we are advancing is fairly rapid, it will take a fairly long time to realize, on a large scale, the industrialization of our country . . . (to build up) a socialist country with a highly developed modern industry, agriculture, science and culture. This whole process will take fifteen, twenty or more years. . . .' Whatever misunderstanding there existed, the Resolution gently put the blame on over-enthusiastic cadres or, perhaps, on even some leaders: '. . . (they) will say that this time is too long. They are good-hearted people in our own ranks, but they are overeager . . . (they hope that very soon) or even now they can dispense with the socialist principle of "to each according to his work" and adopt the communist principle of "to each according to his needs". Consequently, they cannot understand why the socialist system will have to continue for a very long time. Their view, of course, is a misconception, which must be cleared up. . . .'

Once these two delicate subjects were dealt with, the Resolution hastened to assure city dwellers that their turn had not come yet. Though 'some experiments have also begun in the cities' and urban Communes 'in a form suited to the specific features of cities' will be necessary, '. . . this work should be postponed except for the necessary preparatory measures'.[63]

Then, before distributing its concessions to the peasants, the Resolution offered an explanation of another problem which, evidently, caused widespread discontent in the Communes. It concerned the modesty of the cash income of Commune members compared with that of town workers. 'Wages must be increased gradually as production expands. For the present, except the items freely supplied, wage scales in the rural areas may, in general, be divided into six to eight grades . . . but the differences should not be too great; for if they were, they would not conform to the existing differences in labouring skills in the rural areas. . . .' The reasons for the difference in rural and urban wage levels were 'many-sided'. High living costs, money sent to Commune members by relatives or by army-men, among others, were responsible. In any case, the cadres were instructed 'to dissuade . . . members from wrangling about this'. At the same time, however, they were authorized to assure them that their possessions—such as houses, clothing, bedding and furniture as well as their savings—will 'always' remain their private property.

Following these significant preliminaries, the rest of the text was devoted to the appeasement of the peasants.

Difficulties were freely admitted. There was not enough time to consolidate the Communes. '. . . This is because the communes were only recently set up and most of them, immediately after their establishment, threw themselves into the heavy work of the autumn harvest, ploughing and sowing and the nation-wide campaign for iron and steel. . . .' The cadres were to change their methods: '. . . leading functionaries of all levels . . . must look upon themselves as ordinary working people, and treat the commune members in a comradely way. Kuomintang and bourgeois styles of work which coerce the masses are strictly prohibited. Because of the big leap forward . . . some cadres are beginning to get dizzy with success and, unwilling to do the patient work of educating the masses by persuasion, they are exhibiting certain rude attitudes. . . .'

As for the modalities of the orderly retreat, while the aim was the six-hour work-day, 'at present, the system of eight hours of actual work and two hours of study should be put into effect. . . .'

In any event, 'eight hours for sleep and four hours for meals and recreation, altogether twelve hours, must be guaranteed every day and this must not be reduced'. Equally imperative was the order that 'adequate rest must be ensured to women during pregnancy and after childbirth'. Special food was to be provided to the sick, to the children and to the aged and 'it is permissible for some commune members to cook at home'. Instructions in considerable detail specified how the canteens should be run. Apparently confirming news of sabotage through unappetizing food or even through poisoning, there was much insistence on the selection of cooks from politically reliable elements.

Nurseries and kindergartens should be well run so that people should prefer to place their children in them. But '. . . parents may decide whether it is necessary for their children to board there, and may take them home at any time. . . .' Dealing with the reconstruction of villages, there was also clarification on policy towards the family. 'We stand for the abolition of the irrational patriarchial system, inherited from the past and for the development of family life in which there is democracy and unity . . . (yet) . . . attention must be paid to building the houses so that the married couples, the young and the aged of each family can all live together.'

Once these concessions were spelled out, for a brief moment, the dreary, official tone was interrupted by vehement polemics: 'There is now a big bunch of fools in the world who are attacking the people's communes with all their might and main, among them is Mr. Dulles of the United States. This Dulles knows nothing about things in our country but likes to pretend to be a China expert and madly opposes the people's communes. What breaks his heart especially, is that we have supposedly destroyed the marvellous family system which has been handed down for thousands of years . . . the patriarchal system (which) generally disappeared long ago in capitalist society and that was a progressive step. . . .'[64]

Finally, came some detailed prescriptions about the administrative organization of the Communes; about the desirable speed of capital accumulation; as well as about the definition of the 'five guarantees' extended to the aged, the orphaned, the widowed and the disabled or to those who were without means of support.[65]

'The work of checking up on the communes should first be carried out in one or two . . . in each county as an experiment,' the Resolution summed up. 'Every province, municipality and autonomous region should organize its inspection teams consisting of a thousand, several thousands or ten thousand people for the check up, and the first secretaries of the Party committees . . . should personally lead the work. . . . In short, through these check-ups, the work of the people's communes in the country must be generally carried one step forward.'

Thus there was no question of giving up the experiment. It was only to be consolidated. So, one more movement, this time called *Tidying up the Communes*, swept the country with thousands of inspection teams touring it from one end to the other. That the forces of caution were at grips with those pressing for further leaps at any price, could no longer be hidden. Such abrupt and sweeping changes in the life of so many people could not fail to cause acute stress. Moreover, the conflict between the contending forces and the tension it generated, were soon to dominate China's internal as well as external policies.

10 Illusions and Reality. An Interview with Chou En-lai

ON MARCH 11, 1959, when Mr. Chou En-lai received me in Peking, inevitably, my first question to him was about the baffling food situation.

Officially the country lived in the joy of having doubled its food crops within a year. In reality in every city I had visited I passed long queues waiting in every hour of the day in front of food shops and canteens. Each time when I was driven at dawn to catch a plane, I could see sullen lines of people waiting in the dark for the food shops to open. One encountered a thousand symptoms of widespread shortage of food and even of scarcity of rice. In fact, by some obviously unplanned coincidence, quite often the depressing, long food queues were waiting at the foot of giant hoardings displaying production curves soaring past the 375 million tons mark and heading towards the pictorial targets of the 525 million tons of cereals promised for 1959. After the unprecedented results of 1958, China was to perform another advance without precedent in history. Yet the queues were there, waiting, shabby and in macabre contrast with the exuberance of the propaganda overhead.

Foreigners living in Peking, even the best disposed, readily admitted that the official figures were false. Their favourite indoor game was to calculate the probable margin of exaggeration. That all the tremendous efforts of the past year must have led to greater output was generally conceded. But even if the most generous allowance was being made for more seeds, for bigger stocks, for transport difficulties or for more export, there still remained a tremendous and unaccountable gap.

I listed to the Prime Minister what I had seen. If the published figures were correct, there ought to be abundance in China. What was the Premier's explanation? I asked.

First, Mr. Chou En-lai spoke at great length about the past: of famines, of the meatless diet, of inadequate communications and of mismanagement under the Kuomintang régime. Now consumption was more equally spread and was certainly higher than ever before. 'We should never forget the multiplicator of 650 million,' he insisted. 'This is especially important after the establishment of the Communes. Even a slight increase multiplied by 650 million reaches fantastic figures. If you give meat twice a week instead of only once, you have to give it twice a week to all members, to workers, to the old and to the children alike. Six hundred and fifty million times that small piece of meat, how many pigs does that make?' he asked. 'It is obvious that our people eat better and more today than ever in the past. Pre-war record harvests were much smaller than present-day consumption and now we have a surplus for export; far larger quantites of seed are used in close planting and also we stock more. . . . Of course,' he admitted, 'there may be local difficulties in distribution. There is also a certain disequilibrium because industrial production increases even faster than the output of agriculture. But soon we shall reach a new balance and on a much higher per head consumption level than in the past. . . .'

I asked whether growing cereal exports had any important role in the difficulties experienced?

'Exports have increased but this is of no great importance compared to growing home consumption,' Mr. Chou En-lai replied. 'Our primary aim is to satisfy internal demand.'

In view of what could be observed, his answer seemed unconvincing. Yet apparently the Chinese Premier was still persuaded that food-grain output in 1958 had really doubled.

While this conversation took place, inspection teams were still tidying up the Communes. People continued to be driven at a furious pace. The rigours of life in the Communes have barely eased. In all the factories which I have visited the tempo of work was feverish and one needed to be no specialist to note that their equipment was used with no more consideration than their workers. On factory notice-boards rival teams were challenging each other to new labour emulation contests. And one could hardly visit a factory without encountering workers' processions on their way to the management to report, with flags and drums, the overfulfilment of their already excessive norms.

Concurrently there were frenetic new campaigns: for improved agricultural methods; for participation in manual labour of cadres, employees and intellectuals; for better tools; for more stringent labour discipline, or for still more political education. All this was interspersed by nation-wide mass-demonstrations: against American threats; in support of Cuba's revolution; to express solidarity with the Congo's struggle for freedom, or against rightists and counter-revolutionaries hampering the Great Leap's élan.

Then, finally, on March 28, the newspapers announced the rising in Tibet. Shortly after the 'abduction' of the Dalai Lama was admitted. That one of the nationalities so brutally repudiated

China's new order, stung the pride of the régime sharply. Tempers rose and a new, even stiffer tone appeared against both internal and external opponents. Then, on April 27, the second in the official hierarchy was elected as the new head of the State. In Liu Shao-chi China had a new President whose character matched the arduous phase of her revolutionary advance. There may have been a shift of positions behind the façade, but soon it became clear that there was neither any real shift in power nor in any of the policies in process of execution.

The strategy of the break-through was at stake and the economic and social reorganization implied by the Big Leap Forward was to continue.

The Commune's mess-halls, it was reported, were being increasingly used to 'raise (members') ideological standards and (to promote) the leap forward in production. . . . How happy commune members would be if after hard work, they can have good meals, listen to propaganda and take part in studies and cultural entertainment activities. Therefore, mess-halls should gradually undertake propaganda and cultural work. . . .'[66]

The new slogan, *Walking on Two Legs*, too, was being popularized. 'The principle of simultaneous development of industry and agriculture, i.e. the principle of "walking on two legs", is, therefore, intended to make full use of the impetus that industry and agriculture give to each other, to mobilize fully the initiative of the more than 500 million peasants . . . so as to ensure the progress of economic construction in the country at top speed. . . .' And to conclude, Mao Tse-tung was cited: '. . . With the development of agriculture and light industry, heavy industry will be assured of its market and funds, and thus grow faster. Hence what may seem to be a slower pace of industrialization, is actually not so, and indeed the tempo may even be quickened. . . .'[67]

The other instruments of the Great Leap, too, were regularly justified. '. . . Some people have doubts: since indigenous methods are generally rather backward, why then do we advocate their use? . . . In so far as it facilitates full mobilization of the masses and utilization of scattered resources, suits specific natural conditions . . . and can increase production quickly when modern machinery and equipment are lacking, the indigenous methods should by no means be called "backward". . . . Since modern methods of production are something that have been learnt from abroad, they are not often completely suited to the natural and economic conditions of our country. . . . If modern methods are integrated with indigenous ones, they will be further improved and raised to a higher level. . . .'[68]

Above all, the very idea of the Commune appeared to be still under heavy fire. Articles and broadcasts tirelessly extolled its virtues in a way that left little doubt about the widespread lack of popular support. Its critics were endlessly lectured and their observations were dismissed by a mixture of arguments and threats. Then, the natural disasters of the summer provided the propagandists with new ammunition to justify the Communes' existence.

Once again nature was unwilling to collaborate with the impatient planners. The old enemy returned and floods brought danger to life and to crops over wide areas. The worst hit was Kwantung province, in the south; Canton and the Pearl river delta were directly threatened. Organized into shock-brigades the peasants were to harvest the rice quickly before the flood tide. They were to build dykes and, then, to begin replanting in a hurry as soon as the waters subsided. In the meantime, in the North drought and locusts threatened the harvest in five provinces.[69] The Communes' role in fighting the natural calamities was duly underlined and used as a supplementary argument to vindicate them. '. . . The advantages of the people's communes, already amply demonstrated, are being manifested most clearly in the current struggle. With their large size and wide scope of activities, the communes can deploy more rationally the manpower of the countryside and promptly mobilize great forces to defend each threatened point. . . .' Moreover, '. . . the development of small commune-run industrial workshops also contribute to the struggle against natural calamities by turning out a large amount of urgently needed equipment. . . .'[70]

Yet all the oratory notwithstanding, it has become plain that the waves of mass-campaigns, the exhortations or the fantastic figures, were no longer evoking the expected enthusiasm. Calling for heavier and heavier sacrifices, the Great Leap Forward was meeting growing resistance. Food consumption was diving deeper and by the summer of 1959 the shortage of cereals and cloth was nation-wide.

However, the country was preparing to celebrate the tenth anniversary of the new régime. Peking was embellished. The Imperial Palace was given a new coat of splendid paint. The open space in front of the Gate of Heavenly Peace had been broadened and framed by monumental and ornate buildings. By the time the leaders and their guests assembled on the Gate's balcony, they overlooked the world's largest public square. But before history's greatest parade marched past, some loose ends had to be tidied up. Discontent could no longer be concealed. The time had come to reconcile illusions with reality.

The unenviable task was given to Mr. Chou En-lai. He performed it with his customary skill. Speaking to the eighth plenary session of the Central Committee, which took place at Lushan in the first half of August, he began by lavishly praising the Communes. Then, he lashed out at the sceptics. '. . . Those who assert that the people's communes are in an "awful mess" are none other than the imperialists who are violently hostile to our country's socialist cause, as well as some rightists and other reactionaries who are against the people and against socialism . . . (they) maintain that (the Communes) have been set up prematurely and have gone wrong. We would ask: Aren't you afraid of being thrown over the borderline of the bourgeois rightists? . . .'

Upon this stern warning followed the painful effort, richly sprinkled with statistics, to prove that notwithstanding widespread complaints, consumption had in fact increased. The market supply of 'most, important commodities' increased during the first half of 1959. 'Only in the case of about a dozen commodities did supplies drop.' These, however, included meat, egg products, sugar, cotton and leather shoes. 'Our townspeople really have very little justification to blame our peasants whose level of consumption has always been rather low, for eating and using up a little more than usual for a period of time after the great expansion of production . . . .' Some people, in fact, have '. . . alleged that the market was strained all round. . . . A handful of people even said that before liberation one could get every-thing in the market but now nothing was available. Everyone knows that this is . . . a vicious distortion.' It was even less true that exports were responsible for shortages. The inevitable bunch of figures then followed to demolish all these 'vicious distor-tions', yet: 'For a very short period in the spring of this year, grain was in short supply in areas amounting to less than 5 per cent. (of the country). . . .' This was possible '. . . because last year there were natural calamities; there was lack of proper budgeting; the grain crops were harvested in a somewhat hurried fashion; there was lack of planning in consumption. . . .'

Before coming to the major task of his speech, the Prime Minister once again deemed it necessary to preface it with harsh words directed at the Great Leap's opponents: '. . . We absolutely cannot allow reactionaries and right opportunists among the ranks of the people to take advantage of isolated, transient short-comings . . . which have already been corrected, to attack the big leap forward and the people's communes. . . .' One had to identify oneself with the masses, rather than to oppose them. 'Here lies the fundamental difference between the proletarian revolutionary and the bourgeois and petty-bourgeois revolu-tionary. . . .'

After which came the confessions. '. . . due to lack of experi-ence in assessing harvests under conditions of a bumper crop over large tracts of land and sudden increases (in yields) . . .' the 1958 output figures had to be revised. Reaping, threshing, and storing, it was admitted, were badly done last year and the labour force too was inadequate. Moreover, the output of areas affected by natural disasters was also overestimated. For all these reasons '. . . the calculations made of last year's agricultural output were a bit high . . .'.

The 'bit' in question, meant 125 million tons of cereals: the difference between the 375 million tons so loudly and so per-sistently proclaimed, and the 250 million tons now admitted as the quantity really harvested. Other claims also came tumbling down. Instead of 3,350,000 tons, the cotton crop was only 2·1 million tons. Though industrial progress was spectacular, of the claimed 11 million tons of steel 3 million tons—those produced by native-style blast furnaces—had to be deducted as their quality did not qualify for industrial use. Nor would they be included in official statistics in the future. And in the light of these admissions, the targets for 1959, too, had to be severely cut. The figures which Mr. Chou En-lai himself triumphantly announced in April, were quietly dropped. There were to be further increases during 1959, but much more modest and even that, of course, only in comparison with the new, rectified figures. Thus, statistics came down to earth again.[71]

With this delicate passage behind him, the Chinese Premier quickly returned to the charge: '. . . While we are overcoming certain shortcomings in practical work and adjusting economic targets in the light of realities, some people, taking a bourgeois stand, greatly underestimate and even deny the great achievements of last year's great leap forward and of the people's communes. . . . This kind of thinking and sentiment has grown in the past two months. . . . Obviously, if we allow such thinking to continue and grow, without firmly repudiating and correcting it, the initiative of the broad masses will be seriously damaged. . . .' So, '. . . we must (oppose) right deviation and wage a serious struggle against all sentiments, thinking and activities tending in the rightist direction. . . .'[72]

Clearly, then, the overdue confrontation of illusions with everyday reality was not to bring easier times for the common man. Of course it would have been more satisfying to learn that in a world short of basic necessities, even if at the price of terrible sacrifices, a large segment of mankind could double, within a year, the quantity of food at its disposal. Yet the newsagencies of the world were hurrying to spread the news of defeat. Unable to temper the ill-will that colours most Western commentaries on Chinese events, even some otherwise serious journals spoke of a *Great Leap Backward*. According to the rectified figures, however, industrial output in the first half of 1959 was still 65 per cent.

higher than in the corresponding period of 1958. The increase in food crops remained over a third. This may still be an exaggeration. But even when all allowances are made, China's economic progress was faster than achieved at any time in the Soviet Union or in the United States; and was incomparably more rapid than anything ever registered in any of the economically under-developed countries even when they relied on massive foreign aid.

But all this said, a number of important questions remain unanswered.

First of all, did the Chinese leaders know all along that the 'astronomical' claims were false?

One inevitably recalls Mr. Khrushchev's accusations against Mr. Malenkov that, in 1952, when he had declared the U.S.S.R.'s cereal crop as 8 milliard *pouds*, he was deliberately misleading the country for he knew that only 5·6 milliard *pouds* were harvested. Was the distortion in China as deliberate? It is quite possible that even the State Statistical Bureau itself cannot be sure of the accuracy of its harvest figures. The methods of estimating still permit a high margin of error; the area is vast, trained personnel is inadequate, and new production methods as natural calamities affecting large areas, introduce imponderables. Moreover, mass-campaigns and the general atmosphere of fervour which accompany them, tend to encourage local cadres to live up to dizzy targets handed down by their superiors. Town officials, on the other hand, driven by the same determination to please, may pass on figures which they have good reasons to suspect. Inexperience, fanaticism and fear, all combine to confirm wishful thinking. Finally, once spurious additions have obtained the seal of official approval, no one would dare to go back and question their constituent elements.

A more important question is why these startling admissions and the scaling down of targets were announced at that particular moment?

The probable explanation is that the contrast between shortages, the resulting discontent, and the official claims was becoming too glaring. That the steel produced by the village furnaces was left lying on the ground and was no use for industrial purposes, anyone could see. That unwelcome sweet potatoes and coarse grains were making up an ever growing proportion of the daily diet, could no longer be concealed.[73] That long before the natural calamities of the summer, grain rations had been reduced in the towns and that rationing had come to the villages through the use of meal tickets, was equally plain. The tenth anniversary celebrations were approaching and a large number of foreigners were to come to admire China's achievements. The time had come to resort to frankness in order not to abuse any further the confidence of the people.

All this may provide part of the answers. As for the doubts which remain, they are connected with a third question of far greater importance. Did the admissions imply that China's leaders recognized the need to look at the facts of their economic life with the realism which they had been credited with in the past? and if so, why, then, were the attacks continued on those, labelled 'rightists', whose guilt had been merely of saying what the authorities had just confirmed?

In search for the answers, inevitably, one has to move from the economic to the predominantly political sphere.

As the internal situation steadily deteriorated the leadership—and within it, in particular, those most closely associated with the idea of the Commune and the Great Leap Forward—must have been experiencing considerable internal pressure from the opponents of their new policies. This mounting pressure, in its turn, stimulated the virulence of the verbal exchanges between those who favoured revolutionary methods promising spectacular results, and the partisans of steady and orderly economic progress. The admission of exaggerations and the scaling down of targets, on the other hand, have clearly demonstrated that the moderates had proved their points. Though in exchange they seem to have accepted the preservation of the Communes, their political victory was not in sight. In fact, the compromise hammered out at Lushan was evidently not the end of the story. Even if the more glaring illusions had to be abandoned, the rigidity of the party line continued and moderation was far from regaining its respectability. Indeed, the rift appeared to be deeper than the visible, economic part of the controversy may have suggested. Something much more fundamental appeared to be at stake.

While the whole harsh enterprise of the Great Leap Forward was running into difficulties, there was also a corresponding worsening in China's temper in her dealings with the outside world. The new, intransigent tone could be dated from about the same time as the acceleration of the production drive in the spring of 1958. Chinese anger over the American landing in Lebanon and the project of a summit conference without China, created such divergence from Russia as to send Mr. Khrushchev hurriedly to Peking with material concessions. Quemoy was pounded and tension was fanned in the Taiwan Straits each time another round of international negotiations, ignoring China, were in sight. Internal tension and growing external rigidity seemed to reinforce each other. And the common denominator between the two was mounting preoccupation with speed.

In her relations with the rest of the world China had endured far too long indifference, condescension and malice. Year after year, her claims remained unsettled. They were scarcely even taken into consideration. Seeing the Soviet Union busy preparing its rapprochement with the West, China's faith in the reliability of the Russian protective shield may have been shaken. The ring of hostile bases around her territory was continually strengthened. Taiwan, claimed as part of China, remained a dangerous challenge. The wound of Tibet—readily interpreted as the work of foreign interference—was there for all to see. Now, unconcealable internal difficulties may have encouraged external aggressivity even further. Patience and time were running short. The conclusion may have ripened that, more and more, China had to rely on her own force; that she had to speed her industrilization at whatever cost; or that she had to protect her strategic interests as if aggression from outside had become a probability to prepare for.

Under the impact of all these considerations, China's most influential leaders appear to have reached the conclusion that the Soviet Union could no longer be considered as the complete model for the particular needs of their country. By adopting the

Commune and the bold innovations of the Great Leap Forward, they deliberately brushed aside Russia's example and advice and even claimed to have outpaced her in their progress towards Communism. Meanwhile, risking even widespread discontent, the sacrifices imposed on the Chinese masses were multiplied in the desperate hope that spectacular economic results would justify the price.

If, momentarily, this new intransigence had to yield to reality on the home front, it claimed outlets beyond the country's borders with redoubled force. If for so long the world persisted in ignoring that China's temper was turning dangerous, mounting tension convinced at least the more extreme among China's leaders that now they could look after their country's own interests in disregard of world opinion.

So, long before there could be any certainty that counsels of moderation would guide China's internal development back to its former path of realism, she was already moving in the opposite direction in matters affecting her relations with the external world.

11 Reactions to the Situation in Tibet in 1959

COMING FROM Chinese Turkestan I arrived in the central Chinese town of Chengchow late in March. Together with the interpreter accompanying me we went to the local Intourist hotel. It was an austere establishment, though my room was evidently its showpiece. What is more, it had a large and modern radio, made in Shanghai. In China hotel rooms equipped with this amenity were usually reserved for Russian technicians: for the same reason such radios were provided with lavish short-wave bands so that the Soviet engineers could spend their evenings listening to their home country.

As neither the town nor the hotel offered any attractions in the evening, I too began to play about with my radio. My interpreter was with me, sipping tea nearby. Starved for news of the outside world, and turning the dial back and forth, I came upon a station giving an English-language news bulletin. In a minute we heard that there was trouble in Tibet and that the Indian Consulate in Lhasa had confirmed that street fighting was going on around its building. 'There is trouble in Tibet,' I said to my interpreter in that neutral tone I had adopted throughout my stay to provoke the political reactions of my companions.

'What sort of station is it?' he asked. 'If it is American, probably the report isn't true. They keep on spreading rumours. I often listen to the American Forces programme; it's absolutely ridiculous what they keep on saying about events in China.'

I merely remarked that, according to the broadcast, Mr. Nehru had made a statement in Parliament and that he would not have done so had the story been unconfirmed. Whereupon my interpreter turned away from the subject. He usually did so whenever he felt it advisable not to advance personal opinions on ground not mapped by Peking's *People's Daily*.

Four days later, on March 28, we were travelling in the Peking-Canton *Peace Train*, an all-sleeping-car luxury express. As in all trains in China nowadays loudspeakers were blaring the whole day in every compartment and music and 'pep'—talks— produced from the train's own studio—alternated with periods of relays from Peking Radio. About eight in the evening we were sitting in the last coach, the extremely comfortable panoramic car. The armchairs were all occupied by blue-clad passengers, evidently the privileged of the régime; civil servants or cadres on mission, chatting or reading Party literature. Suddenly there was an unusual stretching of necks and clearing of throats as the loudspeakers promised a very special item in a few minutes, and soon Peking Radio's announcer read out a long and solemn communiqué.

'The reactionary clique is beaten,' my interpreter said excitedly, before he had even explained that the statement announced the victorious crushing of a rising in Tibet. The other passengers either sat around with that stolid silence people in dictatorial countries learn in self-defence, or they went on reading their

Party booklets. Their attitude reflected prudence mixed with self-assurance. It had happened; it was over. China was strong.

Next day, my interpreter came to my room with the *People's Daily* in his hand. The entire front page was occupied with the communiqué we had heard the night before. Below the main headlines, in a separate article, was Chou En-lai's reminder to the Indians about non-interference.

'So the radio was right after all,' I remarked.

'All was done from outside,' he answered.

'How do you know?' I demanded.

'You have just come from Sinkiang; that too is an autonomous region like Tibet. You have seen that that province is becoming industrialized, that its people are making progress and that they are happy there. Did the Tibetan students you have seen look dissatisfied? But Sinkiang, of course, has no frontier with the capitalist world; only with brother countries,' my interpreter added with a sarcastic undertone. He then went on translating the articles and his voice was full of genuine hatred whenever he prounounced the words 'reactionary clique' or 'imperialists'.

My interpreter, of course, was the perfect product of official propaganda. He, like millions of others similarly indoctrinated, has been told not merely that the political and especially the economic results of the régime were without precedent in history but also that he was building an entirely new type of society which is already a model for the underprivileged majority of mankind. This new society is more egalitarian and more just than any before; its ideals are new, and in physical labour it has found an unprecedented common denominator to reconcile classes, town and village, labourers and intellectuals, or the élite and the masses. It is an obligation to share the advantages of this new and superior society with the more backward races making up geographic China. It is also a sign of generosity. For such an offer to be refused is logically inconceivable, so any refusal to accept it must be the work of people who are not merely enemies of China but who are also historically obsolete in rejecting this unique passport to progress and happiness.

With all this in his mental background the average Chinese

looks at the map. Along the land-borders where China touches the non-Communist world, Tibet represents the sole really vulnerable stretch. It is the only area populated by non-Chinese and where the Chinese Army is not present *en masse*. If he is particularly well-informed, he would also know that an American mission visited Lhasa in 1949 and that a document for the use of American troops on Tibet, was circulating among the Tibetans and various secret agents in Kalimpong, on the Indian side of the border. He would equally know that, in July, 1951, the Dalai Lama's brother, formerly prominent in his country's politics, escaped to the United States and has been active there ever since.[74] So, our average Chinese might ask whether it is not natural that all those who wish to prevent China building this incomparable new society, should concentrate their efforts on Tibet? Moreover, would it not be logical for them to do so at a moment when China is experiencing the severe strain of her extraordinary effort? India, of course, lies immediately beyond that vulnerable stretch of border: India, then, and whatever Mr. Nehru may say, is an accomplice of anti-Chinese activities. And if the whole chain of argument is not to fall to the ground, the fiction has to be maintained, despite denials, statements or facts, that—even against Mr. Nehru's will—'reactionary' or 'expansionist' cliques have actually done what fits into this prefabricated picture.

In fact, the Dalai Lama was 'abducted' and was received with honours in India. Though a political refugee, he was permitted to engage in political activities. He gave press conferences, received ambassadors and called for foreign help. Mr. Nehru himself went to visit him in Mussoorie and the 'reactionary' and 'expansionist' Indian circles indeed called for intervention in Tibet notwithstanding India's recognition, in 1954, that Tibet was a 'region of China'.[75]

While all this was happening, the fateful contest was growing in intensity between moderates and intransigents in Peking's highest councils. The stand of the prudents was vindicated by economic developments. But the arguments of those calling for a more vigorous assertion of China's external interests appeared to be strengthened by the interpretation put on events in Tibet.

Refugees were moving across the Tibet-Indian border. Perhaps some armed Tibetans were approaching the Himalayan passes seeking refuge on the other side. Chinese reinforcements arrived to seal off the entry points and, after several years of discreet pressure, there followed some serious incidents. In their turn, they provoked the exchange of mutually accusing diplomatic notes. So, all of a sudden, there appeared in South-east Asia a new Chinese export: the country's internal tension forced beyond its borders.

Then, only a few days after Liu Shao-chi was elected to the Presidency—and thus with Mao Tse-tung, the presumed two principal champions of both the Great Leap Forward and of the Communes, jointly held supreme power—the *People's Daily* published an unusually long and significant editorial. It was entitled *The Revolution in Tibet and Nehru's Philosophy*.[76] Its style, as well as the importance attributed to it in Peking whispers, seemed to confirm the rumour that its author was none other than Mao Tse-tung himself.

The lecturing tone of the article was alternating between condescending friendliness and outspoken intransigence. It noted that between March 17 and April 27, the Indian Premier spoke seven times about Tibet before Parliament and has expressed his sympathy with the so-called 'aspirations of the Tibetans for autonomy', as well as his opposition to what he called 'armed intervention' by China. This acknowledgement of Mr. Nehru's great interest in Tibet was then followed by a detailed analysis of the cruel nature of Tibet's 'serf society' only to show that Indians did not understand the situation and thus could not properly appreciate China's action. 'Of course, Mr. Nehru has great confidence in himself, and he has his own independent views on the question of Tibet. . . .' Yet '. . . Obviously there exist contradictions in (his) thinking. But we do not propose to discuss how these contradictions are to be resolved. . . . However, '. . . . the point now is, that a group of Indians, unfortunately including Mr. Nehru, insist that we do things according to their opinions. . . .' But the Tibet question '. . . was China's internal affair, and . . . no foreign interference was to be tolerated. . . .'

The 'smear campaign' of Indian politicians and their press was then compared to U.S. interference in Cuba's affairs. As for Mr. Nehru's contention that Indian reaction is essentially humanitarian and based on cultural contacts, the editorial pointedly asked how Indians would react to similar solicitude for the affairs of some of India's own constituent states? 'The People's Republic of China enjoys full sovereignty over the Tibet region (and) . . . there can be no doubt whatever about this, and no interference by any foreign country or by the United Nations under whatever pretext or in whatever form will be tolerated. . . .'

Though at one point it was conceded that '. . . The argument may have been a bit sharp, because the vital interests of our motherland and the Tibetan people are involved. . . .' Mr. Nehru's good-will towards China was readily admitted. 'China never has interfered and never will interfere in India' and it is hoped that the present argument, once ended, '. . . Will (not) shake the friendship between our two countries. . . .' But, turning once again towards those who are 'trying to continue fanning the flames', the editorialist burst out with intransigence: '. . . So long as you do not end your anti-Chinese slander campaign, we will not cease hitting back. We are prepared to spend as much time on this as you want to. We are prepared, too, if you should incite other countries to raise a hue and cry against us. We are also prepared to find all the imperialists in the world backing you up in the clamour. But it is utterly futile to try to use pressure to interfere in China's internal affairs and salvage the odious rule of the big serf-owners in Tibet. . . .'

During the following months it seemed as if China were indeed not merely 'prepared' to find 'all the imperialists in the world' backing up India, but were actually *preparing* for such a strategic situation.

It was a shock to most Indians when, in the summer of 1959, they were told that a long series of frontier incidents have occurred between their country and its largest neighbour whom, incidentally, they have most consistently supported in international councils. The *White Paper* issued by India brought into the open a long record of Chinese evasions or rejections of

Indian complaints which went back almost to the original Tibet agreement of 1954.

Moreover, the uncomfortable fact became apparent that, even if she were willing to respond with force, India could do little to dislodge the Chinese from the areas they had already occupied. The contested regions, particularly those in Ladakh, are at a height of 5,000 to 6,000 metres; are very sparsely populated, without useful vegetation, and inaccessible from the Indian side over the major part of the year. It is known that already in the autumn of 1958, during his visit to the United States, the C-in-C of the Indian armed forces was particularly interested in specially designed helicopters capable, in an emergency, to transport Indian troops to the Himalayan passes. Yet to hunt down Chinese patrols would be a costly and unrewarding task. On the other hand, to send supplies to Tibetan rebels on the other side of the border, would lead to complications out of proportion with the issues now involved. In the long run, then, and somewhat paradoxically, India may have to assume the romantic, bloody and uncomfortable heritage of frontier policing which that most un-Gandhian of reporters, Rudyard Kipling, had immortalized in a different age and along another border.

But before any more detailed discussion of these events and of their eventual motives, it may be fair to clarify how the Chinese themselves see the issues at stake.

Two widely separated regions of the long Sino-Indian border are involved in the incidents. One is along the frontier between Tibet and the north-east corner of India (known as the North East Frontier Agency, or N.E.F.A.) near the Burmese boundary. The other is on the north-west tip of Tibet where it touches north-east Kashmir, at present occupied by India, and known under the name of Ladakh.

As for the first—in the N.E.F.A. area—the border the Indians claim is the so-called McMahon Line. It was agreed to at the Simla Conference in 1914, between representatives of the British, Chinese and Tibetan governments (as, at that time, Tibet was almost independent). The Chinese Government refused to ratify this agreement and the present Chinese

Government maintains that it had never recognized the Line which they consider as having been imposed as a result of 'British aggressive imperialism'. The Chinese claim that the true 'traditional boundary' between Tibet and India in this region lies well to the south of the McMahon Line.

In the second case—in Kashmir—the Chinese admit that in 1842 a treaty was signed between Britain and China in which both sides agreed to respect the frontier in that area. But the Chinese claim that the border was never exactly defined, and that the Chinese authorities in fact refused subsequent British requests that it should be delimited. Here, too, the Chinese claim that the 'traditional border' lies well to the south-west, in some cases 50 miles beyond, the border marked on most Indian and other maps. Moreover, in addition to these two areas there are other regions (altogether covering some 40,000 square miles) along the Sino-Indian frontier about which the Chinese have put forward similar claims.

As a statement of history many of these Chinese assertions may be reasonably accurate. 'Perhaps the Chinese Government is the more intransigent because it knows that it has a better case for frontier revision than the world has realized,' commented a respected British specialist of Indian problems. 'The quarrel with India is about frontiers which were fixed by the British imperial power, Britain having conquered India, pushed out her frontiers as far as they could be carried without a major war. In doing this, Britain occupied a border area much of which was inhabited by non-Indian peoples. The frontier with China, where demarcated at all, was fixed arbitrarily and surreptitiously, or by treaties which Peking now denies were correctly negotiated with the Chinese Central Government of the time.'[77]

Having said all this, if territorial claims based on 'traditional boundaries' can be put forward with reference to situations a century old, Austria could claim most of Eastern Europe, India might claim Ceylon, or Turkey could ask for rights over the Middle East. Though some of the inhabitants of the disputed areas are Tibetan, the majority is neither ethnically nor linguistically

Chinese. On the other hand, as a multi-racial entity, India herself may claim that the boundaries in question have become 'traditional', established by usage and accepted by international opinion.

But whatever the validity of these arguments, the real question is why the Chinese have been acting as they did and why they have chosen that particular moment to reveal their ambitions and affront the susceptibilities of all Asia?

According to Mr. Nehru, when Mr. Chou En-lai visited India in 1956, he clearly stated that China would be prepared to recognize the McMahon Line. Now the Chinese are explicitly challenging it. Yet they could hardly have felt that the reoccupation of the disputed area was either particularly urgent or that China's honour made their recovery essential.

Why, then, did China flout international opinion at a particularly unsuitable moment, for the sake of a few strips of mainly barren, sparsely populated, mountainous terrain?

Before attempting to list the possible answers, it should be said that one of the first aims of the present Chinese Government after it came to power was to try to re-establish what most Chinese have for long regarded as the traditional borders of their country. China's strength is restored and she is determined to undo the wrongs which she considers were done to her in the past while she had been weak. Full Chinese autonomy was regained in Manchuria; Chinese control of Sinkiang was reasserted; Tibet—considered by even the Chiang Kai-shek régime before and after its flight from China, as part of the country—was occupied; Peking probably sought the return to China of Outer Mongolia, a region towards which flows a large slice of the economic aid China provides outside her borders. Burma—as, later, the smaller Himalayan Kingdoms—were confronted with claims of frontier rectification and, of course, the incorporation of Taiwan is an official claim. Clearly, then, simple irredentist motives provide a conditioning background to present-day official Chinese thinking. This alone, however, does not answer the question.

The most sinister and probably the least plausible explanation is that China is probing the Indian will to resist with the ulterior motive of gaining springboards for an invasion of the Gangetic plain. It is, of course, difficult to see what interest China could possibly have in invading a region representing more problems than advantages, or how such a move would be tolerated either by the West or the Soviet Union itself.

Somewhat more realistic explanations are connected with the Tibetan situation. According to these, Peking needs to confirm its own propaganda picture of foreign intervention behind the Tibetan revolt. China's action may be prompted by revenge for India's asylum to the Dalai Lama, for having permitted him to indulge in political activities on Indian soil or for her toleration of Tibetan 'counter-revolutionary forces' in Kalimpong. China may also have been desirous to seal off the Himalayan passes to prevent the movement across the border of the remnants of armed rebels and, inversely, the infiltration of political agents, or simply to stop the leakage of information concerning the kind and the extent of the cleaning-up operations she undertook in the region.

In an international context, four different interpretations are advanced. According to the first, by provoking the border tension, China's motive may have been to blackmail Russia for increased aid in return for greater co-operation in negotiations with the West. Similar pressure against Taiwan, the offshore islands or, perhaps, in Laos, was discernible each time East-West negotiations appeared near. Another interpretation sees in China's action a means to influence India's internal politics. China, so the argument runs, is impressed by the unmistakable shifting of Indian internal politics to the right; sees no more utility in India's neutrality; and by further hastening this shift in favour of re-action, prepares the ground for the long-range role of India's Communists as the sole alternative. Also, it had been suggested that China may be calling into question all frontiers established by colonial powers all over the world and thus may forge for herself a powerful weapon which by playing on the irredenta of the emerging states in several continents, could be manipulated to her advantage. Finally, and still in the international context, there is the belief that, in the long run, China intends to re-establish her supremacy over the Himalayan border states and thus gain solid strategic footholds south of the Himalayan range.

Two more convincing interpretations remain.

The first claims to detect the signs of inadequate control from Peking over local military commanders. More explicitly, it is conceivable that some local military leaders, instructed to seal off the border, have gone too far in the execution of their orders and have provoked incidents more grave than foreseen by Peking. Going even farther, and considering that the major incidents took place during a period of acute political tension and rivalry within the Peking leadership, it is not impossible that the initiatives of certain local commanders have been planned or have been utilized to further the aims of one or the other of the contending groups. The creation of an atmosphere of international tension to serve the interests of rival politicians was not unknown in Stalinist Russia. Renewed incidents after seemingly conciliatory moves on behalf of Mr. Chou En-lai; the alternation of reasonable and defensively aggressive tones in Peking's notes; together with simultaneous and significant changes in the Army command, do lend some semblance of reality to such speculations.[78]

The most convincing explanation of the events, however, accepts the evidence that the frontier incidents are the result of a deliberate act of Chinese policy to extend control over the disputed areas by force. Five years earlier almost identical tactics had been used in a similar dispute with Burma. There, too, China occupied disputed areas first and then negotiated from a 'position of strength'.[79] To apply the same procedure to the Indian border dispute may have been dictated by two unequal reasons: one strategic, the other mainly political.

The first is connected with a military road China had built in the Ladakh area. It connects north-western Tibet with Sinkiang and renders the reinforcement of the Chinese garrison in Tibet infinitely more easy than through the much longer and much more cumbersome road leading to Lhasa from Central China.[80] Eventual concessions along the McMahon Line, so the Chinese may have argued, could induce the Indians to accept the *fait accompli* in Kashmir and to cede them the area across which their indispensable strategic road runs. Had political passions aroused in India not bound Mr. Nehru's hands, this might have been an acceptable basis for negotiations. In exchange for a region, in Ladakh, without immediate economic or strategic interest to India, she would have obtained at last the recognition of the much more vital north-eastern boundary along the McMahon Line.

This eventual bargain apart, the political reason why China adopted towards India tactics first tried on Burma, may be of wider significance. If the Chinese were prepared to sacrifice the good-will of India as well as that of most of non-Communist Asia—a good-will they have laboriously built up during the preceding years—their reasons must have been wider. They seem to have accepted the desirability of a political and ideological show-down with India and, indirectly, with what India represents in present-day Asia. China appears to have welcomed the opportunity to humble India and thus the efficiency of India's social experiment which is sometimes regarded as an alternative to her own. That the increased defence costs thus imposed on India divert further funds from her economic effort, while it imposes practically no additional financial strain on China, may also have figured in the calculation. That the exploitation of the incidents by the Indian right-wing would deplace the centre of gravity of Indian politics farther towards the right and, to that extent, at least in the long run, would improve the chances of India's Communists, may equally have been considered. Above all, by choosing a terrain where India is physically unable to retaliate effectively, China appears to have profited from the opportunity to impress upon all Asia that she is in a position to make herself respected and, simultaneously, to make it clear that in the expected case of even greater Western military involvement in Asia, she would not shrink from any action intended to defend her strategic interests.

Whatever part some or all the motives enumerated may have played in China's decision, it confirmed beyond her borders the trend which had become noticeable within them. It was merely the external projection of that new mood, born of growing impatience, which appreciated ineffective sympathy less than respect or even fear. Yet outside the country, as within it, the new course was not without its dangers. Together they combined to aggravate still further China's growing tension.

12 Sino-Soviet Divergencies in 1959

IN THE AUTUMN of 1959 the political situation in China resembled a landscape after a major underground convulsion. Extinct volcanoes began to hurl forth lava again, tidal waves of unknown origin were causing havoc, and earth tremors were spreading right across the country's borders. The signs were clear enough. But the epicentre of the catastrophe was not located. Was it in the tensions created by the titanic exertions of the masses? was it, perhaps, in the fear and in the growing incertitude caused by the Soviet Union's reconciliation with the imperialist West? or was it simply in transitory doubts whether the leap over backwardness could really be accomplished with the dangerous methods under way?

Where exactly that epicentre was remains unknown. But the tension at home, and its projection beyond the country's frontiers, showed no signs of abating. While in August, Mr. Chou En-lai revealed the rectified production figures of 1958 and the reduced objectives for 1959, a few thousand Chinese soldiers, moving into small, uninhabited but neuralgic areas in the heart of the continent, were modifying the climate of inter-Asian relations. And if the Chinese Premier's revelations offered convincing proof to support the rightist's case, it soon became clear that his threats to silence and to punish them were only to magnify the crisis.

As an opening to the coming climax, the *Red Flag* summed up the official thesis once again. Only two days after the Premier's speech, it insisted that '... Marxist-Leninists always repudiate the notion that revolution is something in which a handful of people in private work out a formula and then order the masses to act in accordance'. The Communes and the Great Leap, then, were in response to the masses' revolutionary élan. Their opponents, therefore, were both against the revolution and against the masses. They were '. . . hoping in vain for a slackening off of our rate of advance, for the failure and collapse of our cause'. And they, it was hinted, were to be found even in the highest places. They are '. . . always feeling worried lest something may happen and always complaining and even reproaching that "excesses" occur in the mass movement, and being scared of a mass movement as of a conflagration'. Such activities amounted to '. . . criminal activity against the cause of building Socialism'.[81]

These harsh words to the internal enemy were followed by warnings to those with similar fears concerning external relations. Those who are '. . . idolizing America and . . . fear that America (is) unbeatable' were branded as reactionary defeatists. Though Mr. Khrushchev was about to sit down with the American President at Camp David to talk of co-existence, the *Red Flag* assured its readers that 'The international conditions are extremely favourable to the Chinese people's anti-imperialist struggle. As Chairman Mao Tse-tung pointed out, we are now in the great era when "the East wind prevails over the West wind". . . .' Although '. . . to work and preserve world peace is our basic policy' the rest of the article was devoted to the demonstration that the West, and the U.S.A. in particular, were condemned to fail. '. . . with a blow here and a kick there' they could be 'knocked over'. Moreover, '. . . to this day, the U.S. imperialists show no intention of giving up their schemes to attack China from three directions—from our territory Taiwan, from Korea and from Viet Nam'. This external danger, however, can be averted by even greater internal effort. '. . . we can consolidate and win further victories only by forging ahead speedily. If we do not rapidly change our economic backwardness, we will be beaten and there is the danger that the fruits of our victory will be grabbed by imperialism. The Chinese people have been bullied long enough by imperialism. We will never allow it to stage a comeback. . . .'[82]

These explanations of internal and external rigidity barely restated, on September 18, Peking Radio made a laconic announcement of a major cabinet reshuffle.

Marshal Peng Teh-huai, the Defence Minister, was replaced by Marshal Lin Piao, one of Mao Tse-tung's close collaborators, who had just recovered from a long illness. The Chief of Staff of the armed forces, appointed less than a year before, yielded his place to General Lo Jui-ching, for over ten years the head of the Ministry of Public Security. Two assistant Foreign Ministers as well as a string of lesser officials were also to give up their posts, while promotions in several ministries were announced. In addition, in view of the approaching tenth anniversary of the régime, amnesties were granted to certain categories of political prisoners, collaborators with the Japanese, and common criminals.[83]

The most significant of these changes of course were those affecting top military and security appointments. The new Minister of Defence may have sufficiently recovered to direct the impending reorganization of the armed forces. More puzzling was the appointment of the new Chief of Staff. When his predecessor was named, it had been interpreted as a move towards greater political control over the army. Now, a year later, the same argument seemed to apply with even greater force. In fact the new Chief of Staff had been head of the political police for some years. Did this confirm rumoured difficulties between the Party and the armed forces? That the officers and men were unhappy with the campaign sending them to police the Communes, had already transpired from various publications. Or did the changes announced lend weight to the whisper that the army, composed mainly of peasants, was growing restive and was showing unmistakable solidarity with the peasantry's discontent?

Whatever the proportion of truth in these hypotheses may have been, and notwithstanding the amnesty, it seemed clear that rather than subsiding, the conflict within the Party was becoming more acute. Yet after the rectification of economic objectives, and with the reassertion of the Party's control over the armed forces, the first act of the crisis seemed to be over. The time had arrived for an interlude of rejoicing.

Peking's public buildings were floodlit and garlands of electric bulbs shone in the night. On the crisp, sunny day of October 1, a million marchers strode across the immense square in front of the Gate of Heavenly Peace with floats, flags, slogans and large-scale models of China's latest products. They were waving towards the balcony where Mao Tse-tung and Liu Shao-chi stood under huge red paper lanterns, surrounded by leaders of Communist parties from all over the world. And the two rostrums flanking the Gate were crowded with fraternal delegations and visitors from eighty countries. The march-past ended in the traditional Dragon Dance and for two days after the people of China relaxed with the feeling that they well deserved a holiday.

Among the guests on the balcony stood Mr. Khrushchev. He had arrived the day before from Camp David, with only a brief stop-over in Moscow. The night before the great parade, he was guest of honour at a giant banquet held in the brand-new Great Hall of the People. Chou En-lai greeted the Soviet leader. Mao did not speak. Though the Chinese Premier's speech was very brief, he did not fail to underline that 'after several years of searching' China had found her own way of building socialism. Her new methods, the guests were assured, would soon turn her into a strong power which, in the company of the other socialist countries, would 'triumph over capitalism in a peaceful competition'. Then, as if to remind Mr. Khrushchev that there were alternatives to compromise, the Chinese Premier spoke of '. . . the struggle for national independence, for democracy and freedom of the Asian, African and Latin American peoples', a struggle which continues to 'forge ahead' and which 'no force on earth can prevent . . . from attaining victory'.

Mr. Khrushchev's answer was several times longer. Repeatedly he returned to his central theme, the need for peaceful co-existence. 'We must defeat the capitalist countries in peaceful competition, and we will,' he asserted. 'The forces of socialism are already so great that real possibilities are being created for excluding war as a means of solving international disputes. . . .' Elaborating on the change of heart of the United States—the very country which failed to recognize his hosts—the Russian leader redoubled his efforts to convert his audience: '. . . we must think realistically and understand the contemporary situation correctly. This, of course, does not by any means signify that if we are so strong, then we must test by force the stability of the capitalist system. This would be wrong, the peoples would not understand and would never support those who would think of acting in this way. We have always been against wars and conquest. . . . No, we have no need of war at all. The question of when this or that country will take the path to socialism is decided by its own people. This, for us, is the holy of holies. . . .'

There was polite applause. There were friendly greetings when the Soviet leader left Peking airport. But all during his stay neither Mao nor Liu had anything to say in public. They refrained from answering Khrushchev's speeches with as much as a single phrase.

What they might have had to say was already in print in the form of an article by Liu Shao-chi, published the day before. Following on a detailed review of China's achievements, the President turned to their critics: 'Those who find fault with our big leap forward and the mass movement also find fault with our rural people's communes. They maintain that (they) were set up "much too soon" . . . (a) mass movement which conforms to the laws of historical development under the conditions obtaining in China . . . is not something that can emerge because somebody shouts for it, nor will it collapse because somebody opposes it.' And to conclude, he expressed the opinion that China's example may well find imitators in the world.[84]

But the holiday was over. Mr. Khrushchev had gone. The Chinese returned to their daily labours. And in the higher spheres the crisis went on. The anti-rightist campaign restarted with unprecedented ferocity. Notwithstanding the Soviet Premier's advice, or Liu Shao-chi's self-confidence in the right- ness of China's course, the divisions which have been apparent within the Party were assuming the form of a major dispute. They were leading to a bitter fight within the leadership itself.

If the rightists were wrong to point out the dangers of the new course, they were still wrong when events have justified their apprehensions. What is more, they have become responsible for the very opposition which clearly began to manifest itself in the highest spheres of the Party. At this point, however, a new shade was introduced into the debate. In the October 1 issue of *Red Flag*, Kang Sheng, an alternate member of the Politburo, disclosed that Mao Tse-tung himself gave the personal lead to the attack on the 'right opportunists' at the Lushan meeting. In the same article, however, Kang Sheng employed a new tone towards them. Since they were patriotic and opposed to imperialism, he stated, the Party could treat them leniently. In the following months, then, the deviationists have been referred to as 'rightist inclined', implying, no doubt, that the inclination could be corrected given serious self-criticism. But the amnesty no less than this new verbal subtility merely helped to shift official fury on to more precise targets. From now on the campaign aimed less at rightists in general—henceforth the lesser sinners—but rather at unnamed but highly placed members of the Party who were 'undermining Party solidarity and discipline'.

By December 19 an article in *Red Flag* revealed that the issues raised went even deeper and involved the question itself how the Party should be organized. For several months these rightists had been denounced with monotonous regularity. Now a new charge appeared. They wanted to be free to conduct 'anti-Party activities within the Party'. The 'handful' of those constituting this group were accused of 'carrying on factional activities'. They claimed that there was no democracy inside the Party and, of course, thereby paved the way for the return of capitalism. The language employed strongly suggested that the 'handful' were among the highest in the hierarchy, and that more were involved lower down.

The terminology was beginning to resemble that employed in Moscow two and a half years earlier, before the expulsion of the 'anti-Party group'. To those with even longer memories, it may have recalled even the time of Trotsky, Zinoviev and Kamenev, when they had assailed Party bureaucracy. But there followed no purges or expulsions. Foreign observers were trying hard to identify highly placed personalities with one side or the other in the dispute. But persuasion and the astonishing stability of the leadership prevailed. There was no open fissure. Yet, clearly, as in Russia before so now in China, the real question under debate was whether a party wielding dictatorial power could tolerate free discussion within itself.

There could be little doubt whose opinion would prevail. The levers of the Party machine, and therefore of power in China, were firmly in the hands of the few who had ordered the Chinese to achieve all 'within the realm of human possibility'. They were men whose intense pride and contempt for the outside world were growing into an obsession and who, after a quarter-century of success and absolute power, were showing the familiar symptoms of being incapable of tolerating opposition to their opinions. They had become prisoners of the vicious circle they had created. Their case, of course, was solid: China had to hurry. Fast growing population as much as external danger called for bold measures. China could not abandon her new course. External tension only helped to keep it going and to speed the forced march. Any relaxation of international tension implied also the danger that some kind of bargain might be arranged between Russia and the West at China's expense. Soviet *rapprochement* with America was likely to render less dependable the Soviet shield. Yet to consolidate the Great Leap, and to bring under control the internal and external tension it had generated, like the sorcerer's apprentice China's leaders had to find the magic formula capable to provide the issue.

It could not be but in taking over of the leadership of their own opposition. To succeed, the ideological censure of China's allies had to cease and a new inter-alliance relationship was needed to confirm the country's increased stature within the Communist bloc. Yet to rally the doctrinal backing of the Communist world behind Peking's leaders, it was imperative first to change Moscow's current view on the rest of the world. That attempt implied the intensification of the process of readjustment within the Sino-Soviet alliance in the political, the economic, as well as the military field. And the debate which was to accompany it, soon became audible to the whole world.

13 The Search for a United Communist Front 1960

ON FEBRUARY 4, 1960, the leaders of the Warsaw Treaty powers assembled in Moscow to concert their attitudes before the new round of East-West negotiations. The communiqué was mild and optimistic and contained even good wishes for the American President's forthcoming trip to the Soviet Union. However, Kang Sheng, the Chinese delegate, delivered a stern warning. To begin with, he pointedly repeated China's refusal to accept any disarmament agreement negotiated without her presence. He agreed with the other delegates that there was some relaxation in the international situation due to the Communist bloc's growing strength. But from there on his arguments differed. To the Chinese delegate negotiations were not justified. 'The actions of the United States prove fully that its imperialist nature will not change. American imperialism still remains the arch enemy of world peace,' he declared. Peking's press and radio promptly gave great play to its delegate's observations. The publicity organs of the Western Communist states failed even to mention that he had spoken.

The roles were reversed when, shortly after, the Soviet leader set out on his South-east Asian tour and visited the very countries with which China found herself in bitter dispute. While Soviet propaganda heavily underlined Khrushchev's speeches in India, Burma and Indonesia, Peking radio completely ignored the journey during its first week and afterwards contented itself with only very brief references to it.

Peking's growing intransigence seemed to be calculated to appeal to all those within the Soviet Union as in the Communist bloc as a whole who, for one reason or another, were not enthusiastic about Khrushchev's policy of détente. China's insistence that so long as the capitalist system survived sporadic wars at least would be inevitable, could not but please the Soviet officers just packing their luggage to take up prosaic civilian appointments after the extensive reduction of the armed forces. East Germany's request for rockets, in case the Americans gave nuclear arms to the

Federal Republic, was opposed by Khrushchev and was supported by Peking. Kang's arguments may have found attentive ears among the orthodox of the Communist movements all over Eastern Europe. Moreover, there was always the possibility of China creating new tensions, in the Taiwan Straits, on the Indian border, or in Laos, in order to change the climate of Russo-American negotiations. Clearly, China's influence in the domestic affairs of the Communist bloc was increasingly asserted and in a direction unmistakably opposed to that of its recognized leader.

Throughout April, the month before the Paris summit conference, the thinly disguised altercation between Soviet and Chinese leaders was growing in intensity. Gradually it was becoming a match of doctrinal table-tennis with fragments of Marxist scriptures being hurled back and forth between Moscow and Peking.

On the pretext of celebrating the ninetieth anniversary of Lenin's birth, two articles in *Red Flag* and two others in the *People's Daily* offered analyses of the world situation which were barely disguised attacks on Khrushchev's policy of peaceful co-existence. Their theme was summed up in *Red Flag*: '. . . We believe in the absolute correctness of Lenin's thinking: war is an inevitable outcome of systems of exploitation and the source of modern wars is the imperialist system.' The American President was referred to in unflattering terms. One of the articles listed thirty-four hostile acts by the Americans since the Camp David meeting. Lenin was cited to justify the inevitability of war and there were references to 'revisionism' as the current aim of the West to weaken the Communist bloc.

On April 22, Moscow put up its top theoretician, Mr. Kuusinen, to reply. Still within the frame of the Lenin celebrations, he insisted that the Communist bloc's new position of strength permitted to make full use of the new factors acting for peace in order to avoid nuclear war. 'A dogmatic position is an obsolete position', he warned before he underlined that, except during the civil war and the war of intervention, Lenin had always been a champion of peaceful co-existence.

A week later, America's Under-Secretary of State, Douglas

Dillon, made it clear that no concessions could be expected at the Paris meeting and Mr. Herter, the Secretary of State, reiterated the theme a few days later. In another five days, answering them from Baku, Mr. Khrushchev renewed his threat of a separate peace treaty with Eastern Germany but still expressed his hope that the 'spirit of Camp David' might lead to progress in Paris.

On May 5 the Soviet Premier announced the shooting down of the U-2 plane on May 1. Forty-eight hours later he revealed that it was on a spy mission in the heart of Russia, but added that he believed that President Eisenhower did not know of the flight. In another four days the American President accepted responsibility for such incursions and covered the statement that spy flights were official American policy.

The summit conference was to open on May 16. Four days later, after its failure even to be opened, speaking in Berlin, Khrushchev disappointed his East German hosts by fixing no date for a peace treaty with them and rather envisaged renewed negotiations with the West once a new American President was installed.

Something as yet unknown must have happened during the 24 days between Kuusinen's speech and Khrushchev's refusal to agree to the opening of the summit meeting. There were, of course, the speeches by Messrs. Dillon and Herter, the U-2 incident and the President's acceptance of responsibility for it. Considering the Soviet premier's temperament, it is difficult to ascertain to what extent his indignation was genuine or feigned. It is conceivable that he had to give way in face of evidence that within the Soviet Union itself there was response to Mao's manœuvrings to undermine his position. Yet, significantly, he was still careful to stage the Paris break-up in a way calculated not to support the agreement that the policy of negotiations with the West had failed. Only the moment was inopportune.

Whatever the real reasons, Khrushchev seemed to have veered nearer to the Chinese view of the world situation. Peking's pleasure was understandable seeing the West's generous cooperation in its ideological outflanking movement against the

Soviet supporters of the détente. Mao's analysis of the situation proved to be more realistic than Khrushchev's and Peking could congratulate itself on having been right. And there, the first act of the Great Debate came to a close.

But there was a second act to come. It was far more important than the first both for the future policy of the Soviet bloc and for throwing some light on the motives which had brought the first to an end.

Understandably, China was ready to harvest the political dividends of her triumph. The occasion was provided by the Peking meeting of the World Federation of Trade Unions early in June. The editorials accompanying it were uncompromising and the speeches of the Chinese of unprecedented violence. Mr. Liu Chang-sheng, Vice-President of the W.F.T.U. and China's principal spokesman, dealt in detail with the question of war and peace. In barely concealed terms he denounced the Soviet Union as a renegade to the Communist cause. That imperialism would honestly accept disarmament he considered improbable. 'But there are people who believe that such a proposal can be realized when imperialism still exists and that the danger of war can be eliminated by relying on such a proposal. This is unrealistic illusion. . . .' Though the banning of nuclear weapons is an aim worth working for, the Chinese delegate was equally sceptical about its value. The imperialists would not respect it. 'And even if in their own interest (they) dare not unleash a large-scale atomic war, they still can wage war with so-called conventional weapons. Therefore (people should be careful not to adopt) a naïve attitude towards the United States and other imperialists.'

To defend the 'illusions' of those who believed that a nuclear war would be too high a price to pay for 'the truly beautiful future' which the Chinese expected to build 'on the debris of a dead imperialism' and, no doubt, also to defend 'the modern revisionists who are in the service of imperialism', on June 10 the *Sovietskaya Rossiya* of Moscow criticized comrades 'who consider that the smallest worsening of the international situation is proof of the wisdom of their convictions'. But that was only a foretaste of things to come. Two days later, *Pravda* itself lashed out. Profiting of the occasion of the fortieth anniversary of the publication of Lenin's pamphlet *Left-Wing Communism, An Infantile Disorder*, it delivered a vitriolic attack on left-wing deviation within the Communist camp. That infantile disease, *Pravda* warned, is still claiming its victims. Their error was to believe that the policy of co-existence was contrary to the spirit of Marxist-Leninism. Then, to leave no doubt in his readers' minds at whom the attack was aimed, it named a second error: the belief of some Communists that, once in power, they could 'immediately introduce Communism and avoid the historic phases of its development'. And soon it became clear that *Pravda*'s article merely announced that Mr. Khrushchev was ready to get the malady under control.

Yet to understand the essence of the Great Debate, it is worth pausing for a moment to examine the document in the centre of the discussion. The pamphlet in question was a violent diatribe against Communists silly enough to meet the enemy head on rather than to manœuvre and compromise. It had been written while Lenin was still fighting for the very existence of his régime and was aimed principally at uncompromising German and British Communists. It contained Lenin's now classic instructions: '. . . To carry on a war for the overthrow of the international bourgeoisie, a war which is a hundred times more difficult and complicated than the most stubborn of ordinary wars between States, and to refuse beforehand to manœuvre, to utilize the conflict of interest (even though temporary) among one's enemies, to refuse to temporize and compromise with possible allies (even though transient, unstable, vacillating and conditional)—is this not ridiculous in the extreme? . . . It is possible to conquer the more powerful enemy only be exerting our efforts to the utmost and by *necessarily*, thoroughly, carefully, attentively and skilfully taking advantage of every "fissure" however small, in the ranks of our enemies, of every antagonism of interest among the bourgeois of the various countries, among the various groups or types of bourgeoisie in the various countries; by taking advantage of every opportunity, however small, of gaining an ally among the masses, even though this ally be temporary, vacillating, unstable, unreliable and conditional. Those who do not understand this, do not understand even a grain of Marxism. . . .'

Already in February, 1956, at the Twentieth Party Congress, Khrushchev had clearly announced his amendment to Leninist doctrine, that the inevitability of war could be discarded. This was so because the global victory of Communism could henceforth be assured thanks to the new strength of the Soviet Union and without recourse to nuclear war. That time his important statement was overshadowed by the more spectacular revelations about Stalin's terror. Yet the doctrinal change was there and now, in June, 1960, the Chinese had to be reminded of it. And the text utilized to do so was of some significance.

It may have implied that after all Khrushchev did not overrate the capacity of adaptation of Western societies to their changed position in the world. Maybe he had no illusions but, unlike his Chinese allies, he merely considered that clowning, public relations and smiles were more effective than threats, to hasten the process of Western disintegration. By digging up Lenin's celebrated pamphlet, *Pravda* wished to remind Peking that, particularly in the age of hydrogen and cobalt bombs, this was still the wiser policy. And that there should be no mistake about the fact that the power and the will were there to bring the disease under control, the party secretaries of the Communist bloc were called into conclave for the end of June in Bucharest.

The decisive discussions were in secret. The Russian leader reiterated his thesis that Lenin's theory of the inevitability of war was no longer applicable to present world conditions. The Chinese delegate voiced his ineradicable suspicion of the United States and insisted on the complete unity of the Socialist camp. But the final resolution was firm in its attack on 'revisionist, dogmatic and left-wing sectarian deviations', on 'manifestations of narrow nationalistic tendencies', and urged Communists to apply Marxism-Leninism 'skilfully in practice'.

It may well be that Western observers tend to over-estimate the immediate practical impact of doctrinal differences between

Communist countries. It is also possible that the analyses of Peking and Moscow of the world situation had not differed so much as had been believed in the spring, only their preference for the tactics to profit from it. Moreover, during the six weeks between Paris and Bucharest a whole chain of events intervened to give the dispute new context. If Mao's scepticism of Western flexibility was confirmed by American provocations on the eve of the summit conference, international developments during the six weeks following it have even more spectacularly confirmed Khrushchev's faith in the tactics prescribed by Lenin. Ten days after the Paris fiasco there was the *coup d'état* in Turkey. The Koreans revolted against Syngman Rhee and the 'peaceful reunification' of their country became a possibility. The delegates in Bucharest still had in their ears the noise of the Tokyo crowd as it slammed the door in the face of the American President. The main pillars of the world Mr. Foster Dulles had built were visibly cracking while in Cuba the Communists were gaining their first bridgehead in the Western hemisphere. If Mao's suspicion was justified, Khrushchev's smiles were even more paying. And, quite clearly, his position in the Communist world was once again stronger than it had been believed in Paris a few weeks before.

The Bucharest meeting barely over, on June 26, in an article written for Peking's Sunday papers, Mme Soong Ching-lin— Vice-President of the Republic and widow of Sun Yat-sen— ridiculed Westerners who wanted to make believe that China was an aggressive country. 'China is anxious to live in pacific co-existence with everybody, even with the imperialists,' she wrote. Two days later, in its official commentary on the Bucharest conference, the *People's Daily*, though not entirely excluding that war may be forced on the Communist camp, insisted that the forces of Socialism 'surpass those of imperialism' and thus 'the possibility of preventing imperialism from launching a new world war exists and increases with each passing day'.

On August 1, during a surprise visit to a reception at the Swiss Embassy in Peking, Mr. Chou En-lai made a speech which was probably the mildest heard from a leading Chinese personality in recent years. 'Some provocateurs have accused China of having given up the policy of seeking peaceful relations with countries with differing social systems. These are slanders and not at all correct,' he said. Then, he reiterated China's wish to have the best relations with her neighbours 'as well as in Europe and in other parts of the world'. Also he relaunched his former proposal for a zone free of nuclear weapons built on a network of non-aggression pacts in Asia and the Western Pacific in which the United States too might participate. And the fact that he spoke at the Swiss Embassy provided him with an excellent opportunity to hold up as an example to other countries the satisfactory relationship between China and *neutral* Switzerland.

Obviously, somewhere behind the noise of the verbal artillery, a compromise was being worked out. According to all evidence the Chinese have agreed to pay verbal homage to Mr. Khrushchev's doctrine of co-existence but on condition that he applied it with more revolutionary zeal. China, on her part, was to distribute more of the smiles which had been the monopoly of the Soviet leader for some time. Khrushchev, on his part, was to apply Lenin's instructions with less prudence than during the past three years. Thus China will seek to wind up her disputes with her Asian neighbours, to be more accommodating with Mr. Kishi's successors, and to refrain from creating tensions where the Soviet nuclear shield would have to be invoked. To honour his side of the bargain, Mr. Khrushchev already posed China's presence as the pre-condition of any future summit meetings, and he will be moving more boldly in Turkey, in the Congo, in Algeria, in Cuba or wherever else Western policy will continue to provide him with tempting opportunities. And as if to demonstrate his new role, Mr. Khrushchev himself went to represent his country at the United Nations where, with smiles and threats, he applied his technique of simultaneous division and intimidation.

Yet like thunder in the wake of the passing storm, the ideological arguments rumbled on in the journals of Moscow and Peking. The harmful display of differences had to be brought to an end. All during November 1960 the leaders of the world's Communist Parties were holding a secret conclave in the Kremlin. The debates were long and laborious. But the final compromise seemed to confirm Mr. Khrushchev's triumph. Clearly, he obtained his allies' authorization to probe the prospects of compromise with the new American President.

Thus, the second act of the Great Debate was over. Did the U.S.S.R. promise her principal ally further economic aid in order to obtain its ideological collaboration? or did China comply, believing that international developments would inevitably shift Russian positions nearer to her own and thus make any retreat on her part unnecessary?

Whatever the answers to these questions—and whatever concrete economic or military results the bargaining may have yielded the compromise will have moved Sino-Soviet relations on to a new plateau of greater equality. And the certitudes from that new position would permit China to begin the consolidation of the feverish changes of the past three years.

14 Rethinking the Production Plans for 1960/61

WHILE CHINA'S temper had been rising with the approach of the summit conference, internal tension too continued to grow in intensity. But long before the ideological debate had reached its climax, a number of symptoms indicated that China's internal evolution was seeking a new direction.

The daily toil of the masses had not become lighter. On the contrary, it was announced in the spring that the setting up of Communes in the towns was proceeding 'in a big way'. This was rather unexpected. In its December 1958 resolution the Party had indefinitely postponed their formation on the ground that the cities were not yet prepared for it. Now that the decision had been taken it became clear that, in practice, their creation aimed at the total mobilization of labour power still left unutilized in the urban centres. That meant women in particular. Those of working age and still tied to household work were enlisted in handicraft enterprises or in small factories and were given a small wage as members of an urban Commune. The new organization can be based on a group of workshops, small factories or offices in a defined suburban area, with the more modest transforming waste material into elementary consumer goods and the more important ones turning out light industrial products. This involved also the setting up of mess halls, nurseries, old-age homes and clubs and, to that extent, further extended what is usually referred to as 'collective living'. That some of the women welcomed such independence with a modest income rather than to be tied to household work, is possible. That, simultaneously, urban Communes helped to complete the absolute mobilization of the country's labour force, as well as the extension of the State's total control over the activities of its citizens, is certain. Yet in the towns, as in the countryside, the transformation has been gradual. Practice tends to lag behind the Chinese propagandists' inflexible utopia and is still far from the phalansterian visions of some sanguine foreign observers.

In the meantime there has also been an extraordinary intensification of the glorification of Mao Tse-tung. Whatever doubts could exist about his continued pre-eminence at the time of Liu Shao-chi's elevation to the Presidency, they had soon been dispelled. With each new stage of the difficulties caused by the Great Leap and the introduction of the Communes, there had been a compensatory stepping up of propaganda depicting Mao Tse-tung as the infallible leader whose foresight, tactical wisdom, and correct analysis of the future was bound to provide satisfactory ultimate solutions. His essays and speeches were invoked as the mental guide-books of the nation and their study has been elevated into a national cult. To trust his vision of the future was frantically built up into a mass reflex. Remarkable claims were made to extol his clairvoyance and omniscience. Wuhan University had set up a special research institute for the study of the Party Chairman's writings. Even workers and peasants were encouraged to participate in emulation campaigns to see who could better master Mao's texts.

In February 1960 when holding their joint Congress, the two associations of China's former merchants and industrialists declared themselves 'proud to be living in the era of Mao Tse-tung' in a message addressed to him. The real purpose of their congregation, however, had been their mental preparation for more active participation in the country's economic effort. While their resolution emphasized their political reformation, it also acknowledged the State's promise that their further ideological remoulding would be carried on by milder methods rather than through the violent processes of the class struggle they had experienced. Behind the abject style, however, there emerged the outline of a new compromise. In exchange for less manual labour and fewer hours spent with political indoctrination, so it seemed, the skills and experience of China's ex-capitalists were going to be enlisted on a larger scale than hitherto to help provide sound management to the coming new phase of economic consolidation.[85]

Thus, as the denunciation of rightists was slowly petering out, in her own characteristic fashion, China was readying herself for the new course. Having expropriated the arguments of their critics, the authors of the Great Leap were now preparing for the replacement of the past three years' hectic initiatives with more systematic measures.

Yet before the last turn leading to the new road, a final and symbolic ritual sacrifice became necessary to drive home the dangers of nonconformism, however rational its arguments, in contrast to the safety of obedient orthodoxy. It was announced in the middle of April that Professor Ma Yin-chu, at the age of seventy-six, had been dismissed from his post as president of Peking University. His last article still arguing his thesis for population control had appeared only a few weeks before. His dismissal marked the end of a long drawn out debate. By now the Government seemed convinced that, notwithstanding rapid growth of population, it could fully develop China's industrial power without risking a dangerous lowering of living standards.

The plans were ready. Everything was set for the new departure.

It may be that assurances of Soviet help and solidarity had been obtained before the ideological debate was finally called off. In any case, the hope that through a series of feverish telescoping processes China could achieve full Communism within a few years was visibly giving way to more sober calculations. The errors to which doctrinaire impatience could lead at home and abroad had become apparent. Still, the most urgent aims had been realized. It was announced on January 22 that most of the 1959 production targets had been fulfilled. Thus the main aims of the second Five-Year Plan had been achieved three years ahead of schedule, by the end of 1959 instead of in 1962. Now the time had arrived for rationalization. For months China's leaders had been touring the country, personally supervising the work of modification and adaptation in factories and Communes. Mao Tse-tung himself had not been seen in Peking from October till the end of March. The self-assurance which for some time had seemed to be shaken, was gradually being re-established. The machine which had floundered towards the end of the first Plan, had been overhauled and was doggedly pushing forward again. The direction had slightly changed and the speed was readjusted. But the ultimate aims remained the same.

About this time, in the April issue of the specialized Party organ *Planning and Statistics*, a highly significant article appeared. It announced the details of a plan for the basic re-drafting and consolidation of China's industrial and agricultural expansion during the next three years. The outline, it transpired, was based on the findings of 'reports by Soviet experts in Peking'.

Wrapped in technical language, the project heralded the extension on a national scale of the principles which had governed the recent reorganization of the Communes. Just as their centralized control had been dispersed along three levels—the production brigades, the units comprising them, and the original central planning organ—so a similar decentralization was to be applied to industry and to other economic activities as well. While the central planning authority was to continue to control key enterprises, the Soviet experts urged, whenever possible power over small and medium enterprises should be transferred to local bodies. In place of irregular leaps, they advised the gradual mechanization of agriculture. Furthermore, the report counselled still greater dispersal of heavy industry, particularly towards the north-west and the south-west. Finally, to wind up their report, appropriately Lenin was quoted to the effect that: 'A balance which is regularly maintained indicated that it has been well planned.'[86]

When, on March 30, the production plans for 1960 were announced, the new trend became clear. It revealed a new and healthy reluctance to repeat the errors of 1958. The rate of industrial expansion, of course, was to remain high. That of heavy industry even spectacular. Yet the prescriptions for agriculture betrayed a compromise with reality. The growth called for was still far higher than in most underdeveloped countries. But it seemed attainable. Significantly, however, where once all the drive lay with industry, now some of the impetus was shifting to agriculture. The role of industry in the modernization of the countryside was repeatedly emphasized. Above all, a timetable for the gradual mechanization of agriculture was announced. 'The target we are striving for is to achieve a minor solution in four years beginning from 1959, an intermediate solution in seven years and a major solution in ten years,' the chairman of the State Planning Commission declared. 'We must strive for the basic realization of agricultural mechanization and extensive building of water conservancy works throughout the farmland in around ten years, and for a considerable extent of electrification by that time too. Our policy is to simultaneously introduce mechanization and semi-mechanization, simultaneously use the modern and the indigenous methods and, in the next three years, to put the main emphasis on improved and semi-mechanized farm implements.'[87]

And so, another May Day parade marched past the Gate of Heavenly Peace. China's remarkably stable leadership weathered yet another storm by the time the news came from Paris that their analysis of the world situation, and not that of Mr. Khrushchev's, was proved to be right. The doctrinaire altercation was wound up. Gradually it became known that 1960 was once again a hard year for Chinese agriculture and that there were unprecedented calamities playing havoc with production targets. There were hints that a third Five-Year Plan—sober and realistic —was in the making. Mr. Chou En-lai was preparing to put once again his considerable flexibility and personal charm at the service of his country's diplomacy. Mr. Lu Ting-yi, a deputy Premier, addressing a writers' and artists' congress in Peking, even told his audience: 'We must continue to persist in carrying out the policy of letting a hundred flowers blossom and a hundred schools of thought contend in the days to come.'[88] And it was noted that for the first time a Peking evening paper has reported a simple, ordinary murder—without completing it with a Marxist-Leninist moral.

'There is only one kind of genuine theory in the world,' Mao Tse-tung once remarked, 'that is the theory drawn from objective reality.' Deviating from his advice and then returning to it again, his country has accomplished its take-off. And the tide of China's revolution continues to rise, drawing its energy from the apparently inexhaustible reservoir of the awakened pride, the ambitions, and the limitless endurance of the Chinese quarter of humanity. The steel plants and all the other factories are busy reproducing themselves. The Communes are being consolidated and through them Peking is able to control and to direct the country's population and resources to a degree that is likely to produce even greater results. 'The course of development of the national economy is always from imbalance to balance, and again to imbalance,' Li Fu-chun said in his latest report. 'Every time this repeats itself it raises production to a higher level and the national economy advances uninterruptedly in these wave-like movements.'

Thus, China's tensions will continue to wax and wane. The Chinese people will have to get used to them. As for the rest of the world, it will have to learn to live with a powerful neighbour following those wave-like movements.

PART TWO

The Neighbour

DISTANCE USED to offer a comfortable alternative in international relations. Far removed from each other people could either ignore or misunderstand each other. They could choose one or the other without serious danger to their interests. One of the less obvious consequences of technological progress is the end of this alternative. Henceforth, one is obliged to try to understand the needs, the fears and the aspirations even of far away peoples just as if they were neighbours. No country can afford any longer to ignore or to misunderstand any other without grave risk to its own interests and security.

Today, one can breakfast in Peking and sleep in one's own bed in a Western capital the same night. Missiles cover the distance much faster. All the other instruments carrying ideas need no time at all. In fact, developments have been so fast that there can be no time to make up for all the neglect accumulated in the past. Yet there is probably no more urgent case for rectification than that of China. This is not so merely because the Chinese make up a quarter of the human race who live under one strong, central government. Neither is this the case merely because China is fast becoming a great industrial and military power. The main cause of the urgency is that China is bound to play an increasingly important role in international relations in the very near future.

As for the Chinese, history has been forcing them to familiarize themselves with important aspects of Western ways and means. The West, on the other hand, could afford to interest itself in only those features of Chinese philosophy, culture and other activities which it wished to know. To make up for our lack of knowledge of each other is becoming unpostponable. And it is forced upon us in the least favourable moment for the West.

Dimensions, linguistic difficulties and lack of communications had already conspired to make China almost unintelligible for Westerners. Her cultural background had still less in common with that of the West than that of either Russia, the Moslem world, or the mental universe of the Hindus. But this initial remoteness was only the starting point. Upon it came layer after layer of misunderstanding until, today, any effort at comprehension has to go beyond even detached objectivity and needs to rely on sympathy as its driving force.

After his disastrous encounter in the nineteenth century, the white man too easily convinced himself that China was being Westernized. As in many other parts of the world, we have taken respect for our technology for acceptance of our civilization. Perhaps in no other part of the world has this misunderstanding led to a greater reversal of Western fortunes than in China. Yet by the time this happened, our generalizations about China—as about many other parts of the world—had already been made on the basis of our contact with that tiny and unrepresentative minority who indeed accepted the supremacy of Western civilization.

Such generalizations about Chinese character, motives and aspirations left the West totally unprepared for China's coming choice of her emancipating ideology. It stunned the West when it discovered that the enthusiasm with which China embraced her new faith revealed also the unsuspected violence of her anti-Western feeling.

So, already vaguely conscious of the enormous difference in cultural background; then, bitterly disappointed by the brutal exposition of the superficiality of its generalizations; and, finally, deeply offended by such enthusiastic adhesion to an anti-Western creed, the West began to view China through the distorting prism of contemporary political passion.

And while looking at this already distorted picture, it was still further blurred by the techniques appropriate to the historical phase through which the Chinese have been passing. The means at the disposal of contemporary authoritarian régimes can, within a few years, bring about greater changes in people's traditional characteristics than had been possible in the past over centuries. Such techniques, in proportion to the tasks undertaken, are being wielded in present-day China with unprecedented concentration. Thus, even the puzzling and inscrutable picture of the Chinese of 1948, has become almost unrecognizable for most Westerners only a few years later.

Thus, though distance has been shrinking and, for the first time, China and the Western world have become neighbours, the gap of incomprehension continued to widen. It is indeed possible that China and the Western world had more reliable knowledge of each other when they had to rely on no more than the, often sympathetic, descriptions of rare travellers than in our days of controlled, but usually maliciously angled, information spread by mass media.

And to complete the tragedy, helped by Western humiliation in the past as much as by its condescending hostility as a deliberate instrument of policy, at present, the Chinese authorities themselves are now presenting their citizens with a picture of the West that is at least as distorted as are most Westerners' ideas about China's contemporary acts, methods and ambitions.

I The New Great Wall of China

ABOUT 170 MILLION Chinese have been born since the Communists came into power in 1949. There are some 200 million others who have reached mental maturity since that date. Thus it is probable that, at least in its main outlines, the thinking and the notions about the rest of the world of this half of China's population follows the officially inspired picture. Moreover, most probably, a great many of the remaining half too have been influenced by it.

The rough outline of that picture is easy to trace.

To begin with, little effort was needed to fold the past into the required shape. The great majority of Chinese are convinced that the West had exploited their country's past weakness, treated it with merciless inhumanity, humiliated its citizens, imposed on them unequal treaties, and offered in exchange even less than to their colonies where exploitation went hand in hand with at least a certain degree of responsibility for the satisfaction of the masses' elementary needs.

As for the more recent past, the majority of living Chinese have had first-hand experience of the régime that governed China before 1949. They have cause to remember its injustice, its inefficiency and incompetence, as well as its subservience to foreign interests. They know of the corruption and high-handedness of its leaders and officials. They have not forgotten that this same régime was generously aided by the West, and in particular by the United States; that there was no moralizing interference to improve its methods; and that, finally, no aid or effort was spared to maintain it in power even after it was clearly repudiated by a great majority.

In contrast, even those with grievances against the present régime would admit that it has put an end to corruption, maintains order, banished famines, ensures full employment, and has to its credit some very impressive material achievements. They know equally well that the same Powers which have desperately tried to salvage the previous régime, refuse even to recognize the existence of the present one notwithstanding all the advance it incontestably represents over the discredited past. Moral arguments in support of this ostracism can carry no real weight in the eyes of people who had direct experience of the immorality of the very system the present critics helped to prolong. They can concede even less that China now constitutes a military threat as their country's growing strength appears to them a satisfying guarantee against the repetition of past humiliations. As for the wilful misunderstanding of even their most positive achievements, they could hardly interpret it otherwise than hostility to everything that is flattering to Chinese national pride.

It is not to my purpose to discuss here the validity of this picture. It may be noted, however, that Chinese propaganda had a relatively easy task. We have already reached the tragic situation where Western attitudes perhaps even more than Chinese propaganda have managed to convince the majority of Chinese that anything they consider as their country's achievement must automatically be against the will and the interests of the West.

This conviction may or may not be justified. Yet in dealing with contemporary realities it is advisable to note its existence. In fact the accumulated deposit, as it were, of past and present grievances mixed with the ideological cement of Communism, have provided all the raw material needed to build China's new Great Wall of mental separation. And this new Great Wall constitutes today a more effective barrier to intercourse with the rest of the world than the old one ever provided against the invasions of the barbarians.

Again and again, in ordinary conversations, I have heard the Opium War mentioned with such bitterness and passion as if it had happened the day before. Visiting the Summer Palace with a young Chinese, I was treated to a description of its looting and destruction as a natural illustration of Western 'imperialistic behaviour'. Another Chinese, showing me around in Hankow's former international settlement, commented on the period with astonishing vehemence. His voice trembled with hatred as he spoke of real or alleged atrocities committed in his country by foreigners with extraterritorial privileges. And memories of the cruelty and of the corruption of the last years of the Chiang Kai-shek régime are unfailingly associated with Western interference and backing.

This artificial nursing of past grievances, however, takes on an even more frightening aspect as one sees it merged into contemporary distortions. Together they add up to a mental outlook in which past and present are moulded into a passionate and aggressive national resentment. Being shown workers' homes or factory canteens one is promptly assured that capitalist society could never provide such amenities. Daily headlines which report insignificant strikes in Western countries are referred to as proof of the insupportable misery of the workers groaning under capitalist exploitation. The slightest observations about long hours of labour in factories or in the Communes provokes angry retorts about Western bourgeois society's contempt for physical labour. The countries of Western Europe are pictured as decaying lands exposed to the rapacity of American monopolists, with both sides condemned to early doom. And when I once remarked on the Chinese internal airlines' objectionable habit of remaining on the ground each time a cloud appears in the skies, I was lectured about the West's inadmissible callousness about human life.

The rigidity and uniformity of mental outlook and even of verbal expression, as much as the tendency to preach with unctuousness on any subject, is bound to try the patience of even the most tolerant. Arguments, even the most factual, are met with that blank look of complete incredulity. And whenever drawn into the dreary enterprise of rational polemics, one soon reaches the point where there is the unmistakable frontier in the process of discussion. One can push just so far before coming up against one of the Big Certitudes tenaciously planted in Chinese consciousness.

This new Chinese neighbour, then, the product of humiliation and of the tendentious interpretation of both past and present, is apparently devoid of any sense of humour; is obstinately convinced that there can be only one side to any question; rejects all qualifications as inadmissible deviations from Absolute Truth; has all the admirable but irritating optimism that proclaims higher production and wider education to be the key to all human problems; and this is rendered even more formidable by his unshakable sense of mission. Less than fifteen years after the triumph of his new creed, he is confident in his country's growing power and influence in the world. This confidence is manifested in his increasing indifference to foreign opinion, in his understandable pride in the achievements of his government, and in a new nationalist tone, bordering on arrogance, which treats technical experts even from Communist countries with an unmistakable shade of condescension. In one word, after a century of helplessness, visibly, the new Chinese enjoys being feared.

The real question is, how much of what the Chinese leaders want their masses to believe, do they believe themselves? How much, in other words, are they misled by their own propaganda?

There is, of course, no sure answer. All one can say is that such attitudes have already caused China to misjudge both Western and Asian reactions to her acts.

It may be observed that similar tendencies have been discernible in the Soviet Union; that revolution, foreign hostility, enthusiasm for a new ideology, coupled with great exertions and isolation are bound to produce the same psychological results. Even if the parallel were complete, the Russian example would suggest that another quarter-century may pass before Chinese mental rigidity would begin to mellow. Even in that case the rest of the world would have to prepare itself to live for a good many more years with a dangerous China whose power and influence would probably grow. But the parallel is far from complete.

Unlike the Russians, the Chinese have been living in an age-long isolation from the rest of the world and even in periods of national weakness have maintained their vigorous sense of superiority over countries and races outside their borders. There are also important differences in the experiences of the two revolutions' leaders. The most influential of Soviet revolutionaries had spent long years of exile in Western capitals and were almost a cosmopolitan group of intellectuals in comparison with the majority of Chinese leaders whose guerilla schooling and complete lack of physical and intellectual contact with the outside world allows for only two or three exceptions. Nor is the situation comparable in the field of foreign relations. Once intervention was defeated, for over a decade no serious military menace challenged the existence of the Soviet régime. In China's case, war in Korea and then the climax of the fighting in Viet-Nam could be interpreted as direct threats. Moreover, ever since the establishment of the régime, a rival authority is being maintained which, even if politically discredited, is generously equipped with modern weapons by a foreign power. Next to all these factors likely to strengthen tendencies of isolation from world opinion or of aggressivity as a permanent posture, there is, in addition, the fatal weight of China's experience during the past hundred years. Though Russia had suffered repeated invasion from the West, she at least had the psychological satisfaction of having victoriously repelled them. She never experienced on her body the greed of the colonial age. Nor did she ever know the prolonged occupation and separation of important portions of her territory. Her hatred of the West and its contemporary ideology, therefore, could never be nourished from such deep and rich roots as China's revenge and ambitions have at their disposal.

These are perhaps too grim conclusions. Technological imperatives or a more understanding attitude of the outside world may yet temper the heritage. But history is very sparing in examples of self-restraint by the strong. So, for many years to come, China is bound to remain a difficult neighbour. How difficult, may depend on answers to a number of questions. How effectively does the régime that leads the country to meet its new destiny mould the minds of its citizens? on whose alliance and on what kind of aid can China rely? or, how effective is her military machine and how modern are its arms?

The answers, however tentative, may help to complete the balance-sheet of China's achievements. And the balance-sheet, in turn, may give the real measure of the shadow she already casts over three continents.

2 A Machine to change Men's Minds

IN EVERY CITY I have visited in China I have stayed in a new, large and imposing hotel. In all of them the first two floors were reserved to foreign visitors or technicians. The rest of the building was filled to capacity by crowds of blue-clad men with a small minority of women among them. They were young or middle-aged, with delicate features or, especially in smaller places, men with heavy boots and with the manual workers' hands. They may have been employees, administrators or factory workers or, as in Sinkiang or Inner Mongolia, heavily built peasants in padded jackets, wearing fur hats with ear flaps, evidently used to village mud.

They usually lived two to four in a room. Each of them had their indispensable two fountain pens in their breast-pocket and whenever one met them they carried sheaves of mimeographed reading material under their arm. Twice a day they descended in dense columns to the dining-room to take their free meals and spent the time in between listening to lectures or participating in discussions in the larger reception halls. After the evening meal and a short walk, they returned and, in smaller groups, crowded into smoke-filled individual rooms where they continued their debates late into the night. At the end of one or two weeks, they dispersed. The rooms were aired and cleaned and new men, in identical blue suits and with the same purposeful expression on their faces, came to fill the same hotels.

All over China and all through the year—from Shanghai to Chungking and from Harbin to Urumchi—those blue men and women gather, listen, debate, learn and obey. They absorb arguments and explanations, listen to criticism and offer self-criticism, and then descend on the villages with a new set of slogans. In every corner of that immense land they interpret the Party's latest decisions, adapt them to local conditions where necessary, and see to it that the orders are carried out to the full. They are the tiny vehicles on which the Supreme Will travels down the slopes of the administrative pyramid to the hundreds of thousands of villages forming its base. Simultaneously, they serve also as the Party's sensitive microphones which register and pass on the pulse of the masses. It is through them that Peking dictates the tempo of the forced march or distributes its pacifying concessions. They are perfect cogs, their strength lies in their utter dedication to the ideals and the methods of the Party. It is on them, on the *kan-pu*, the Party's trusted cadres that rests the colossal task to persuade, to cajole, to educate or to threaten into its new mould the Chinese quarter of mankind.

The authority behind them is the Chinese Communist Party together with its auxiliary organizations. The Party itself has 14 million members while the auxiliary organizations—mainly those of youth and women—account for another estimated twenty-five million. Together they form, what may be called, the unconditional base; about one person for every seventeen Chinese. It is in the name of this hard core that the cadres act. The Supreme Will of the Party together with the *kan-pu* personifying the mechanism of transmission, constitute a perfect piece of apparatus which has transformed the inert Chinese masses into an alert, disciplined and highly organized society geared to the execution of imposing tasks.

Even after the Communists' final victory, the majority of cadres were not Party members. The largest segment of Party membership has always consisted of peasants, many of whom were illiterate. Though they usually possessed the required competence, they often needed several years of training and responsibility in the course of which they could acquire the intellectual equipment qualifying them for admission. Hard work, education and selective recruitment, however, are gradually filling the gap. The proportion of non-member cadres is in decline and the majority of top leaders in village and industry are by now cadres who have already qualified for Party membership.[89]

While in the Soviet Union non-Party technocrats play a growing role in public life, in China there is the opposite tendency to extend the Party's direct control over key-posts. But the most significant difference in the role of Soviet and Chinese cadres is in the peasant origin of their majority in China. Moreover, unlike in the U.S.S.R., large areas administered by the Communists long before their final triumph, have provided them with valuable experience both in organization and psychological approach. In addition, cadres have also been recruited among minority nationalities and so their organization and indoctrination did not have to rely on only racially 'alien' personnel. It was for all these reasons that the Chinese Communists' organizational web over the country could be spread much faster and with far greater smoothness than was the case in the Soviet Union. For the same reasons, contact with the peasant masses was much closer than in Russia after the October Revolution. The Soviet Communist Party's hold on the peasant hinterland was very slender indeed compared to the Chinese Communists' close ties with the villages. In Yenan first and during the anti-Japanese guerila struggle after, the Chinese Communists' opportunities for close and organic contact with the peasantry were further enhanced. Their collaboration could rely on both nationalist and ideological incentives. It is not without significance that some of the organizational methods utilized in present-day 'battles' against nature, or in large scale construction projects, still rely on wartime experience down to even the wording of the slogans employed.

But wartime collaboration between the masses and Party-cadres bequeathed even more important legacies, destined to condition the basic organizational principles of Chinese Communism. The requirements of guerila warfare—to maintain the ideological unity of scattered guerila forces—called for an organization which could ensure both absolute obedience to the supreme command, and flexibility and independent initiative on the part of dispersed guerila groups. In fact, it was under those conditions that the decisive and highly original 'dialectical' character of the organizational principles of Chinese Communism was shaped.

The two dominant conceptions which emerged from this heritage, were *the theory of contradictions* and the belief in *democratic centralism*. Both are notions which recur in official Chinese thinking and in Party phraseology. They condition the Party's action and, owing to their historical and theoretical inaccessibility for most Westerners, are either misinterpreted or receive inadequate attention.

The theory of contradictions, underlying the Party's every action, is decisive in Chinese Communist thinking. In a sense it merely codifies in Marxist terms a mode of thinking with deep roots in China's cultural heritage. Its principal Communist exponent has been Liu Shao-chi himself and his writings on organization have anticipated Mao Tse-tung's definite formulation of the theory in his celebrated speech in February 1957.[90]

Though that discourse was prompted by topical considerations —like the Hungarian revolt and growing bureaucratism—it outlined a theory which provides an indispensable analytical instrument for the understanding of Chinese action. Mao spoke of two types of contradictions: antagonistic and non-antagonistic. The first are the well-known contradictions defined by Marxist ideology, between classes and hostile social systems, which cannot be resolved but by force. Yet there are also non-antagonistic contradictions which occur within Socialist society. Unlike in the Soviet Union, these are considered as more than mere technological discrepancies. They act—as in Arnold Toynbee's chain of challenge-answer-new challenge—as stimulants to progress. They can be resolved through non-violent means with the help of persuasion, through 'discussion, criticism and education'. The basic contradictions and strains between the leaders and the led, then, maintain an almost welcome tension. It is both dissolved and prolonged through a permanent effort of purposeful confrontation. By resolving old tensions, this ceaseless confrontation is *designed* to lead to new tensions. The result, it is implied, is a forward-moving process constituting progress.

Given the fact that contradictions are objective, as are the laws of history seen through Marxist eyes, for each contradiction there is only one *correct* resolution. What, in a given moment, the *correct* resolution is, is determined by 'the fundamental consensus as to the interests of the People'. What that interest is at any given moment, is determined by the supreme authority of the Party. To ensure that the Party's decision is indeed 'correct' there is the safeguard of another organizational principle, equally built on flexible duality, that of *democratic centralism* or, more faithfully to Chinese usage, democracy *and* centralism, in which the word democracy has nothing in common with notions attached to the word in the West.

Centralism needs no elaboration. As in the Soviet model it implies hierarchical structures with defined leadership at all echelons, united in obedience under the will of the controlling organization at the top. As for 'democracy', its organizational functions are the dialectical opposites of 'centralism'. Its essence seems to be *positivism* and creativity or, more precisely, *creative obedience*. Opposed to blind obedience, then, the Party expects from its members the qualities of leadership, adaptability and initiative. In other words not merely the ability but also the will to take responsibility and to improvise in harmony with the intent and purposes of Party resolutions.

The two concepts—the theory of contradictions and of democratic centralism—find, then, their common denominator in a self-imposed and continuous purge; a process designed to identify the Party member ever more closely with the instincts, as it were, of the Party which, in turn, is the expression of the People's will.

This double principle, aiming at what may be called harmonized tension, inevitably reminds of the age-old Chinese concept of Yin and Yang: the two symbols which evoke both the cosmic rhythm and the fundamental duality of things. It schematizes the tension each individual has to resolve for himself. Such forced alternation of interdependent phases and ideas—transplanted into the contemporary Communist context—serves a double purpose. It tempers with flexibility the fundamental rigidity of Communist organization, and maintains it in a permanent revolutionary fermentation capable of resisting fossilization.

It is against this background of, what one may call, the metaphysical convictions of Chinese Communism that the individual is intentionally exposed to conflicting forces. In actual practice Chinese Communism assumes that if an individual can be forced to participate in organized and controlled group-activity, he automatically becomes exposed to tensions inherent in Socialist society. The resolution of those tensions is bound to improve his quality and lead him towards closer identification with the Party's intentions. 'Discussion, criticism and education' thus deepen the commitment. Nor are they to remain purely verbal. They have to be completed by action. Talk and work, together, produce the pressures which call for greater identification. And to enmesh ever greater numbers in this cycle of action and interaction—in the cycle of tension-resolution-new-tension —particular importance is attached to mass movements. Being the great catalysers of the individual's identification with this cycle of action and inter-action, mass-movements are also believed to counter-balance excessive centralism. They do so because the multiplicity of individual interests and interpretations involved add up to that 'democracy' which militates against excessive 'centralism'.

In two separate passages of a recent article by Liu Shao-chi, these concepts are exposed as applied to practical problems.[91] '... All types of contradictions that exist in society will inevitably find expression in the political and economic life of our country and in our inner Party life. Therefore, we must learn to recognize and handle (them) correctly. Only thus can we thoroughly eliminate the hostile anti-socialist forces, complete the transformation of members of the bourgeoisie and the upper strata of the petty bourgeoisie and their intellectuals, adjust the relations among the people, and carry our cause forward successfully. In socialist . . . and communist society, the unity and struggle or contradictions and the resolution of contradictions are still the driving force of social progress. . . .' As for mass movements, the urge for change 'is transformed inevitably into action. . . . With correct leadership, such mass movements can certainly become the most dynamic and constantly operating force propelling . . . forward our country. Our mass movements are carried out under the centralized guidance of the Party. Party guidance means integrating political work with economic work, integrating the political education of the masses with material encouragement and placing politics in command, making it the guiding force. . . .'

It was this doctrinaire attachment to the fertilizing characteristics of mass movements which was probably the root-cause of the great 1959 debate. The protagonists of continuous mass movements were in conflict with those who advocated more rational methods of economic action befitting at least the activities of the more advanced industrial sectors. As usual, however, the ideological arguments prevailed.

Yet this attachment to the basic principle of harmonized tension provides Chinese Communism with its most characteristic features. The veritable orgies of criticism and self-criticism, as the other instruments of the great rectification campaigns, are reminiscent of the methods of psycho-analysis. They are intended to provide the individual with an opportunity to overcome his insecurity and—through study and creative struggle—to resolve his contradictions which create tension. The same principle gives also its highly original and puzzling characteristics to China's conception of penal labour as a means to offset 'crime' with reforming identification.

On the occasion when he received me, I tried to have Mr. Chou En-lai's views on this attitude. He was categoric that in case of 'political crimes'—as distinct from ordinary 'criminals'—only the therapeutic of manual labour was applied. 'Our conceptions are different . . .', he said. 'We believe in re-education through labour. Only manual labour can enrich people or society. In our society work is never forced because it is for your own future. . . . We enable prisoners to remake themselves through work. The notion of forced labour is inapplicable in these cases. . . .' In fact, like other observers before me, I too was impressed by the intense political studies people undergo in prisons. I heard more than one prisoner express his hope of liberation in terms of his political reformation. Dubious as the sincerity of such declarations may be—especially in the presence of guards—there are too many reports, even by Westerners who had the misfortune to be in Communist Chinese prisons, to underline the method and even the philosophical consistency of such treatment.[92]

Irremediably antagonistic contradictions, to use Mao Tse-tung's definition, are dealt with in Chinese practice with the same merciless logic as they have been dealt with in the Soviet Union or, for that matter, under any authoritarian régime. Yet the flexibility reflected in the concept of 'non-antagonistic contradictions' or in the professed desire to harmonize 'centralism' with 'democracy', have broadened Chinese Communist practice with an approach which, if the expression is permissible within the framework of so harsh an enterprise, is relatively humane. It is this relatively humane component that makes the Chinese organizational model both dynamic and perplexingly monolithic, as well as simultaneously flexible and rigid. In practice, it is this basic concept of duality which tempers the system's oppressive absolutism with a degree of subjective tolerance.[93]

That in present-day China there must be widespread discontent with excessive labour, with material conditions or with the rigours of discipline, is only natural. In the improbable case of a change of régime, there would certainly be enough people to line the streets to hail the new rulers. Yet the great majority of Chinese not merely comply but contribute to realizations in a fashion that mere fear could not explain. The numerical importance of the unconditional and indoctrinated hard core, the quality and devotion of the cadres, as the organizational virtuosity which enmeshes greater and greater masses in constructive activities, supply only part of the answer. Pride in achievements, a sense of purpose, together with the evenly spread, even if slight, material improvements, help to complete it. There is also the permanent external threat which inevitably helps to galvanize patriotic feeling around leaders who visibly render China strong and respected. Moreover, to stand up to the formidable apparatus that directs the country's activities, an opposition ought to have faith in a practical alternative.

Return to the humiliating past is unthinkable. The refugees on Taiwan are, in Chinese eyes, mere instruments of foreign interests. The West offers but scorn. Not only does the omnipresent Communist organization tolerate no crystallization points for organized opposition, but, as some penetrating observers believe, Communism, adapted to the Chinese heritage, may even suit Chinese temperament.[94]

Thus, both the solidity and the competence of Chinese Communist organization render probable the continuity of its present aims. To that extent the intractability of our Chinese neighbour promises to be lasting. But that isn't all. Western self-indulgence tends to perpetuate the fiction that only the Communists' obstinacy prevents their subjects returning to those co-operative attitudes which—while Western supremacy could impose the desired behaviour—the West came to regard as 'natural'. With that supremacy over, and Communist organizational techniques involving ever-growing masses in new psychological and economic relationships, such a return is increasingly illusory. We rather face a rapidly growing proportion of Chinese whose radically altered scale of values will frustrate every attempt to rediscover that—artificial and now extinct—'natural' Chinese interlocutor.

In fact, the longer Western inertia postpones the effort objectively to assess the fears, the motives and the methods of the new China, the more it will become prisoner of its own totally negative approach. And that sterile approach, rather than preparing an understanding with China, condemns the West to seek nothing more positive than misunderstanding between China and her present allies.

3 No Alternative to the Soviet Alliance

AT THREE O'CLOCK every afternoon the loudspeakers of Peking's new railway terminal begin to play the *Sino-Soviet Friendship Song*. While an enthusiastic baritone sings that *From Peking to Moscow Everything is on the March*, the new daily Peking-Moscow express slowly moves out of the station. Notwithstanding the daily air-link between the two capitals, the train evidently did not lack passengers. In its compartments officials and tourists installed themselves for the seven-day journey. Then, as we moved towards the north and across Manchuria, at every station I could see delegations of Chinese workers and functionaries saying farewell to Soviet technicians whose service in China had come to an end. Usually there were bouquets and tearful handshakes and the feelings shown seemed genuine. Next to them, workers and students got in, probably on their way for a period of training or study in the Soviet Union. And on its way back the express carried a comparable load, composed of officials, technicians and students, though that way with a predominance of Soviet citizens.

If one could know more about the experiences, the feelings and the thoughts of those passengers, one would be nearer to answering what is perhaps the most intriguing political problem of our days. There are indeed few imaginable developments in the world today which could more completely alter the existing balance of forces than the eventual drifting apart of the two major Communist Powers. For the same reason, there are few subjects on which, based on so little concrete evidence, so much speculation has been built. If, at the beginning, fascination with the immense impact of the Sino-Soviet collaboration tended to discount signs of disagreements now the danger is rather that, under the influence of political mystery literature, the importance of existing differences may be vastly exaggerated.

Yet if the mood of China or the durability of her ideology are essential features of the country's new personality, it is of no lesser importance to assess the solidity and the nature of the ties which identify her with the Communist bloc. To do so, and for the lack of any more reliable information than what is available to other observers, there is no safer method than to sketch the evolution of Sino-Soviet relations and to see to what extent they are likely to condition their future.

To begin with, it may be useful to presume that Communist states respond to similar impulses in their relations as those between others with different ideologies. Communist ideology in itself does not necessarily short-circuit the power rivalry which characterizes the relations of all countries. Such power rivalry, however, has always been influenced by historical, ideological and economic considerations.

'The Chinese revolution,' Liu Shao-chi wrote in 1959, 'is the continuation of the great October Revolution.' But if the 'New China joined the socialist camp headed by the Soviet Union', the same article explained, that was because '. . . None of the Chinese bourgeois political parties could put forward a programme of thorough opposition to imperialism and feudalism (or) could carry the Chinese democratic revolution to the end'. Though it had been maintained that China's Communists were establishing the dictatorship of the proletariat while, in practice, they were relying almost entirely on the peasants, Mao Tse-tung had been even more outspoken about the function of ideology as a mere tool to further Chinese Communists' national aims. 'We study Marxism not because of its good words, not because there is any magic in it, as if it were a kind of charm to cast out devils,' he wrote. 'It has neither good looks nor magic. It is only very useful. There are people who think that it is a kind of magic with which we can easily cure any disease. Those who take it as dogma are that kind of people. We ought to tell them that their dogmas are more useless than cow dung. For dung can be used as fertilizer, while dogma cannot.'

Bearing this approach in mind, and simplified to the extreme, Sino-Soviet relations may be divided into four phases. They begin with Moscow's complete mastery over the Chinese Communist movement. The second phase, during which the individuality of Chinese Communism is increasingly asserted, opens after 1927 with Mao's independent experiments in peasant organization, and lasts until the establishment of China's new régime. The next phase, the shortest, covers the interval between 1949 and Stalin's death. Since then, the fourth and present phase, has been dominated by China's unconcealed desire not merely to assert her equality within Communist councils but even to be in a position to impose on them decisions which serve primarily her own interests.

Plans for China's Communist revolution, as for other parts of Asia, were first outlined by Lenin and M. N. Roy, the Indian revolutionary, at the Second Congress of the Communist International in 1920. It was to further their plans that Michael Borodin was sent to China to advise Sun Yat-sen's national revolutionary government in Canton. At that time the Chinese Communist Party was a loose and tiny group dominated by intellectuals, insignificant both in numbers and in power. Their aim was merely to penetrate the revolutionary Kuomintang under Dr. Sun, considered by Moscow at the time as the sole force in

China which was both anti-imperialist and had a chance to conquer the whole country. These plans were complicated not merely by rifts between the Chinese Communists themselves or by the differences between them and their comintern advisers, but also by parallel disputes in Moscow, about China policy, between Trotsky and Stalin. Trotsky believed that, working alone, the Communists could seize power against the will of the bourgeoisie. Stalin, trusting the letter of Marxist doctrine, maintained that the chronological revolutionary order had to be respected and that the triumph of the bourgeoisie was an indispensable preliminary to the victory of the proletariat. The doctrinaire view prevailed and Stalin's directives imposed on China's Communists almost suicidal tactics.

But the aim, to secure for the Communists the hegemony within the Kuomintang-led coalition, misfired. Chiang Kai-shek, the successor of Dr. Sun, was unwilling to play the game. His coup in March 1926 drastically curtailed the power of the Communists within the alliance and, in April 1927 his brutal massacre of Communists in Shanghai revealed that he was ready to use the most ruthless methods in order to eliminate their influence from the régime he was establishing.

Undaunted by the failure of their China policy, Stalin and his advisers ordered several other ill-fated moves. When, as a result, the action of Li Li-san's peasant troops against the cities failed to rouse the proletariat, once again the Chinese were blamed for Moscow's miscalculations. Nevertheless, all through these years Moscow was in complete command of the leaders and of the shaping of the Chinese Communist line. In the Kuomintang-Communist alliance both sides tried to use the other for its own advantage. The tragedy of the Communists was that they stirred up enough trouble to alarm the Kuomintang, but acquired too little influence in the Army when the show-down came. In fact, all through this period Comintern policy in China got stranded on the central issue of the Kuomintang's monopoly of military power. In the international context Stalin evidently overestimated the extent to which Chiang's nationalism committed him to hostilities with Britain and Japan and thus kept him in line with Communist aims. And the Chinese Communists paid a high price for these mistakes when, after 1927, they were dispersed or forced into underground activities.

Discouraged perhaps by this succession of failures, Stalin's interest in Chinese revolution had markedly declined after 1927. Yet in the meantime a very different kind of Communist movement was taking shape in China from that which Comintern doctrinaires still expected. Mao Tse-tung, an agrarian commissar at the time of the Kuomintang–Communist alliance, and driven to the hills with some troops after the 1927 Shanghai massacres, was developing in the borderlands of Kiangsi and Fukien provinces his own rural Soviet experiment. Difficulties of communications between his movement and Shanghai, where the official Party still functioned underground, gave him a free hand. In practice there were during those years two different Communist movements in China: the first, under continued Comintern direction, operating from Shanghai; and the second, following a totally different line, in Mao's Kiangsi Soviet. While the first continued to obey Moscow's orders, the second, cut off from the outside world, was experimenting with land reform and was building up its own army and police force.

Then there came the Long March and the new beginning in Yenan. By the time the Communists re-emerged as a serious political force, their methods and their leaders were tested in action and were, in a sense, rebels against Moscow's will. There was a comparably decisive change in the international situation. When the world became conscious of the existence of a well-organized Communist movement in the north-west of China, both Japan and Germany were already casting their threatening shadows over the two extremities of the Soviet empire. By then, Stalin and his advisers were more preoccupied with meeting that menace than with directing the manœuvrings of what must have seemed to them a minor political movement in a country whose actual government looked like a potential ally.

Japan's aggression and the second World War only confirmed Stalin's conviction that Russia's interest lay in collaboration with Chiang's régime. And his attitude had not changed even after the end of the war. As reported by Harry Hopkins in his diary, Stalin told him in 1945 that he did not consider the Chinese Communist Party a serious factor and that he continued to recognize the Chiang Kai-shek government. Though events later convinced him of his error, as late as 1948 he still found it natural to issue instructions to his Chinese comrades and to advise them to seek a compromise with Chiang and even to dissolve their army.[95]

Though Stalin and his advisers persistently under-estimated the chances of China's Communists and their final victory was for them not merely a surprise but even a rebuff to their instructions, the Communist triumph was accepted with understandable haste. The Soviet Union recognized the People's Republic of China the day after its proclamation.[96] Within a week most of the Communist states followed the example. Moreover, only a few months after, on February 4, 1950, Mao Tse-tung and Stalin signed in Moscow the Sino-Soviet Friendship Treaty which was soon followed by a series of trade pacts and other agreements.

The Soviet Union renounced a Russian sphere of influence in Manchuria which dated from 1905 and had been formally re-established by treaty with the Chinese Nationalist Government in 1945. Russia was to return to China the industrial equipment which she dismantled there as 'war booty' after Japan's defeat. The U.S.S.R. also recognized Chinese sovereignty over Manchuria and guaranteed to return Port Arthur, Dairen and the Changchun Railway into Chinese hands. The Treaty also established a military alliance between China and the Soviet Union, pledging mutual assistance not merely against Japanese aggression but also against 'any other state' which might unite with Japan, directly or indirectly, 'in any act of aggression'. These pacts were accompanied by Moscow's first slice of credit and promise to supply China with industrial equipment. These advantages for China were compensated by nothing more than China's acceptance of Outer Mongolia's independence; an acceptance the more easy as it had already been a state under unconcealed Soviet protection and was peopled by non-Chinese races who had repeatedly rebelled against Chinese rule.

On April 20, 1950, further agreements were concluded, this time involving the exchange of commodities and the establishment of joint Sino-Soviet corporations, especially for the development of mineral resources in Sinkiang.[97]

The March-April agreements, seemingly much more advantageous for Moscow than the original February deal, were followed by the entry of Chinese 'volunteers' into Korea in November 1950. If in February, armed with all the prestige of his recent victory, Mao could obtain real concessions from Stalin, three months later Russia's terms already appeared to be more harsh. Another seven months and China was at war. Though her performance on the battlefield certainly helped to enhance her prestige in Asia, nevertheless, the truce deadlock as much as the cost of the war—as China had to pay for weapons supplied by Russia—appeared to make China and her armies increasingly dependent on the Soviet Union for diplomatic backing as much as for supplies and arms.

That some hard bargaining and manœuvring was going on between the new allies seemed to be further confirmed by the prolonged negotiations which were to take place in Moscow from August 18 to September 23 in 1952. The joint announcement revealed that steps were being taken towards the promised return of the (Manchurian) Changchun Railway, but that Peking had 'requested' Moscow to delay the withdrawal of Russian troops from the naval base of Port Arthur until treaty relations could be established between the two countries and Japan. Dairen was not mentioned but, so it was believed, that city too would remain under Russian control.

Once again Stalin appeared to be dictating his terms to a China caught in the Korean trap. By 'requesting' the continued presence of Russian troops in Port Arthur, China seemed to be relinquishing, and without compensation, something she had gained in 1950. And it is hardly surprising if, with the joint companies, with the flow of Soviet technicians into China, and with Russian advisers in key posts, the question was being asked whether the Soviet Union was not discreetly reasserting its supremacy over China and her Communist Party?

But Stalin's death in 1953 clearly marked a turning point in Sino-Soviet relations.

Their reversal, still in process, began in that moment. Stalin always acted on the assumption that he knew better what was good for China than the Chinese Communist leaders knew themselves. There can have been little love lost between two so remarkable and powerful personalities as Stalin and Mao Tse-tung. And if Stalin had not done much to help Mao's struggle, he did just as much as was absolutely necessary to assure Mao's collaboration after his final triumph. Stalin was the senior leader of Communism, one proven in war. Even Mao could defer to him without much loss of prestige. Yet while his power was being consolidated, there now developed a crisis of Soviet authority brought about by de-Stalinization. Mao, with his own road to Socialism, and in power without the aid of Soviet arms, was gaining in influence in proportion to the hesitations of Moscow's new leaders. What is more, in trying to consolidate their position as Stalin's successors, the Soviet Union's new masters were increasingly in need of Chinese support. Far from the time when Stalin could make and break Chinese Communists, more and more, the giant Chinese ally's political weight could henceforth stabilize or weaken whoever wished to assume Stalin's former dominant position.

Nothing could have better illustrated the changed equilibrium than China's appearance, for the first time in history, on the European political scene. After the Polish rebellion and the Hungarian uprising in the autumn of 1956, it was Mr. Khrushchev —in the process of consolidating his own position—who called on the Chinese to help mend the shaken authority of the Soviet Communist Party in Eastern Europe. By asking Chou En-lai to interrupt his tour of Burma and to fly to the Polish and Hungarian capitals in order to lend China's moral and ideological authority to Moscow's decisions, Moscow had spectacularly abdicated its hitherto undisputed leadership of the Communist world.

That ideological turning point, however, was preceded by other, not less significant events informing the world that a new phase had begun.

Most important among them was the new Sino-Soviet Treaty of October 1954. Significantly for the first time the Chinese did not go to Moscow but a Soviet delegation headed by Khrushchev and Bulganin travelled to the Chinese capital. Of even greater importance was that, this time, all the concessions appeared to be in China's favour. The U.S.S.R. promised to evacuate the naval base of Port Arthur by May 31, 1955,[98] relinquish its shares in the controversial Sino-Soviet joint companies,[99] and assist China in the construction of two new strategic railroads, both linking her network to the Soviet Trans-Siberian line.[100] Finally, Russia was also to advance a further loan to China.

But the increased stature of China, implied both by the circumstances of the negotiations and by the concessions, tended to conceal an additional new element making its appearance at this crucial juncture of Sino-Soviet relations.

The political core of the communiqué, when compared to the Russo-Chinese Treaty of 1950, implied a change of policy towards Japan. From the status of a dangerous aggressor she was promoted to that of an unwilling victim of American imperialism and both sympathy and trade were offered to her. This change of attitude towards the very Power against whom, almost exclusively, the 1950 military alliance had been directed, had significant implications. It appeared to modify the use to be made of the alliance, especially with reference to Taiwan. In the very moment when China was proclaiming her determination to liberate Taiwan by force, her interest would have been to have the content of the alliance reaffirmed and broadened in terms independent of Japan's attitude. Such a revision would have warned the Americans that any counter-blow against China would automatically bring the U.S.S.R. to her ally's defence. It would have given China the green light for war in the Taiwan Strait. Instead, China's attention had been directed to the wooing of Japan and to the need for an early end to the Korean War. More explicitly, though concessions acknowledged the power shift in favour of China, her external ambitions—rather than being encouraged—had been restrained. In one word, the reliability of the Soviet atomic shield was left intentionally vague.

That pattern, set in 1954, has been operative ever since. China's prestige and power within the alliance is still gaining. Accordingly, the readjustment in Sino-Soviet relations continues. Yet China's material and military dependence still permits the Soviet Union to make Peking accept its restraining influence in exchange for the aid Russia can no longer afford to refuse. How long that dependence will last or how much longer Russia can impose her moderating advice, is gradually becoming the central theme of Sino-Soviet relations. And the nearer comes China's material and military independence, and the more limited grows Russia's moderating influence, the sharper will grow the ideological rivalry both for leadership within the Communist bloc and for the direction of its policies towards the rest of the world.

The divergencies arising out of this process of readjustment may or may not break through the verbal curtain. When they do become audible, they may take the form of intervention in each other's internal politics; of different attitudes towards neutral and decolonized countries; or of differing appreciations of the Communist bloc's strategy in international relations.

While Khrushchev exploits the revulsion against Stalinist excesses to consolidate his own power, Russian Stalinists who oppose that change may enjoy a measure of encouragement from Peking. Inversely, it is probable that the moderates within China's Central Committee—who have been opposing methods leading to internal and external tension—could rely on a corresponding backing from Moscow. If Peking ostentatiously refrained from joining the demolition of the myth of Stalin, or applauding reconciliation with Belgrade, Moscow made even plainer its scepticism concerning the Communes and the mass-movements which were destined to telescope decades of evolution into a few bold moves able to place China ahead of Russia in their advance towards full Communism. And if both sides recoiled before the prospect of dissolving the ideological unity of the Communist world into a Titoist Right, a Maoist Left and a Khrushchevite Centre, and—as Khrushchev announced at the Twenty-first Party Congress in Moscow—the compromise was reached that Communist Parties must not interfere in each other's internal affairs, the rivalry and mutual irritation have since found outlets in other fields.

It may be that, sensing the dangers of such ideological rift, Mao's resignation as the head of the State was indeed prompted by his desire to concentrate his energies on Party work and, in particular, on the mending of differences with the Soviet Communist Party. It is equally possible that in exchange for Khrushchev's promise to refrain from criticizing China's way of building socialism, Peking is reluctantly paying its verbal homage to Moscow's 'undisputed' leadership. But such compromises in one field merely announce renewed bargaining in others where each side may still expect concessions.

It is that way that time and again differences become conspicuous in Russia's and China's attitudes towards neutral and decolonized countries. They have repeatedly differed in their appreciation of the value of neutrality, each according to the phase through which their internal development has been passing. While Russia had seemed uncompromising and even sponsored insurrections all over South-east Asia, China—still weak and hesitant—was successfully bidding for their sympathies. Later on, having become confident in her growing means to gain friendship through economic aid, Russia changed her policy. In the meantime China—by then stronger and anxious to protect her strategic interests—also changed her line but in the opposite direction. By 1960, but particularly during Khrushchev's February tour of South-east Asia, it appeared as if Russia was not merely anxious to repair the damage done to Communism by China's bellicosity but was actually trying to recruit friends in an area which would seem more in China's than in the Soviet Union's direct sphere of interest. The way the Chinese press almost completely ignored that trip clearly showed that it did not have Peking's blessing. As for the border incidents with India, not merely was Russia's attitude one of direct neutrality but Khrushchev pointedly expressed his hope in public that they would not recur.

But China's growing weight within the alliance steadily broadens the field of rivalry. Instead of mere internal political probings or of regional differences, China will tend to extend the bargaining to even more fundamental issues.

A mixture of national pride and manœuvring for power may induce her to challenge the Soviet Union's ideological leadership of the Communist third of the world. And by attempting to direct the power strategy of the entire Communist bloc, China may gain control of bargaining levers far more powerful than have hitherto been within her reach.

Ever since, in the summer of 1958, Peking openly vetoed Russia's attempt at a rapprochement with the West, no ideological arguments have been spared to prove that the Communist bloc's ultimate triumph could be more effectively assured without concessions. There were moments when China seemed to believe that by first opposing the détente with the West and then acquiescing in it, she may force further Russian concessions. Then, again, the fear seemed to predominate that the détente might loosen Russia's commitment towards her. Under the influence of the latter attitude Peking may have offered further encouragement to Khrushchev's internal opponents and thus, perhaps, may have contributed to the failure of the 1960 Paris Summit Conference. Much-publicized Chinese declarations have been designed to give credence to the macabre calculation that in a nuclear war the Communist bloc, and China in particular, would inevitably win by sheer weight of numbers. Yet when considering the gravity of such verbal belligerence, it is well to remember that the key to the Chinese Communists' final triumph had been their willingness to gamble and, even in the most desperate situations, to take great risks. Moreover, throughout the debate nothing contradicted the thesis that Khrushchev simply avoided invalidating the impression that his hand had been forced by China, because his decision to act in accordance with his own good reasons, may already have been taken.

Inevitably, one deals with hypotheses built on insufficient evidence. All that seems certain is that throughout these manœuvrings the Chinese have been building up a coherent doctrine of their own; one which implicitly challenges Soviet leadership on the ground that it under-estimates the revolutionary possibilities of the

Communist bloc. The accusing twist of this assertion marks a further and significant stage in China's ambition. It poses not merely her claim of being the depository of Marxist orthodoxy, but also of being the genuine vanguard of Communism's revolutionary potentialities in the present world context. The ascendancy of this doctrine within the Communist bloc, demanding its inflexible unity as a guarantee of ultimate success, may, in the long run—*and depending on Western attitudes*—eliminate just as effectively its opponents within the Communist countries as Stalin's 'Socialism in One Country' was instrumental in ridding him of his own rivals within the Soviet Union.

But we are not yet quite there. As matters are today, China is still too dependent on Russian aid and the advantages of the alliance are too obvious to both sides for either to risk it by any reckless action. In fact, every new factory or barrage built in China at the price of great sacrifices, is bound to make her more prudent. For many years to come, then, rivalry and its attendant pressures will continue to be mere phases in the inevitable readjustment to the changing balance of power within a mutually advantageous alliance which is still without any alternative.

However, under the impact of the transformation of Soviet society, as much as under the influence of China's own preoccupation with the consolidation of her achievements, disagreements are likely to shift more and more to the economic field. It is probable that economic issues have already been decisive behind the political and ideological disputes. It is almost certain that, for some years at least, they will grow to condition them all.

4 The Limits of Russian Generosity

ONE ENCOUNTERS in China many visible signs of close Sino-Soviet collaboration. No conversation is complete without reference to Russia's unlimited and brotherly aid. Among translations, the works of Soviet authors are most numerous. Cinemas often show Russian films and Moscow's opera and ballet pay regular visits to China's big cities. Russian is the first foreign language and in the library of Peking University I could see many students reading Russian technical text-books with the aid of Sino-Russian dictionaries. There are thousands of students and workers completing their training in the U.S.S.R. and most of the new Chinese Universities have visiting Soviet professors on their staff. Though always insisting on their dwindling numbers, Chinese factory managers readily admit that Soviet specialists have been indispensable in building and getting into production their plants. It is barely possible to board a plane without finding Soviet technicians among the passengers and most big cities have special buildings where, together with their families, they are housed. Above all, when visiting the brand-new factories from Manchuria to Sinkiang, and walking around in their veritable forest of Russian-made machine-tools and other heavy equipment, it is impossible not to be impressed by the Soviet Union's massive contribution to China's economic transformation.

All this said, however, there is perhaps no more striking aspect of Sino-Soviet relations than the surprising modesty of Russia's effort to share the financial burden of China's tremendous effort. In fact, the more one examines the available data, the more obvious it becomes that the volume and especially the nature of that aid must have been the chief bone of contention between the two countries.

Facts in this case speak more eloquently than any possible interpretation.

From 1949 up to this day, as far as it is known, the Soviet Union has not given China a single free economic grant. The loans extended, altogether, do not surpass the equivalent of about $430 million. All the rest of the considerable amount of equipment and services supplied by the U.S.S.R. had to be paid for by the export of Chinese commodities which, quite often, have been in very short supply to Chinese consumers.[101]

The framework of Sino-Russian economic relations was established during the 1950 Treaty negotiations when Moscow granted China a $300-million loan. There was, however, no further loan until after Stalin's death. Then, on the occasion of the Khrushchev-Bulganin visit to Peking in 1954, a second loan amounting to about $130 million was offered.[102] That is all as far as *loans* go. The story, of course, is very different concerning Soviet commitments for the supply, on a barter basis, of specified quantities and kind of machinery and other equipment or of technical assistance. These are negotiated in the form of 'aid projects' which imply equipment, technical aid, training facilities as well as agreed delivery dates for the realization of entire industrial enterprises. As for these, up to the end of 1960, altogether 336 of them have been contracted.

The first such engagement was accepted by the Soviet Union during the initial 1950 negotiations, for the construction or the rehabilitation of 50 projects. Soon after China entered the Korean War and large scale military aid flowed from the Soviet Union to China, though its volume or value was never revealed. In the meantime China launched her first Five-Year Plan, Stalin died and the stalemate in Korea was reached. Waiting to adjust the final shape of the Plan to the situation in Korea and perhaps even more to the availability of Soviet equipment, after prolonged bargaining in the autumn of 1953, China was assured of Soviet collaboration on a further 91 large-scale projects. Then, a year later, on the occasion of the Khrushchev-Bulganin visit and the offer of the second loan, the number of aid-projects was raised by another fifteen. These 156 'key-projects', then, formed the backbone of China's first Five-Year Plan.

In April 1956 barely two months after Khrushchev's revelations about Stalin before the Twentieth Party Congress, Mr. Mikoyan, visiting Peking, promised to raise the number of Soviet aid-projects to 211. Of these over 140 were scheduled to be started, and 60 to be finished, before the end of the first Plan.

As China's second Five-Year Plan got under way, Moscow pledged help to build further major industrial enterprises. In the autumn of 1958 another 47 projects were agreed. Then, after the Communes had been launched and Peking's tone was growing increasingly radical, the Soviet Union signed its hitherto largest commitment. It involved 78 major projects, implying supplies worth $1,250 million to be sold to China between 1959 and 1967, or till the projected completion of China's third Five Year Plan.[103]

Altogether, then, since 1949 the Soviet Union agreed to help build in China—before 1967—a total of 336 major industrial projects. Very approximately, the value of Russia's contribution may be evaluated at $3,250 million. But with the exception of $430 million worth of equipment covered by the two Soviet loans, all the rest has to be paid for by China's ordinary commercial exports.[104]

To pay for all these supplies Peking has to raise the volume of its exports to the utmost. The bulk of them being agricultural products, including foodstuffs, it is inevitably the Chinese consumer who is most directly affected. That Russia's contribution to lighten this effort does not surpass 13 per cent. of its total cost, is the more surprising as loans of greater importance have been offered by her to mere neutrals. Egypt, Iraq, Indonesia or India benefit by large Soviet credits. Against the $430 million loan hitherto accorded to 680 million Chinese allies, India has been offered nearly $700 million. Even Indonesia—with only 90 million population—has obtained Soviet loans worth $370 million since 1950. Population taken into account, then, Soviet aid to Middle Eastern or to South-east Asian neutrals represents greater generosity than what has been shown towards Russia's major ally.

Before looking for political explanations of this attitude, however, two factors have to be considered.

The first, understandably shrouded in mystery, concerns military supplies. The second, demands the objective evaluation of the importance and usefulness of the Soviet Union's total commitment to China.

Although, officially, only the 1950 and 1954 Soviet loans were announced, in the middle of 1957 the Chinese authorities stated that from 1949 to 1957 they had received 'loans and credits' from the U.S.S.R. worth about $2·24 milliard. At the same time they also let it be known that $1·31 milliard of this total had been received during the first Five-Year Plan. The fact that, with the exception of the $430 million loans, none of this sum has ever been publicly accounted for calls for explanation. The only convincing one is that the $1,810 million not accounted for, represented other receipts than current economic aid. Chinese leaders have let it be understood on several occasions that they had to pay for all the military equipment Russia put at their disposal during the Korean War. This may offer part of the explanation. But next to aid in the form of arms, part of the sum mentioned may have been received also in the form of the transfer of Soviet shares in the Sino-Soviet joint companies which were turned over to exclusive Chinese ownership in 1955. Provided these suppositions are correct, the mysterious $2·24 milliard 'loans and credits' referred to, change nothing concerning the niggardliness of the genuine, economic loans officially announced.

Yet even if Russia shoulders only a modest part of China's *financial* burden, the importance of her contribution to China's economic modernization could not be over-estimated.

'On the 156 industrial projects which the Soviet Union is helping us to build,' stated, in 1955, Li Fu-chun, Chairman of the State Planning Commission, 'she assists us through the whole process from start to finish, from geological surveying, selecting construction sites, collecting basic data for designing, directing the work of construction, installation, and getting into production, and supplying technical information on new types of products, right down to directing the work of the manufacture of new products.' Such overall aid, presumably, has been available for all the other projects signed and begun after that date. In addition, through the Sino-Soviet Scientific and Technical Co-operation Commission—established in 1954—China had received from the Russians blueprints for factories and machines as well as all sorts of patents and production licences whose value could hardly be estimated and which, alone, may be considered as a grant of immense importance.[105] Moreover, up to the end of 1959, a total of 10,800 Soviet and 1,500 Eastern European specialists went to work in China[106] and about 10,000 Chinese students and almost an equal number of workers, technicians and factory administrators had received training in the U.S.S.R. The Russians, however, have not only sent technical experts to work on major projects but Soviet advisers have also played an important role in the institutional reorganization of industries, the planning mechanism, the tax system, as in numerous other fields. Equally, they have also aided the Chinese in the reorganization of their educational system so that, on the Soviet model, it now concentrates on the formation of technicians.

Formidable as this assistance is already (and even if most of it is paid for), Soviet aid has a further important aspect not measurable in monetary terms. Every underdeveloped country is familiar with the difficulties represented by the lack of stable markets for its limited range of exports; by the uncertainty of delivery dates once it manages to contract the desired industrial equipment; or by the frequent refusal to supply it with machinery of the really latest design. The synchronization of Soviet and Chinese economic plans eliminates such difficulties to an extent that is hardly possible between countries with liberal economies. In fact, instances are known when domestic output of certain commodities was reduced in the Soviet Union by 2 to 3 per cent., in order to facilitate the absorption of corresponding Chinese exports.[107] In reality, the existence of the Soviet bloc market and the Communist countries' willingness to collaborate, have enabled China to develop her exports with exceptional rapidity and to be assured of a steady and safe market for them. Inversely, this same close collaboration enabled China to obtain all the essential machinery and other supplies in the required moment, so as to permit the fulfilment of the Five-Year Plan targets. Moreover, China was assured of the most up-to-date capital goods produced by Russia and could thus launch her industries on a basis of technological equality with the most advanced industrial powers.

Notwithstanding the tremendous advantages for China of such collaboration, the fact remains that its cost has been straining the country's resources to their utmost limit and that, proportionately, the Soviet Union did less to lighten the financial burden than she had done for some neutral countries. Actually, from 1956 onwards China's repayments and her servicing of past loans has been higher than the credits she had obtained. Budget figures reveal that against $50 million credit remaining in 1956, and only

$10 million in 1957, China's repayments and servicings amounted to $260 million and to $271 million in those two years. By 1957 all credits were exhausted and since that date China had to export enough not merely to cover her current purchases but, in addition, to run an export surplus in order to pay off past obligations towards the Soviet Union. [108]

There is no sure way of answering why Russia makes no greater *financial* effort to lighten China's exertions. That grants, distributed by the United States on a large scale, are opposed by the Soviet Union as a matter of principle, may be defended on rational grounds. Trade is more likely to steady the self-confidence or to stimulate the productive efforts of an underdeveloped country than reliance on gifts.[109] That Russia extends loans only to cover military supplies, is contradicted by her long-term credits offered to Egypt and Iraq, among others, *both* for military and industrial equipment. As for the argument that the volume of equipment furnished to China already imposes a heavy burden on Russia, it is borne out neither by the known resources of Soviet industry, nor by the obvious fact that important quantities of industrial equipment are still diverted towards neutral countries.

It is difficult indeed not to conclude that there seems to be a certain reluctance on Russia's part to facilitate still further the acceleration of China's industrialization and, therefore, the shortening of the period at the end of which she might become not merely very powerful but also self-supporting. With over three-quarters of China's foreign trade with the Communist bloc; with her capital equipment almost exclusively supplied by Communist countries; with most of her heavy armament and her petroleum supplies coming from the same direction; and with her commercial, industrial and strategic integration with the Communist bloc still increasing, the Russians may consider that they are running no great risk by not extending any further the aid they already offer their principal ally.

But even if economic issues overshadow the process of continuous readjustment in Sino-Soviet relations, China's dependence renders unlikely any radical change in her basic orientation. True, China's aims are becoming clearer. Yet neither the most fanatical nationalist, nor the most rigid doctrinaire can ignore obvious facts. The differences and the disputes, important as they may be, develop against the background of a thick network of reciprocally advantageous activities.

There are people who foresee overpopulation driving China to the conquest of empty Siberia, though they never ask themselves why, for that purpose, instead of provoking war with a military giant, the Chinese would not rather go towards the sparsely populated rice-surplus lands of South-east Asia where they would encounter no serious military opposition. Others, more reflective, think of the distant future of the Central Asian border lands where, on the two sides of the Sinkiang frontier, the same races live divided by the Sino-Soviet frontier. But far fewer are those who consider the durable external interests existing between the two countries. The immense strategic advantages of their joint domination of the surface of Eurasia they equally share. Then, to prevent the renewal of Japanese aggression or, eventually, to bring Japan's industrial potential within the Communist bloc, is a common Sino-Soviet interest built on the mutual experience of Japan's past irruption. Moreover, to eliminate the United States from the Western Pacific, together with the menace which America's advanced bases represent to both Soviet and Chinese security, is bound to remain a joint preoccupation for the foreseeable future.

The outside world's understandable interest in the detection of the symptoms of discord inevitably leads to a distorted picture in which dissension is magnified at the expense of the much more important field where there is coincidence of interests. To mistake the occasional creakings of the Moscow-Peking axis for symptoms of deep-seated conflict is, and is likely to remain for many years to come, a dangerous miscalculation. The image of a Russia frightened by a reckless China is a poor substitute for a coherent Western policy in Asia. The illusion that the West can thrust a wedge between the two allies is likely to remain fashionable for some time even though its victims continue to do their utmost to weld the two countries even closer together.

When China and the Soviet Union meet it is not merely to

bargain but also to concert their action. And as long as the renewal of Western hegemony over the world will appear a real possibility to the non-Western majority of mankind, the power struggle with the United States and its allies will continue to override any antagonism China and Russia may feel towards one another.

In the meantime, with the passage of years, the only factor that might significantly alter the balance of power *within* the alliance, could be in the military field, particularly by China's acquisition of her own, independent atomic arms together with the means to deliver them beyond the oceans.

5 From the Umbrella to the Bomb. China and the U.N.

THE RISE OF China as a modern military power is the least known but probably the most extraordinary chapter in the story of the country's amazing transformation. From the contempt in which the soldier's profession had been held to the adaptation of strategic thinking to the needs of nuclear war, an enormous distance has been covered within a few short years.

Barely a century ago, the indiscipline, the low morale and antiquated equipment of the Chinese armies were notorious. The Chinese soldier, armed with his spear or musket and carrying an umbrella or a fan, inspired the derision of westerners. The Chinese themselves proudly professed to be pacifists and they had been too readily accepted as too wise and intelligent and generally too civilized to bother to make war. The guerilla exploits against the Japanese invader and then the Korean war have quickly eclipsed that picture. Though still ill-equipped, the modern Chinese soldier displayed both initiative and unlimited endurance. Not fighting any longer under unscrupulous leaders for unscrupulous ends, he emerged as a courageous fighter often politically indoctrinated and conscious of an ideal.

Foreign instructors and advisers have tried to hasten the process. The Russians first, beginning at Canton's Whampoa military academy. Then, after the Kuomintang's break with the Communists in 1927, it was the turn of the Germans. They stayed until 1938 when Hitler withdrew them to placate Japan. Between 1938 and 1941 there were Russian advisers again until, finally, the Americans took over, headed, among others, by Stilwell and Wedemeyer. During all these years, however, China knew small, private armies—belonging to warlords or to Chiang Kai-shek—always distinct from the troops pressed into service against the Japanese. What may be called the first national army was established on August 1, 1927, and developed in Yenan after the Long March. This, the People's Liberation Army or P.L.A., relied on volunteers, was trained for guerilla warfare and was built up gradually as the Communist sphere of action steadily expanded.

During the trials of the Long March, the Party and the Army became undistinguishable. Everyone was a soldier as much as a civilian. The Party leaders, with Mao Tse-tung at their head, were both its generals and its theoreticians. And the Party leaders who survived the Long March and set up the Communist system in Yenan, retained their joint military-political status throughout the period of intermittent warfare up to the end of the civil war in 1949.

Yet once final victory achieved and the guerilla war over, the P.L.A. was suddenly confronted by totally new problems. It spread out over huge areas, controlled cities and could rely on modern industry and communications. The former guerilla forces had to be turned into a regular army applied to new tasks. To begin with, the country was divided into five vast military regions each occupied by a field army whose commanders were also civilian governors. Each field army was made up of a number of army groups which, in turn, were divided into armies and divisions. But barely was this reorganization completed when the P.L.A.—a guerilla force only three years before—found itself in battle with one of the world's best equipped and most mechanized war-machines.

The shock of the Korean War provoked another large-scale

reorganization. From 1954 onwards the system known before China's entry into Korea was drastically overhauled. In September, 1954 conscription was introduced on a regular basis.[110] The Army was reduced in size from 5 million to about half that number and simultaneously a reserve militia was created. Conscripts were to receive a small monthly salary while the officer corps was reorganized and given standard ranks and uniforms.[111] At the same time the country was divided into smaller military districts on the Soviet pattern and separate tank, artillery and airborne corps were set up. Gradually the naval arm too was being developed. The help of the Soviet Union was becoming more and more important; not merely in instruction and reorganization but also in the building up of China's own armament industry. In fact, from 1954 onwards China was already assembling her own models of Soviet designed jet fighter-aircraft.

The *People's Daily* spoke at the time of officers who were required to make the safeguarding of the country 'their long-term job or even their career'. Thus, for the first time in modern times, China was to have a class of professional officers. This, together with the other changes in the military sphere, did not fail to produce problems comparable with those with which the Soviet Union has been grappling during the past forty years. There were vast questions of morale, politics and administration to be settled. There emerged problems concerning everyday relations between the population and the professional army, henceforth, less close to the masses than in the old guerilla days. But long before all these questions could be settled, the revolution in armaments called for both the theoretical reorientation of the armed forces and for another and sweeping reorganization. This time it involved mechanization and probably also preparation for equipment with nuclear weapons. And long before it was clear whether the atomic arms would be supplied by the Soviet Union or would have to be developed by China herself, there appeared perceptible differences between the political authorities controlling the Army and the professional officers within the General Staff.

In the background of these pressures and rivalries has been

evolving the compromise between ambitions and means. Each stage of that compromise in Chinese strategic thinking, however, marked also a phase in Sino-Soviet bargaining in the military field. And that bargaining, in its turn, has gradually become almost as important in the continual process of readjustment in Sino-Soviet collaboration, as have been the two partners' economic relations.

The main themes of this evolution unfolded simultaneously on the internal and external planes. Internally, they involved the professional army's attitude towards the economic and political activities of the population, as well as its hesitations between its essentially revolutionary or its purely professional vocation. Externally, the central issue has been all along the adaptation of China's ambitions and her strategic posture to the degree to which the Soviet Union's thermonuclear shield could be relied on to be at their service. All these themes have been intertwined and, quite understandably, little information about them was permitted to reach the public or the external world.

It has become known, however, that by 1957, if not earlier, the problem of the relations between a huge standing army and the civilians was causing headaches to the Party. In fact, widespread complaints of the high-handedness of Army officers and men have driven the Party to apply the rectification campaign of 1957 also to the armed forces. At that time the Army's journal referred to 'acts of violence' and an attack was launched on 'commandism' within the forces. Another article referred to 'contradictions' between the Army and the people. Though it blamed it on a few diehard officers, a campaign of criticism was encouraged both within the Army and on behalf of the civilians coming in contact with it. When Marshal Zhukov fell from favour in Russia in 1957, Marshal Liu Pocheng seized the occasion to launch a bitter attack on 'excessive professionalism' in the Chinese Army, and on those who wanted to divide the Party from the armed forces. Clearly, China too had come up against the old problem that the man who is quickest to master a new military technique has the least time for politics.

About a year later, the July 1, 1958, issue of the *Liberation Army*

Newspaper revealed that some officers, impressed by the suddenness and complexity of modern warfare, had openly opposed the Party's grip over the P.L.A. arguing that it impeded the indispensable concentration of command. Replying a few weeks later, Vice-President Chu Teh himself attacked those who overemphasized the exclusive importance of the requirements of national defence, and, to that extent, minimized the decisive priority of economic construction.

By 1958, then, the basic issues under debate have become clear. They were, first of all, the definition of the armed forces' revolutionary objectives; priority in the allocation of limited resources; and, above all, relations between the Army and the Party. Imperceptibly, however, the debate widened and touched upon foreign policy, Sino-Soviet relations, as well as upon the growing preoccupation with nuclear armaments.

Shaped by Mao Tse-tung's writings as much as by guerilla experience, Chinese strategic thinking was along the lines of protracted war, of strategic withdrawals and most of all, of the subordination of military to revolutionary political considerations. The implications of atomic weapons collided head-on with these inherited conceptions. That military technology was essential, or that an initial blow could determine the outcome of war, found Chinese military thinking unprepared and without a reply. This, no doubt, explains why no authorized discussion of nuclear warfare is traceable in Chinese publications up to the beginning of 1955. After that date, however, the debate could not be postponed any longer.

China's willingness to end the Indo-China war short of complete control of the country and, even more, the manner in which the risks inherent in the 1954 Taiwan Strait operations were appraised, were the first indications of a changing Chinese attitude. For the first time the deterrent power of nuclear weapons seemed to be taken into consideration.

It is not without significance that this alignment on Soviet strategic thinking was soon followed by China's call for negotiations with the United States at the Bandung Conference.[112] During the following months the discussion of the subject of atomic war grew wider. It was during that period that two schools of thinking crystallized: one represented by the Ministry of National Defence, and the other by the professional soldiers expressing themselves through the General Staff. The first, with Peng Teh-huai, the Defence Minister, as its spokesman, continued to stress the importance of manpower and resources and, by implication, the long war of attrition. The professional officers, on the other hand, emphasized the need for mechanized, mobile forces, including a strong air-defence system able to reduce the danger of a surprise blow. In a wider context, the dependability of the Soviet deterrent was involved. The first group, taking the shield for granted, gave priority to economic over defence construction, approved growing Party control over the P.L.A. and the Army's participation in construction work. The second group, however, called for maximum independence in China's defence, minimized the importance of political control over the Army as being at the expense of technical competence and, implicitly, questioned the Soviet military commitment towards China.

The Mao-Khrushchev talks in Moscow, in November 1957 seem to have marked a new departure. They followed closely upon Russia's spectacular successes in the field of long-range arms.[113] The Soviet Union was in a new position of strength. Inversely, the Chinese must have found themselves still more dependent within a stronger alliance. The first result—implying Russia's refusal to supply her ally with atomic arms—was China's support for the concept of an Asian atom-free zone. This acquiescence, however, became hesitating and seemed to be over by the spring of 1958. On May 10, in an interview to a German newspaper, Chen Yi both reaffirmed China's support for the Asian atom-free zone and predicted that she would have atomic weapons in the future. Two weeks later, on May 23, the Commander of the Air-force, writing in the *Liberation Army Newspaper*, was even more outspoken: '. . . China's working class and scientists will certainly be able to make the most up-to-date aircraft and atomic bombs in the not too distant future,' he wrote. 'By that time . . . we can use atomic weapons and rockets . . . in coping with the enemies who dare to invade our country. . . .'

The renewed probings in the Taiwan Strait in 1958 were against this background. They were to determine whether China could exploit her advantage in conventional forces while the new Soviet posture neutralized the American threat of nuclear retaliation. Once that military match ended to China's disadvantage, she appeared ready to revise her assumptions about Western weakness. The first reaction was greater reliance on available means. More desperate efforts in the field of economic construction were accompanied by decreasing preoccupation with nuclear strategy. The Army was even more intensely utilized for construction—particularly in railway building and the settlement of border areas—as well as in the policing of the Communes. Simultaneously the 'generals to the ranks' programme was enforced with new vigour. Moreover, in October 1958 the Chief of the General Staff was replaced by the Vice-Minister of National Defence, himself a member of the Party Secretariat.

In the meantime the Soviet Union seemed to perpetuate the intentional uncertainty concerning the availability of her nuclear shield. China's reply to this ambivalence has been her growing reluctance to accede to a reduction of world tension and to call with growing insistence for a more aggressive policy towards the West. As several times since, China's reaction to the renewed evidence of her weakness within the alliance was verbal truculence designed to force the Soviet Union's more open commitment.

Yet these episodes in bargaining within the alliance were not without their effect on inter-Army relations. The professionals, resentful of continued dependence and, perhaps, pointing even to the poor performance of the Chinese forces during the latest Taiwan Strait crisis, reiterated their points. By participating in construction work the Army's strength was being dissipated to the detriment of professional training.. The obligation upon officers to serve with the ranks was harmful to discipline. And the role assigned to the Army in the Communes, so they argued, was likely to undermine the morale of their troops. As for the Party, it was aware that the rank and file, predominantly of peasant

origin, had little enthusiasm for the Communes and that, indirectly, it was taking sides against the Great Leap's 'mass line'.
Clearly, the time had come to reaffirm once again the subordination of the General Staff to the Ministry of Defence. That is why,
on September 17, it was announced that the Defence Minister was
replaced and that the Minister of Public Security became the
new Chief of the General Staff. The causes which had prompted
the changes in October 1958 have evidently become still stronger
a year later.

The new Defence Minister, Lin Piao, was not identified with
either side in the debate. He had been out of active politics for
some years due to illness. High in the Party hierarchy, with close
contacts with the Soviet Union where he had spent several years,
and with the reputation of a strategist, he seemed better suited to
reconcile the Party's aspirations with the opinions of the professional soldiers than had been his predecessor.

Only two weeks after his appointment, addressing the officers
and men of the People's Liberation Army in an article written
on the occasion of the tenth anniversary celebrations, Lin Piao
revealed that his first task was to re-establish harmony between
the diverse shades of opinion within his forces.

The Army 'has advanced from a single arm to a modern
combined force of different arms' and, as a consequence, 'we are
confronted with a series of vital problems', he wrote. 'Is it still
important for politics to be in command at this stage of the
modernization of the army?' he asked. 'Concretely speaking,
what place has political and ideological work? What attitude
should the members of the armed forces adopt towards the
country's economic construction and the mass movements?
What is the correct way to handle inter-Army relations and to
strengthen still further the Party's leadership in the army?'

Though he dealt in detail with the complaints, divisions and
criticism of governmental decisions, his answers were unequivo-
cal. 'None of the work of our army, including its modernization,
can be divorced from (the) ideological struggle. . . . The Party's
absolute leadership in the armed forces and the staunch Party
character of the host of cadres of our army are the best guarantee

for victory. . . . The Party should be obeyed absolutely; no personal ambitions are permissible. Discipline should be strictly observed in all circumstances, importance should be attached to the unity of the Party and nothing should be done behind the back of the Party. . . .'

The militia was justified as a 'force of several hundred million people' which 'in co-ordination with the standing army . . . can engulf the enemy in the flames of an all-out people's war . . .' Even if, due to their peasant origin, some officers and men pick faults with the Communes and the 'mass movements', the P.L.A. is '. . . firmly for the full mobilization of the masses' and participates in their work seeing in it the people's 'magnificent success'.

Though '. . . some comrades take the view that modern warfare differs from warfare in the past, that since the weapons and equipment available (in the past) were inferior, we had to emphasize dependence on man. . . . (Now) they attach importance only to machinery and want to turn revolutionary soldiers into robots . . .' , the Minister insisted that '. . . Men and material must form a unity and men must be made the leading factor. . . .' As for the practice of officers serving as rank and file soldiers for a period of a month each year, '. . . we have always held that the only difference between officers and men is one of division of labour within the revolutionary ranks . . . (and) there is no distinction of high and low . . .' .

Lin Piao then recalled Mao's dictum: 'Our principle is that the Party commands the gun and the gun will never be allowed to command the Party.' And having clarified that much, he reiterated his assurance that the strengthening and the modernization of this disciplined and politically controlled Army would, henceforth, proceed parallel with the leap forward in national economy.[114]

Simultaneously—as General Lo Jui-ching, the new Chief of the General Staff declared on May 10, 1960—China is forming 'a colossal reserve force' from which 'in response to a single order, hundreds and thousands of divisions will rapidly be formed'. The armed forces, reinforced by this immense militia, will guarantee the country against invasion while, presumably, the Soviet deterrent would neutralize the American thermo-nuclear threat. This, reinforced perhaps by renewed Soviet assurances after the failure of the Paris Summit Conference, ought to provide China with new margins for external manœuvring.[115] In the spirit of Lin Piao's article, then, the task of the period ahead will be the harmonization of military means and political objectives. In more concrete terms, the realization of China's ambitions— within the alliance as much as beyond her present borders— would have to await the acquisition of arms capable of serving the desired ends.

That China intends to equip her forces with nuclear arms has been stated on several occasions. That the Soviet Union, though debarred by no undertakings to others, has been reluctant to supply them is equally clear. Although it has been Russia's policy in Eastern Germany to copy step by step the rearmament of the Federal Republic, notwithstanding repeated requests from the East German Government for nuclear missiles, the U.S.S.R. failed to oblige. The main cause of this restraint is probably to avoid the precedent which would force the Soviet Union to provide with nuclear weapons also its Chinese ally. Thus, to realize her declared ambition China will have to manufacture her nuclear arms herself.

It is known that China operates experimental reactors and that she trains scientists and technicians in the atomic field in large numbers. She has eminent specialists trained both in the Soviet Union and in the United States. In 1959 it was announced with unmistakable publicity that Chien Hsueh-san, the well-known American-educated specialist of missile propulsion, was among the intellectuals who had recently entered the Party. It is generally admitted among specialists that Chinese science is on the necessary level of attainment and that the country commands the human, the natural and the industrial resources required. Given China's political system, the authorities can certainly effect the diversion of resources to this end whatever its social price. In fact, the scientific report on which the British Labour Party relied in 1959 in framing its 'non-nuclear-club' proposals, listed China among the nations which could make nuclear weapons within five years. Some scientists estimate that the period may be even shorter.

We have then to reckon with the probability of a China armed with nuclear arms within the next few years. This, no doubt, will create a changed world situation.

To any impartial observer it has been long obvious that neither lasting détente nor progress towards genuine disarmament were possible without China's participation. If this was the case while China possessed but conventional arms, it will be even more as soon as she is in command of nuclear weapons.

That, however, isn't all. Every increase in the number of states possessing nuclear arms makes the world less safe. With every extension of their numbers grows not merely the possibility of accident, miscalculation or reckless decision, but also the danger that agreed and controlled disarmament becomes even more difficult to negotiate. Moreover, the two Great Powers now equipped with nuclear weapons are, in a sense, satisfied Powers. They are not sufficiently dissatisfied with the present division of the world to risk nuclear war in order to change it. China would be the first dissatisfied Great Power equipped with nuclear arms; the first one opposed to the idea of the consolidation of the existing *status quo*.

It is not necessary to presume that China would intentionally unleash a nuclear world conflict. Nor is it indispensable, in this context, to examine how far her grievances are or are not justified. Even less is it relevant to calculate how many additional years China would need to develop the full range of missiles to deliver her nuclear charges beyond the seas. What is decisive is that, within the foreseeable future, a dissatisfied Great Power will have atomic bombs in its armoury. This means that even if China is not planning aggression, she may, at any time consider her prestige or her interests so intolerably humiliated that the resulting impulsive miscalculation could ignite world-wide disaster.

As matters stand today, and because the West willed it so, no international organization is on speaking terms with China to provide her with means other than recourse to force for the satisfaction of her justified aspirations.

Over a century of experience has convinced China of the effectiveness of physical power as the supreme argument. In all probability by now it is too late to prevent China manufacturing her own nuclear arms. Yet it is still possible to employ every expedient to bring China within the mechanism of international negotiations. In fact, to do so would remove the most obvious weakness of the organizations created for that purpose. China's inclusion would certainly render them more realistic and thus enhance their chances to promote world peace. And in pursuit of that aim, for the first time, the Soviet Union would have its own good reasons whole-heartedly to collaborate with the West. It may indeed become one of the paradoxes of our times that the very country which will have provoked that new approach, will have been the one whose very existence her future negotiating partners have been trying to ignore with such suicidal and futile obstinacy.

Yet once that stage is reached—and whatever the damage delay will have caused—China will have become our neighbour not merely because of the reduction of distance and of her technological backwardness, but also because she will have found her rightful place among those who are clearly destined to determine and to maintain the world's emerging, new balance of power.

PART THREE

The Balance-Sheet

PEKING'S LAST blanket of snow was just melting away as a messenger of spring descended along the rays of the March sunshine. It was a Sunday morning and people were filling the gardens and the streets to greet it. Joining them I drifted through a side-entrance of the Imperial Palace into the Workers' Park of Culture, the part of the gardens now open to the public. We walked over the delicately sculptured white marble bridges, along the winding lanes, past statues and bill-boards filled with illustrated statistics, until we came upon one of the palaces. Its gracious yellow-tiled roof rested lightly on the red lacquered columns and little cushions of snow were still hidden in its curved corners.

A little further away, in front of a gilded pavilion, I sat down on a bench next to an old lady with a wrinkled, nut-like face. She was reading a booklet illustrated with brightly coloured drawings and she wore the light blue pyjamas of olden days. It was only later on that I noticed that she had tiny bound feet curiously resembling goat-hooves. All around us children were frolicking in the over-brilliant sunshine and, at regular intervals, a tiny boy ran up to her to exchange a few words. He looked at me with unconcealed curiosity and then, like a billiard ball, he darted off again to tell about the odd stranger to his screaming comrades. He was barely five years old, in a thickly padded overall and only his radiant little head bare, illuminated by a pair of wondrous eyes looking like two enormous black cherries.

Relying on my meagre Chinese, we came to exchange a few words. The grandmother was all smiles. Her son worked in a Ministry and they lived not far from the Palace. As for the rest, she was understandably reticent. To most of my questions she had only one answer. 'Times have changed. . . . Times have changed . . .', she repeated, wrapped in apologetic smiles.

The next time when the boy ran up to us I asked what profession he would choose. They lovingly consulted each other and the boy pointed at the large model of a Diesel rail-coach displayed in front of the Palace. Then they looked at the hoarding facing us, showing a moon-rocket lifting a red production curve into space. 'Engineer . . .', she said. 'He wants to build machines. . . .' Then, she laughed again as the boy ran off. 'Times have changed. . . . Times have changed . . .', she repeated.

Later on, after polite nods, they decided to go. Soon I could see them disappearing along the lane, she hobbling along on her crushed feet and the boy circling her like an impetuous satellite. What a prodigious life-span she must have had. When her parents had been lovingly binding her feet to make her beautiful, those gardens had been part of the Forbidden City and no ordinary mortal could hope to see them. Among her childhood memories must be glimpses of the brocaded ladies of the Manchu nobility, fairy-tale-like processions converging on the giant red doors of the Gate of Heavenly Peace, rumours about the Empress Dowager's schemings behind the forbidding Palace walls or, perhaps, even scenes of the massacres and the mass-suicides which accompanied the looting of the capital by the 'long-nosed' foreigners. Now her grandson wants to build moon-rockets and she is reading history illustrated by brightly coloured images which reshape the very past she had known.

Indeed, times have changed. But what would the balance-sheet be like which she could draw from such a prodigious life-span? and what could it be when attempted by an outsider unaffected by all the events and emotions which have been shaping the world in which she now has to live?

China's recorded history covers four millennia. The present régime is only twelve years old. Its achievements may be measured in objective terms: how, at what speed, and at what price were the country's resources put to constructive use? but could that balance-sheet be objective if not held up against the collective memory's subjective image of the past? could the scale and the ruthlessness of China's revolution be comprehended without that double effort? or could one hope, without their aid, to understand the methods of the rulers or the revolutionary fervour of the ruled?

The sufferings and disorder of past centuries have yet to be put on record by historians. For the time being one can but choose among odd fragments.

An investigator tells us that, on the basis of records found in local files, there were 67 peasant revolts within a period of some 180 years (1448-1627) in one small border region between the provinces of Kiangsi and Fukien.[116] Then, a recent book by an expatriate Chinese historian provides unexpected information. It deals with the unexciting subject of population.[117] After exhaustive studies it comes to the conclusion that several Chinese provinces actually had a larger population a century ago than today. And the reasons, if one examines them, may go a long way to help Westerners to grasp China's present mood.

During the Taiping rebellion, between 1851-64, more than 30 million people perished and those thirteen years may represent the most destructive period of warfare in human history. About as many people lost their lives again in the Moslem rebellions in the North-west in the sixties and the seventies of the last century with barely a tenth of the population surviving in some counties. Then there were the great natural disasters. In the 1877-79 drought in north China nearly 15 million people lost their lives. Famine in 1920 and 1928, then flood in 1931, claimed again millions of lives.

In Szechuan province alone there were over 400 civil outbreaks since the fall of the Empire in 1911. Between 1932 and 1934 more than a million people lost their lives from that cause in that province alone. Civil war between Kuomintang and Communists from 1928 to 1934, together with savage reprisals by Chiang Kai-shek's forces, continued to pile up the dead in millions. The figures only mounted with the coming of the Japanese. Together with disease, caused by rotting corpses, the losses of this period are evaluated at nearly 20 million. The renewed civil war, between 1946 and 1949, again claimed deaths up to 3 million.

Another observer, perhaps less scientifically documented, claims that nearly 50 million people died violently in China during the twenty years of Kuomintang rule.[118]

It is a century of frightfulness to look back upon. Can the significance of discontent over the Communes, over the inhumanity of forced labour, or over the stringency of rationing be dissociated from the welter of blood and suffering from which China is just emerging? or can the methods and the feverish drive of the country's present rulers be comprehended independently of the sense of suffering and injustice in which their ideals have ripened?

Any attempt to answer would inevitably lead to arguments of a theological nature. Yet to judge the present one has to keep in mind the past. And only that past could give its real measure to the balance-sheet on which China's future is now being built.

I Equality in Austerity

NO MAGIC COULD have changed in a few years the misery inherited by the Chinese masses. Those, in a few big cities, who had known civilized living standards, never amounted to more than a tiny fraction. The destitution of the majority had been such that even if all the increase in production could have gone to alleviate it, the results would still be meagre. But, in fact, most of that increase was devoted to long-term aims rather than to the quick expansion of consumption.

The possibilities of observation of a visitor to present-day China, already limited in the cities, are totally inadequate in the countryside. There, one visits selected sites, sees other regions from the train or at odd points where the plane or the railway stops, and remains without first-hand impressions about immense regions of the size of several European states. How, then, can one generalize about the way of living of China's 500 million peasants?

Most of them are by now to all intents and purposes labourers employed by the State. In exchange for free meals, some basic necessities and a modest wage, they have to supply all the labour they can stand. As for their women-folk, nine out of every ten of the able-bodied among them are now working in agriculture too.[119]

Careful calculations by foreign specialists conclude that between 1953 and 1957 individual consumption of food grains in the rural areas had slightly increased. In 1957 and 1958, during the Greap Leap, however, there was a marked decline amounting, in some regions, to as much as one-third. In 1960, so it seems, there has been some improvement though it is by no means clear whether consumption is already back to its 1957 level. But these generalizations call for qualifications. Official statistics and foreign estimates agree only on an increase in *basic* foodstuffs. In other words, China's rural population is provided today with more staple food than ever before but at the expense of other food which, in the past, was unequally distributed. Articles like vegetable oil, meat or fresh vegetables, ample in the past for those able to pay for them, have become scarce. Today they may be available for all though in very modest quantities only. The situation is similar with cotton–cloth. In 1957-58 the ration had gone down from seven to six metres and there is no doubt that larger quantities would be needed. The basic change is again that most villagers now have the cash to purchase what is available on the market while in the past often greater variety and larger quantities were available for only the minority who had been able to buy.

Official declarations do not tire of repeating that, in monetary terms, rural consumption has considerably increased. Indeed it is established that larger quantities of staple food and some necessities—such, for instance, as rubber shoes—are being sold in the rural areas. But such figures do not reveal the growing proportion of cereals and coarse grains sold instead of more nutritive food stuffs. Nor do such official figures bring out the fact that a great deal of what the peasant household used to grow or to produce for its own use has now to be purchased through commercial channels. The higher quality foods which people used to grow in their back-gardens are now bought through the Commune's shop and go to inflate *monetary* estimates of peasant spending. The same applies to articles like straw-shoes, dresses or hand-woven cloth which used to be made at home before women were made to join the labour brigades.

On the other hand, a number of valuable services now freely available to all Commune members could not have been had, even for money, in the past. Health services, schools for the children, not to speak of the advantages of new roads, better communications, or, perhaps, electric current, are not measurable in money terms. These, added to other satisfactions, like greater security against natural disasters, the knowledge that education opens new opportunities before one's children, or that life is progressively freed of the miseries of avoidable disease, may possibly compensate for the simplification of the peasant's diet.

The situation, of course, is very different in the cities. The food situation has probably not been better than in the rural areas. Transitory shortages may have affected them more than the villages, as the long queues in front of food-shops and canteens eloquently prove. As for the basic rations of cereals, they seem to have been regular and adequate. Moreover, from 1951 onwards, a system of social security was introduced for urban populations. It offers a wide range of benefits. State enterprises have to contribute about a sixth of their wage bill to finance these welfare services and they represent an innovation totally unknown in the country on any comparable scale. Workers and employees obtain free medical assistance, cost-of-living subsidies, educational privileges for their children, and factory workers can draw sick and disability benefits. From 1958, even a system of retirement insurance was put into effect thus providing *urban* workers and employees with a range of social security almost comparable to that existing in the most advanced Western countries.[120]

As if to counter-balance these new privileges, the worker and the employee is entirely at the mercy of the State concerning the choice of his job or the place of his employment. He is liable to be shuttled about the provinces and be sent to remote construction sites where his skill may be needed. The building up of the interior and the creation of new industrial centres only accentuates that possibility which may often cause real hardship in dispersing families for long periods. Redirection from urban to rural work is equally a possibility and that involves also the sudden loss of privileges going with living in towns.

Notwithstanding such difficulties—hardly avoidable in a country where large regions are being peopled and put to economic use for the first time—urban employment offers further advantages. Industrialization and urbanization imply multiple services which, even if they are not measurable in monetary terms, represent tangible benefits to the consumer. Collective welfare services from better equipped schools and hospitals to electricity, water supply, sewerage and other municipal amenities, represent a degree of comfort unknown over most of China's countryside. These, together with wider opportunities for amusement and the utilization of leisure tend, in China, as practically all over the world, to attract people from village to town.

In daily practice, most town dwellers eat in canteens. The meals I have seen were plentiful though often very simple and without meat. But even the lowest paid worker could afford them at a price of 15 to 20 yuan a month for a daily three meals.[121]

Differences in income are smaller than in any other, even Communist, country. The range is rarely wider than one to seven. An apprentice working in a factory earns about 35 yuan a month. An unskilled worker, from 45 yuan upwards and the officer worker not much more. The skilled worker's pay may rise from 80 to 120 yuan. On the other hand, the manager of an important plant would rarely earn more than 150 or 180 and only in exceptional cases—like those of specialized engineers or of directors of great 'combines'—earn salaries surpassing 200 yuan. As a whole, doctors, engineers, scientists and artists are today China's best paid people and their income is usually ahead of that of senior officials in Ministries or of Ministers themselves. I was told that China's most popular film star, the idol of the country, earned the 'fabulous' salary of around 300 yuan.

With the exception of some spectacular housing projects near new industrial complexes, there is a great deal of overcrowding in the cities. Apartments built for foremen and factory managers which I have visited, though shown with understandable pride, were austere constructions. The privacy of their one or two rooms, however, represents luxury in comparison with the homes in which the majority live. Housing could hardly have kept pace with the growth of urban agglomerations.[122] Rents, however, are controlled and, as a rule, represent only 5 per cent. of the occupant's wage. Thus, the two basic necessities of food and housing do not absorb an unreasonable proportion of the earnings of the average urban Chinese.[123]

The clothing situation is very different. Inspecting shop-windows in several cities, I kept on wondering how the Chinese managed to buy even essential items, apart from the always neat and attractive garments of their children. A pair of trousers may cost up to 50 yuan. A cotton shirt is priced around 6 yuan. A metre of the simple printed cotton for women's pyjama-like garments, costs around 5 yuan, though for a Western housewife its quality would seem shoddy. The price of men's or women's leather shoes ranges from 20 to 40 yuan but at work most Chinese wear either rubber-soled tennis-shoes—which are plentiful and cheap—or the traditional felt slippers which they can buy from 3 yuan a pair.

Looking at these prices one understands why most Chinese prefer the blue uniform invented by Sun Yat-sen. Consisting of a cotton-coat and a pair of trousers, it costs no more than 8 yuan. Made of better, tweed-like material, it still is not dearer than 12 yuan. No wonder then if most consumers, whether men or women, prefer to be neatly, even if uniformly, clad in those celebrated and mass-produced utility suits.

Yet they are symbolic of the general price policy. The aim is to provide the largest possible number with basic necessities at an accessible price. The model Chinese wears the blue tunic, eats in a canteen, lives in a rent-controlled room and equips his home with only mass-produced utensils, which are more plentiful in China's shops than they used to be in Russia during the first two Five-Year Plans of that country. If he permits himself no greater luxuries than an occasional visit to the cinema, a fountain pen (a cheap local imitation of the *Parker 51*), some books, or here and there a packet of cigarettes (from 15 to 60 cents for 20)—he may even find himself with some surplus cash. That he may spend on a surprisingly wide variety of articles, including semi-luxury goods, on display in state-stores. Every time I changed money in a bank, I was surprised to see people queueing up with their savings books. In fact, with some patience, our model Chinese may save up enough to buy one of those shiny objects usually behind glass cases in the state-stores of the bigger towns. Their prices often surpass the skilled worker's earnings over several months. They may be radios, electric record-players, cameras or bicycles, all manufactured in China. In the more modest range, the luxury may be no greater than a small mechanical toy, a record (78 r.p.m., 10 cm. for 1.20 yuan), or simply a 100 gr. bar of chocolate priced at 2 yuan.

The inevitable result of all this is that most people in towns dress the same way and buy the same narrow range of goods. And the almost complete lack of any effort to present the available articles in an attractive way, merely underlines the general air of austerity. The luxury of the few is certainly over. It has been replaced by the very modest uniformity of the many. Yet even that modest uniformity must already represent progress over what the majority of town-dwellers had known in the past.

It is evident that the Chinese of all walks of life are made to work very hard and that the State literally commands their waking hours. That life in the Communes is tough, no one would contest. That China no longer knows large-scale famines or the natural disasters which used to claim millions of lives is equally clear. Yet, inevitably, the Chinese peasant is still desperately poor. If their majority has experienced any improvement in its living conditions, it must have been slow and slight. Compared to the villagers' lot, however, town-dwellers are in a favoured situation and the industrial workers' growing purchasing power and expanding social security already marks them off as a new élite.

But the only measure by which may be judged the living standards of urban and rural populations alike is in terms of their own past. That comparison, for the vast majority, is unlikely to be unfavourable. Only too painfully visible in a number of Asian countries, I have seen in China no evidence of malnutrition. People as a whole, and children in particular, look healthy and vigorous. There is no unemployment and no one goes around in rags. There is no rich or privileged class and that, no doubt, renders uniform austerity more bearable. Then, even if incited into action by ruthless methods, it must be a totally new and welcome experience for most Chinese to have an inspiring objective. Peking has created a collective society which offers to countless millions security in a new and powerful China. And what that society offers in terms of national pride or of freedom from hunger or violent death may seem to most Chinese of more immediate interest than even elementary liberties for the individual which the majority of them never really knew.

Those unable to fit into this new pattern are inevitably ruined. The small minority of intellectuals are probably unhappy in their strait-jacket. But the overwhelming majority, whose material conditions have probably never been better, may well consider acceptable things as they are. And the impressive changes all around them may induce the hesitants to be patient and to await the dividends of their present sacrifices.

2 The Great Shift in Power to the Hinterland

AN IMAGINARY line from the North of Manchuria to the Burmese border in the South, cuts the map of China into two unequal halves. It reveals two very different Chinas. Density of population to the right is ten-times of what it is to the left. To the right, on the side of the Pacific Ocean, spread the fertile plains, there are the crowded river deltas, the big cities, and almost all that is relatively modern in the country. To the left, towards the heart of Asia, spreads empty China: enormous regions barely populated, without cities of importance, without railways or roads, and with uncharted natural resources buried in the ground. Against barely 100 million people thinly spread to the left of that line, more than 500 million Chinese crowd the much smaller outer half which faces the sea.

There are several reasons for this disequilibrium. Deserts, mountains, invasions, and history in general have contributed their share. Moreover, all over Asia, Africa and Latin America, contact with the industrialized West has acted like a magnet. It has drawn people, enterprise and resources towards the coasts. It was there, in mushrooming cities, that the raw materials of the interior have been exchanged for the industrial goods of the West. It was through those windows opened to the West's mercantile economy that came the mass-produced, machine-made products which have destroyed the prosperity of artisans inland. And it was in those new ports that a tiny middle-class, ready to adopt the West's ideas, crystallized around the new, commercial activities. Equally, it was from those new coastal centres that roads and railways groped inwards, though usually no further than was just necessary to fill the waiting ships. The life of the deep interior remained untouched by the fertilizing contact. Its resources were unknown, its order was uncertain, and whatever prosperity it had known in the past, it withered away through isolation.

One of the most spectacular aims of the new China is to obliterate that imaginary line. And the reasons for it are as numerous as were the causes which have brought about the present disequilibrium.

As a reaction to past dependence on the external world, there is the desire to build an independent economy which can rely on its own resources and is capable of supplying the country's needs. That implies the mobilization of indigenous resources, modern communications, power to feed industries and new cities where their workers would live. That implies also the opening up of new land to support the new urban centres and, above all, the movement of settlers able to perform all the required new tasks. The ultimate aim is a new equilibrium: the shifting of the country's centre of gravity from its present, artificial situation towards a new and more natural position.

It is an enterprise that may take a century or more to accomplish. It is at its beginnings only. Yet already it begins to modify the picture of China as it has been known during past centuries.

Though the purpose and the motives behind this momentous enterprise are clear, it is difficult to gain a reliable picture of its progress. One reason is distance and lack of communications. Another is secrecy, dictated, perhaps, by strategic considerations. The third one is simply in the paucity of reliable statistics which, even when they do exist, are not always released. Moreover, the density of Chinese statistics declines in proportion with distance from the Pacific coast. Thus, attempting to follow the process of this great transformation, one has to peep through key-holes, as it were, through the rare openings left by selected statistics or by the restrictions on travel in China's interior.

China's future economic plans depend primarily on the availability of natural resources. Spurred on by their grandiose plans of industrialization, China's new rulers undertook a vigorous prospecting of the country in search of unknown wealth buried in its soil. Geologists have been trained in great numbers, in the Soviet Union first and at China's own universities later on. A Ministry of Geology was established in 1952 and its staff of a thousand specialists is busy analysing the samples sent to them from every corner of the country. In 1959, so I was told, the Ministry had over 4,500 prospecting teams in the field, scattered in Sinkiang, in Tibet and in the mountainous regions of the South-west. All provinces have their own geological bureaux and geological colleges are being set up in dozens of towns. All these institutes send their students for more or less prolonged periods to join teams in the field and even Communes are said to have organized their own prospecting groups. As a result of all these efforts the picture of China as a country poor in raw-materials is being rapidly modified. 'An unprecedented bumper harvest was reaped (in 1958) in the discovery of mineral resources', reported the Minister of Geology on April 28, 1959, while the press regularly publishes news of important new discoveries though, as a rule, neither their exact location nor any quantities are disclosed. From speeches and articles, however, a few basic facts are beginning to emerge.

Already known to possess considerable reserves of coal, China can now be considered as the country with probably the most extensive proven reserves. They are now estimated at around 10,000 milliard tons. As for proven iron-ore reserves, believed to be before 1949 about 3,000 million tons, they are now reckoned at a level four times that high. Large and varied resources have been discovered also in the field of non-ferrous metals and rich deposits of uranium were located in Sinkiang.[124] With the exception of cobalt, nickel and one or two other minerals of importance, China now seems to command the mineral resources to justify the scale of her industrial plans. Moreover, oil has been discovered in three new regions surpassing in importance the old Yumen fields.[125]

These new discoveries, of course, will decisively influence the location of China's future industrial centres. Next to Manchuria and a few coastal cities—the old centres of modern industry—it is possible already to foresee at least four new regions which will become, and are already being transformed into, great industrial zones.[126] The first, in Szechuan province, will extend into Yunnan to the south. The second will be in Inner Mongolia, based on the new steel-works at Paotow. The third is taking shape in Kansu and Chinghai provinces, between the cities of Sining and Lanchow, with the latter fast emerging as China's largest inland industrial centre. Finally, a fourth industrial region is emerging in Sinkiang, based on both the petroleum and mineral wealth of that Autonomous Region. Medium-sized steel-plants are projected for all four of these industrial zones, while the two further steel-complexes of the Anshan size (with a yearly production of 3 to 4 million tons)—foreseen in the latest lot of Soviet aid-projects—may be located in Sinkiang and in the Szechuan-Yunnan areas each.

These plans, to mature by the end of the third Five-Year Plan around 1967, are already taking shape and, patchy as available information about them may be, one may follow the process along three different planes.

In the first place some figures are available concerning the proportion of the new factories built behind the coastal areas. There is also the large-scale movement of people from the over-crowded coastal provinces to the new industrial regions. Finally, there is China's policy towards her ethnic minorities. As already in Inner Mongolia, so in Tibet and in Sinkiang as well, they may soon find themselves doubly minorities: in China as a whole and in their own areas where the influx of Chinese settlers and industrial workers may turn the newcomers into a majority within a few years.

As late as 1952 more than 80 per cent. of the productive capacity of China's iron and steel industry was located in the coastal areas. For the textile industry the proportion was nearly 90 per cent. Of the total value of factory products, three-quarters were manufactured in the coastal areas and the remaining eighteen provinces and Autonomous Regions contributed one-quarter only. The declared intention of the first Five-Year Plan was to lessen this disequilibrium. The aim, as its text said, was 'to locate industries as close to sources of raw materials and fuel supplies as to consumption centres, when the interest of national security is served . . .'. And, of course, railway and highway development too was to be adapted to that aim.

Results were quick to emerge. In fact, initially, the neglect of coastal industries and the parallel encouragement to inland location was so energetically pursued that the trend had to be slightly reversed. For a brief period in 1950 there was even some encouragement to move certain light industries from coastal to inland areas. Security considerations have played a certain role. But official sentiment against the big ports as citadels of both capitalist enterprise and of the class and of the way of living which were condemned to disappear may have been equally important. As a result there was calculated neglect of certain industries in big cities like Shanghai. Soon, however, it was admitted that productive capacity had to be put to maximum use wherever it was found. The turn of the tide came late in 1956 when, for instance, the attempted depopulation of Shanghai was definitely abandoned to give way to a new policy of the expansion of the city's existing industries.

During the first three years of the first Five-Year Plan three-quarters of all investments in new enterprises were made behind the coastal areas. After 1956 development was more evenly balanced. Yet even so, of the 825 big industrial projects initiated during the first Plan period 530, or two-thirds, were located in the interior. Both of the large iron and steel combines begun during those five years were deep inland: one in Inner Mongolia at Paotow, and the other at Wuhan in Central China.[127] During these same five years the value of industrial production in the coastal areas about doubled while inland the increase was nearly threefold.[128] Though little precise information is available, this trend continues and it is likely to gather momentum in the coming years. As Paotow and Wuhan come into full production, their subsidiary industries alone will represent a considerable increase in inland output. Moreover, most of the heavy industry complexes planned for the future would be located in the vicinity of the newly discovered coal and oil deposits or near the hydro-electric projects under execution, nearly all deep in the interior.

Such changes in China's economic structure inevitably involve also large scale migration towards the new industries and to newly opened up land. During the first Five-Year Plan alone 26 new cities had been built, 20 others were extensively reconstructed, and another 74 were remodelled.[129] Even a foreign traveller can see that a number of formerly insignificant provincial towns are fast growing into large industrial conglomerations. Their new population comes mostly from the coastal provinces and it is becoming a mass movement. Up to 1956 development in distant areas drew labour mostly from large towns, from Shanghai in particular. After that date the internal migration was more systematically organized. It seems that by now certain provinces help to people selected inland regions. Honan, for instance, sends its pioneers to Chinghai, China's 'wild west' adjoining

Tibet, bigger than Britain and France combined though with less than 2 million population. Other provinces send their pioneers to Kansu or even further inland, for example, to Sinkiang.

How far this migration is voluntary it is difficult to tell. The press carries exhortations calling on the young to go to the 'border regions'. Their patriotism, their 'socialist consciousness', as well as their sense of adventure are appealed to. In all probability the familiar mixture of enthusiasm, persuasion and force is being applied and, in fact, it is known that on several occasions people have drifted back to their place of origin after their first contact with the bleak highlands. Now things appear to be better organized and the migrants join communities of their own kind into which they can fit more easily. Higher wages and better stocked state-stores await them and even 'comfort missions' are being organized—composed of propagandists, entertainers and welfare teams—busy to smooth the integration of the new-comers. More and more frequently entire army units are settled in border areas after their demobilization and, after a period of two or three years, their families are encouraged to go and join them in their new homes.

How many have already moved or will do so in the future is still difficult to ascertain. In the three years after 1956, from Honan province alone about 80,000 young people have gone to Chinghai and it was announced that each year 100,000 would move from that province alone. It is reasonable to suppose that comparable numbers are involved in the migratory movement from the other over-populated coastal provinces. That particularly in the areas peopled by ethnic minorities this is bound to pose special problems is only natural. In Inner Mongolia, the Chinese already outnumber the Mongols by seven to one. With rapid industrialization the proportion is bound to grow even less favourable for the Mongols. In fact, it is probable that, in the long run, the fate of most minorities will be similar to that of the Manchus. Under the Manchu empire, Chinese immigration to Manchuria was allowed only after the mid-nineteenth century. Today, about 95 per cent. of Manchuria's population is Chinese and the Manchus as a separate entity have almost disappeared.

Particularly instructive is the example of Sinkiang. Mr. Mehmed Ismail, Secretary-General of the Sinkiang Government, told me in Urumchi, the capital, in March 1959 that Sinkiang's population—about 4 million in 1949—was by then slightly over 6 million.[130] When I remarked that this signified a yearly increase of over 4 per cent., a rate too high even for a Moslem population, he quickly added that this was due to vast improvements in health conditions. 'Look at the new hospitals, at the number of doctors, and you will understand why our population grows faster . . . ', he said. Yet even if one took the highest probable rate of natural increase, let's say 2·5 per cent., this figure still implied that at least 80,000 people a year must have come from outside to swell that Autonomous Region's population. How many Chinese actually came, he professed to ignore. Industrialization, however, caused a shortage of labour, he said, and the Sinkiang Government asked Peking for help. The capital, he confirmed, agreed to 'mobilize the young people of Hupeh, Anhwei and Kiangsu provinces' and, as a result, 200,000 of them were expected in Sinkiang in 1959 alone. As a matter of fact I have found in Urumchi's auto-repair works that 60 per cent. of the workers were Chinese. Although the local authorities were making a genuine effort to train foremen and technicians of local people, both the land and factories needed Chinese immigrants.

As it happens huge and sparsely populated areas inhabited by non-Chinese peoples contain much of the natural wealth now being discovered. Inner Mongolia, Tibet, Sinkiang and some smaller areas in the south-west, are the most important among them. 'Less than 5 per cent. of the people in China occupy more than half our territory,' Mao Tse-tung was reported to have said in 1957. 'They are National Minorities, tribesmen once regarded as not part of the Chinese race. We must convert them and convince them they are Chinese.' And to do so has become a double necessity: to find room for the fast expanding Chinese population, and to provide the manpower needed to put the areas inhabited by minorities to constructive use.

But how to convince them that they are Chinese? Like all

contemporary great powers China too is a multi-racial State. Within her borders live some fifty minorities. About a dozen among them number each more than a million. Yet, as a whole, China was more favoured in this field than was the Soviet Union. All the non-Chinese races within her borders add up to no more than 6 per cent. of the country's total population.[131] On the other hand, they occupy vast border regions which are only beginning to be connected with the rest of the country through highways, railways and internal air-lines. In some cases they pose stiff problems. The Tibetans took up arms. The Miaos of the south-western mountains had for long fought the Kuomintang. Their neighbours, the Yi—numbering over 3 million—were in 1949 still taking slaves and their primitive agriculture rested on slave labour. Of the big minority peoples only with the Chuangs of the far south-west (about 7 million), the Turkic peoples of Sinkiang (about 5 million), and the Mongols of Inner Mongolia (over 1 million), could the new régime rely on good relations almost from the start.

China's basic approach to the problem has been similar to the one experimented with in the U.S.S.R. The official belief is that the traditional nationalism of the minorities will gradually give way to a super-national loyalty to the socialist, multi-racial state. The old patriotism of the ethnic minorities, so it is expected, will be slowly supplanted by a new, ideological allegiance. This allegiance will be stimulated both by cultural and material improvements, as well as by the mutual advantages accruing from the common enterprise of the industrialization and the modernization of the powerful, joint motherland. In fact, in a sense, the present Chinese régime has done more for the advancement of the minorities than any Chinese government in the past. It has created autonomous regions, departments and districts (rather than Federal Republics as in the Soviet Union) for even small ethnic groups.[132] It built more schools, hospitals and theatres than they ever had before. It helped to make scripts for revived and half-forgotten languages. It publishes newspapers and books in tongues which have never been printed before.[133] But the suspicions left behind by past oppression, by savage reprisals, or by the fear of Chinese colonization, are still strong enough to counterbalance much of the benefits from material and cultural progress. Actually so it would seem, even some of the people who had been chosen for training in Institutes of Nationalities allow their nationalism to overcome their ideological indoctrination once they return to their own regions. Attacks are made both in speeches and in the press against 'local bourgeois nationalism' on the one hand, and against 'Great Han chauvinism' on the other— *Han* being the Chinese's own word for their race. While the first implies the reluctant admission that nationalism is not merely an aberration of the capitalist phase of societies, the second implicitly admits that even now there are still Han settlers and officials who think of their role in terms of condescension and racial privilege.

Yet official policy is to encourage the formation of minority cadres and to provide the nationalities with genuine opportunities for self-administration. Actually, the more numerous the local cadres and, as a consequence, the more likely that the local authorities would follow Peking's leadership, the greater is the likelihood of a minority obtaining the status of autonomy. To what extent this policy will fulfill the hopes attached to it, is difficult to say. Some of the minorities are too small and their cultural heritage too vague to withstand for long sinicization in an age of mass-communications. For them, the loss of their identity will be the price to pay for their admission to twentieth-century civilization. Some others, like the Mongols, are already half-way to the fate of the Manchus. Tibet constitutes a special case. There, geography poses entirely different problems. The homogeneity of Tibet's religion, its social structure, and its way of living practically unaffected by outside influences over centuries, combine with climatic difficulties and lack of adequate communications to render Tibetan nationalist resistance both more vigorous and probably more lasting. But with highways across the mountains, with the railway to follow, and with the new social and economic structures imposed, the cohesion of the old order is bound to crumble. Moreover, it is quite possible that at least a section of the young may become supporters of social change. And whatever the heroism of national resistance may have been, sooner or later, Tibet too may yield to the onslaught of sinicization and eventually even to the influx of Chinese settlers.[134]

Technological progress allied to the contemporary desire to integrate the resources of ever greater areas into centrally directed units, heralds in China, as in many other parts of the world, the end of the distinct personality of peripheral peoples.

None of China's minority areas, however, is so clearly destined to play a major role in the country's transformation as Sinkiang. It has much potentially fertile land and its natural resources are considerable. Its strategic situation as the future marshalling-yard of Central Asia makes it already prominent in Chinese plans for the future. And it is there that the immediate consequences of the great shift in China's national power are the most spectacular.

3 Sinkiang, the New World beyond the Jade Gate

NOT SO LONG ago to venture beyond the point where the Great Wall petered out in the majestic Jade Gate was a risky enterprise at the traveller's own risk. To be permitted to go to Sinkiang, the old Chinese Turkestan, still spells adventure even if one sets out on an *Ilyushin 14* of the Chinese airways. For hours, in the Gobi Desert, one is followed by the incredible loops of the Great Wall: an appropriate reminder when in search of the future that the Chinese have always been capable of fantastic feats of labour and endurance.

At the end of the first day's flying the plane turned southward and descended over a sandy basin, surrounded by barren mountains. There, following the Yellow River, it flew in over Lanchow, descendant of the *golden city* of the silk caravans over 2,000 years ago. Lanchow is well to the west of that imaginary line which divides the two Chinas. As late as 1950 it was a shabby little desert town with a population of less than 200,000. It was nearly 400 kilometres from the nearest railway, without paved streets and with nothing more to offer to the outside world than its fruits and tobacco, or the sabres, the saddles, and the cheap woollen fabrics of its artisans.

Now all that was visibly changed. As I left the plane the Blue Danube waltz was pouring from the airport's loudspeakers, a symbolic warning, no doubt, that the West's technology has already crossed China's invisible internal border, even if from the East. Along a broad auto-route we drove to the imposing new hotel to arrive just in time to meet the usual crowd of blue-clad cadres descending from their lectures to the dining-room. Later on I walked around the city's new quarters, along streets lined with spacious new public buildings, by tall blocks of apartments, cinemas, theatres, hospitals and schools. Everything was on the move. Wide asphalted roads were being laid across condemned old quarters, chunks of which still survived, criss-crossed by dirt-lanes. I met marching columns with shovel on shoulder, following a red flag or banners with uncompromising slogans. Sturdy trucks shared the new avenues with caravans of mules and Chinese made autobuses—pulling two or three brightly coloured trailers—were hooting their way through masses of workers busy on construction sites or literally carrying away the remaining hills which still obstructed the spread of new buildings. A faded red-lacquered temple sheltered timidly on a tiny hill and already a blustering *Palace of Culture* trespassed over its gardens. Then, there was particular animation in front of the new railway station. Lingering in the motley crowd in front of it, I could see groups of immigrants leaving the building—Mongols with fur caps, giant tribesmen, or broad-featured Hans from the coastal provinces. They put down their load, stopped, and looked around with amazement over the tumultuous new world where they had just arrived to spend the rest of their lives. Some of them stared at me with the honest curiosity of people who have never seen a white man before. And behind them, the robust locomotives which hauled them that far, whistled with clumsy indifference before they began to move the still packed coaches and clattered on still deeper into Central Asia towards even more remote stations of China's unfolding adventure.

To have a full view of this fascinating world, one afternoon I climbed up on the surrounding mountains in the company of a young cadre-member. He was one of the genuine pioneers who had left their native Shanghai in order 'to build the interior'. And he was a devoted and unquestioning product of the new régime.

All around us incredibly sterile mountains ringed the horizon and there wasn't a blade of vegetation in the soft sand on their slopes. 'You see those steps and the tiny saplings along them?' my companion asked pointing at the fantastic terraces carved around the mountains. They were barely distinguishable in the yellowness of the lunar scenery. For several years now, tens of thousands of volunteers, workers, students and ordinary citizens have been giving their free day to sculpture those mountains and to plant trees along the terraces. A few of them were already visible if one looked hard. Many more were still below ground, in struggle with the inhospitable soil.

We moved on and arrived at a promontory which offered a splendid view over the valley. Deep below us to the end of the horizon was spreading Lanchow. On our left, jutting out over the precipice, stood an old temple and a slender pagoda. They were sadly deserted in their mountain solitude. Along the walls encircling them, painted in giant red characters, an inscription beaconed to the city: *Spare No Effort Go Ahead with Socialist Construction.* And below us, in its yellow cradle, twisted the sand-coloured river which earned the name of *China's Sorrow.*

'It's here that it becomes yellow. There are no trees left to stop the water and pouring down the slopes it washes the soil into the river. But all that is now the past,' the cadre explained. 'Afforestation will put an end to it. Besides, from an enemy of the people, the Yellow River will be made its servant,' he said, and immediately supplied the facts and figures in the style of China's un-romantic pioneers. Several multi-purposes projects, 46 dams and 24 reservoirs will do the taming. They will irrigate millions of hectares and will generate energy to drive new industries. A great deal of it was already under execution. And much has been done by the naked hands of workers and volunteers.

Deep below us were the new bridges. Next to the dilapidated span dating from 1909, there were four wide, new ones. In the eastern suburb the sun was sparkling on the metal towers of the new, automatic refinery which alone occupied a site larger than had been the whole town before 1949. It was to serve the Yumen oilfields and its output (over 1 million tons) already exceeded that of all of China's pre-war refineries put together. On the other side of the two sprawled the huge machine-building plant, soon to supply all the equipment needed by the region's chemical and oil installations. It was already turning out ultra-modern heavy drills, able to bore to a depth of over 3,000 metres. We could see also the new power station, the large university buildings, and all the smoking chimneys of Lanchow's 355 modern factories built during the past few years.

'When did you have your last day off?' I turned to my companion at the end of his explanations.

'Perhaps two months ago,' he said after some hesitation. Then, as if to forestall what I might have wished to say, he quickly continued: 'For centuries nature and events have shaped our fate. Now, for the first time, it's we who shape events and the future.'

'And your life?' I asked. 'Just occasionally, you and the millions like you, wouldn't you like to stop to attend meetings, to read Party literature, or to stop volunteering for extra work—and just relax for a while?'

'Our lives? what do our lives matter when there is so much to do?' the cadre said. Then, his usually alert face suddenly turning static and meditative, he looked around the lifeless mountains and slowly he added: 'We are terribly late. . . .'

Having, for weeks, listened to codified and dutiful enthusiasm of the same kind, that little conversation would not have seemed unusual had its surroundings not lent it such a spectacular and convincing frame. Somewhere to the south-west, far beyond the yellow hills, lay Tibet with the promise of all the wealth of its mountains. Towards the south-east a new industrial region was taking shape around the wartime capital of Chungking. To the left, deep in the Gobi Desert, was arising the Inner-Mongolian steel centre, already spreading its satellite industries. To the east lay coastal China with its giant markets and its inexhaustible reservoir of labour. Behind us, in the north, were the Yumen oilfields and, to the north-west, well beyond them, spread the almost empty and fabulously rich province of Sinkiang. Below us we could see railway lines radiating in all those directions, locomotives hauling long trains where only a few years before there existed no modern transport. Not far from Lanchow, in the Liuchia Gorge, an immense hydro-electric station was under construction to supply the town and its surroundings with all the energy their industry and agriculture would need. Lanchow, with its population climbing over a million, was building China's largest water-works, big enough to supply with drinking water a city of ten million people. Evidently, we were overlooking one of those enviable regions of the world where history and geography combine to provoke bold answers to a challenge, able to provide a whole generation with a broad and satisfying purpose.

Yet Lanchow was but like the mountaineers' base-camp whence they climb on to even more remote peaks. Those who left it by train for the West, rolled on for several more days along new, acrobatically winding railways, through mountains and deserts, past Sining and the Yumen oilfields, to enter Sinkiang at the end. Already deep within its borders, there the line is still under construction. By 1961 it will reach Urumchi, the capital. Beyond, it will grope on to Alma Ata and to Aktogai on the Soviet side. It will bring new life to Sinkiang and will provide Asia with a second trans-continental railway far south of the Trans-Siberian.

That new world, the Sinkiang Uighur Autonomous Region, covers a sixth of China's total area and is bigger than France, Germany and Italy combined. Its 6 million people are composed of thirteen nationalities among whom the Uighurs are by far the most important.[135] Tibet is along its southern borders. In the north are the Soviet Republics. Afghanistan, Kashmir and Pakistan are neighbours. And Sinkiang's Turkic peoples are Moslems in their large majority.

High Tartary or Chinese Turkestan—as Sinkiang used to be called—had been a dangerous region to cross for caravans trading between East and West. As late as the beginning of this century some explorers never returned from its arid and hostile interior. As the power of the Manchu dynasty gradually declined, both British and Tsarist imperialism competed for its strategic advantages. Under their protection rival adventurers had consolidated their influence and revolts and extravagant cruelties punctuated Sinkiang's recent history. But divided from China proper by deserts and lack of communications, Sinkiang seemed destined to be drawn into the Soviet economic orbit.[136] Then, with the Soviet Union's power strained by the second World War, in 1942, Sinkiang turned against it. Handicapped by its crude methods of sinicization, however, the Kuomintang never really managed to extend its effective control over the area. Moreover, barely two years after the change, in 1944, a revolt broke out in Sinkiang's three north-western districts—the richest in mineral resources—and led to the creation of a pro-Soviet East Turkestan Republic with its own Kazakh-Uighur army. Thus, when in 1949 China's revolution flooded into Sinkiang it came not so much as an invading army—as in Tibet—but rather as a relatively peaceful reinforcement of an already strong popular movement which had been inspired and encouraged from across the Soviet border.

But China's modern, westward urge, now being given concrete form, is not a Communist innovation. In his grandiose projects of railway building and industrialization, as early as 1921, Sun Yat-sen himself advocated the building of a trans-continental railway to reach to the Altai Mountains in Sinkiang. 'The colonization of Mongolia and Sinkiang is a complement of the Railway scheme . . .' , he wrote. 'If within ten years we can transport, let us say, 10 millions of people from the congested provinces of China, to the north-western territory to develop its natural resources, the benefit to the commercial world at large will be enormous. . . .'[137] Yet, as in so many other spheres, what the Chinese had been dreaming of during the first half of this century, their present rulers are actually implementing with a vigour and with means such as the Kuomintang never had at its disposal.

After the establishment of the joint Sino-Soviet companies for the exploitation of oil and non-ferrous metals and the influx of large numbers of Soviet technical experts, it seemed as if Russian influence might remain paramount in the Region. After all, the same ethnic minorities which people Sinkiang had their own Republics across the border. Yet, with the gradual readjustment in Sino-Soviet relations, after Stalin's death, the joint companies were handed back to the Chinese and by October 1955 China felt herself sufficiently in control to grant Sinkiang the status of an Autonomous Region. Even if this falls far short of full self-determination, it provides wide opportunities to the local populations and permits them to play a considerable role not merely in cultural and economic matters but even in the political field. Yet, notwithstanding the 'autonomous' label, in Sinkiang too, there have been occasions when both 'Great Han chauvinism' and 'dangerous' Uighur separatist tendencies had to be branded and even ordered to be treated through a 'rectification campaign'.[138]

Notwithstanding such occasional difficulties, Sinkiang, according to all evidence, is a showpiece in multi-national relations for the rest of China. One significant reason for this apparently satisfactory co-operation between Chinese and minorities—as well as for happy inter-minority relations—is in Sinkiang's political past. Though the Regional Government is in the shadow of the Sinkiang sub-bureau of the Chinese Communist Party, one of its four secretaries is an Uighur. Then, at least half of the province's 100,000 cadres are of local nationalities.[139] Moreover, Sinkiang being underpopulated, there is no real rivalry between local agriculturists and new settlers and rapid economic progress offers tangible benefits to all the races.

When the *Ilyushin* lands at Hami, the first stop inside Sinkiang, one gets a superficial first impression of this collaboration. Compared to Lanchow, this is already a very different world. All the races of Central Asia mingle in the crowds which fill the streets. Massive Uighur, Kazakh and Kirghiz tribesmen shop in the state-stores, children wear motley, embroidered skull-caps, bearded Moslems like those one encounters in the Middle East form the majority, and behind them all rise the bulbous domes of mosques apparently too numerous for such a small oasis town. Yet scattered among the dilapidated old houses, tall new structures stand: schools, hospitals and administrative buildings with, here and there, a factory in the making. The teacher and the officials, Chinese and Moslems all mixed up, speak with equal enthusiasm of growing production, of new canals and, in identical style, they illustrate their story with the usual charts and rising production curves. Then, pointing at the wandering donkeys and camel caravans in the streets, they proudly show the new railway station, barely completed and awaiting the first locomotive. Shortly after my visit to Hami the railway reached it, bringing all the hope attached to its coming. In the meantime, once known only for its famed melons, Hami now lives half-way between its dusty past and the technical age coming in concrete.

From Hami it is a few more hours of flying towards the west to reach Urumchi. It is a tough and splendidly impressive journey. The plane's tiny shadow effortlessly glides across the spine of awe-inspiring mountains. The Altai to the right and the snow-capped peaks of the Tien Shan branch of the Tibetan ranges to the left, form a majestic corridor of bare and sharp peaks glittering with snow and growing taller and taller like furious waves. Not far from the end of the voyage, they reach a terrifying supreme exclamation in the legendary Bogdo Ola, its summit, over 7,000 metres, and with icy clouds floating around its neck like some fantastic Elizabethan collar of lace. All the time, however, almost permanent storms blow down from the passes and play ball with the *Ilyushin*, driving half the passengers in painful search of their paper bags. Then, at last, the plane descends. Below us, with the snowy ranges on one side, and the boundless Jungarian Steppe on the other, lies Urumchi, the evil Tihwa of the past, the city that was China's place of ultimate exile.

After Lanchow and all the other big cities in feverish trans-formation, Urumchi's metamorphosis is on a relatively modest scale. It is of course punctuated by building sites and its wide new avenues are already lined by large public buildings. The new Petroleum Institute, the Exhibition Hall, the schools and buildings of the Medical College are on a scale indicative of the shape of things to come. New factories go up on the outskirts and air-conditioned cinemas dominate large squares laid out in place of dismantled old quarters. Yet what renders Urumchi different from the other inland towns is the visible coexistence within its walls of several, still distinct layers of the past.

In the old parts of the city one may easily have imagined oneself in the Middle East. Past wretched wooden buildings, Moslems with astrakhan caps rode on mules with legs dangling on one side. Others carried buckets of water on shoulder-poles up steep lanes leading past tiny mosques glued to the mullah's modest abode. Urumchi had no fewer than fifty-five places of worship and they ranged from mosques with onion domes to others, brightly coloured and distinguishable in style from Chinese temples only through the crescent at their gates. Artisans' shops displayed local carpets and mixed in the crowd of Moslems moved giant Kazakhs and fur-coated Kirghiz tribesmen melancholically leading their long line of heavily packed camels tied to each other by light chains.

In other parts of Urumchi, again, the lingering traces of Russia's presence provided the curious amalgam of Siberia with Islam. Troikas rattled down streets whose architecture ranged from the red-brick Siberian country-houses to dignified Russian-style mansions with their colonnaded fronts. There were also statues and busts of Stalin at public places and in front of factories: images which, so I was told, have already disappeared at Alma Ata and at Aktogai across the Soviet border. Further away, in the new quarters, in the three storeyed state-store pretty Uighur girls were selling kitchen utensils, bicycles and radios and there was a conspicuously wider range of attractive goods than I had seen anywhere in the rest of China. In front of the new buildings Skoda buses tried to break through the maze of mules, camels and troikas while, a little further away, former tribesmen now in factory overalls queued up for their canteen meals.

The President of the Islamic Association, a shrewd man in

astrakhan cap, received me in his modest office, sitting cross-legged on a sofa behind which Chu Teh and Mao Tse-tung were shaking hands on a tapestry framed by Chinese and Arabic texts. Our conversation concluded on a long explanation why, at that particular moment, I would have had difficulties in buying a copy of the Qurân in Urumchi. When leaving the building, I came upon a long line of joyous Moslem girls running in red overalls, training for the forthcoming athletic contest among the Region's different nationalities. The wall-journals of the textile factory on the outskirts were illustrated with caricatures of American leaders identical with those I had seen in coastal China, thousands of kilometres to the east. On street-corners bearded Moslems were frying *shishkebab* and behind them, on mural paintings, ridiculous imperialists were on the run, or the usual sputniks hauled production curves into dizzy heights. And in the first workshop of the new tractor plant, the Uighur, Tartar and Kirghiz technicians, just completing the first machine tool ever built in Sinkiang, answered my questions with the same statistics and slogans as did their Chinese colleagues in Manchuria or in Central China.

Then, one morning I found Urumchi in festive mood. There were triumphal arches along the main avenues and school-children waving Chinese flags were lining the streets. In front of the tall Petroleum Institute delegations had been waiting since early morning and, to warm themselves, the bands were rehearsing the tunes they would be playing when the moment arrived. Across the streets and over the triumphal arches streamers carried greetings in Arabic and Chinese: *Welcome to the Pioneers who Come to Help Build Sinkiang.*

By midday a long convoy of lorries arrived, each crowded with uniformed young men. And as they rolled by slowly, they were accompanied by the music and the cheers of the flag-waving crowd along the pavements.

They were the new settlers Sinkiang had been asking for, as Mr. Mehmed Ismail, the Secretary General of the Sinkiang Government had told me. More exactly, they were soldiers whose hour of demobilization had arrived and who were now being transformed into labour corps of the 'army of production'. This was an original experiment with several years of history behind it. In the past the coming of Chinese colonists inevitably had meant expropriation for Sinkiang's native oasis-dwellers. Quite often this had meant bloody clashes and still greater hostility between the races. To do away with such dangers, from 1949 onwards the People's Liberation Army was called upon to turn its energies to construction in 'economically backward or distant regions'. By a decree of January 20, 1950, about half of the 193,000 P.L.A. troops stationed in Sinkiang were charged with productive work. From 1954 onwards they were organized into 'production units' and a year later they were withdrawn from Defence Ministry control and paid at civilian rates. They have been engaged in agricultural work, in transport and railway building, water conservancy and construction. While individual immigrants came as technicians, factory workers or for other urban work, the main task of the 'production units' has been to expand the irrigation system and to found State farms on reclaimed land. Being gradually turned into civilians and being regularly replenished by newcomers, the 'production units' are passing under a State farm administration while they still remain the disciplined vanguard of Sinkiang's agricultural expansion.

So far they have reclaimed nearly half a million hectares on the fringes of the Takla Makan desert and the Jungarian steppe, and have built enough canals to permit the cultivation of many more. By 1961, so I was told, State farms alone would cover about one million hectares of new land or nearly as many as were under cultivation in the whole of Sinkiang before 1949. A target three-times higher was foreseen for 1967, the end of the twelve-year agricultural plan. This would be about half of what is considered as Sinkiang's total arable area.

The tempo of change is swift in Sinkiang's countryside. With more and more immigrants coming and with production targets being constantly raised, most of these figures may already be out of date. There is, however, a natural brake to count with. The two vast basins north and south of the Tien Shan range—covering most of Sinkiang—are very poor in water. Not even all the reservoirs and irrigation canals now being built or under planning could significantly change that fact. Yet the railway is coming and soon heavy equipment will be more readily available for large-scale hydraulic works. Moreover, experts believe that modern dry-farming methods could make large tracts of the arid plains as productive as are the Canadian prairies. If one day all the 6·5 million hectares—now designated as 'arable'—could be brought under cultivation, that would amount to about a sixteenth of all of China's cultivated land now feeding nearly 700 million people. On the basis of such crude arithmetics, then, in the foreseeable future Sinkiang might support a population of some 30 to 40 million people.

Though the aim is to render Sinkiang self-supporting, next to stock-raising and wheat and rice production, the great expanse of the Region's uncultivated land is also being transformed into one of Asia's major cotton-growing areas. The textile mill on Urumchi's outskirts—with 3,500 employees, about a third of whom are non-Chinese—already supplies half the needs of the whole Region. But in a new town, north of the capital, a much larger textile factory is now being completed, perhaps not merely in order to keep up with growing local demand but eventually even to export to other parts of China. Yet given the natural limitations on expansion on the land, the more vigorously are pushed forward Sinkiang's projects of industrialization.

Urumchi is transforming its old truck-repair works into a far larger tractor plant. A factory for the production of machine tools, one for electrical equipment, and a whole string of lesser ones for light industrial products are in active preparation. All around the great Takla Makan desert, modest industries are beginning to change dusty oasis towns like Kashgar, Ili, Turfan and Hami. Moreover, '. . . the (P.L.A.) production-construction units,' as Saifuddin, Sinkiang's Vice-President declared in 1955, 'will also give energetic aid to the large-scale industrial construction in the Region after the Lanchow-Urumchi railway is open to traffic'.

The old caravans had almost vanished. Some 10,000 lorries, churning up dust along the desert roads, have taken their place.

When that first train rolls across Sinkiang in 1961 the tempo of development will move into higher gear. And in the meantime, China's geologists are confirming what had been suspected in the past, namely, that Sinkiang has all the raw materials needed by a modern industrial power.

Though little precise information is released concerning Sinkiang's mineral wealth, enough has been said to show that they are considerable. Already before 1949 it was known that the Region held large coal deposits. Since then, new and important discoveries have been made. One official release spoke of 'vast reserves' of iron-ore and non-ferrous minerals; copper, manganese, lead and many other raw materials for chemical industries. Such claims, as a rule, are not made without justification.[140]

But perhaps of even greater importance for China's economy as a whole are the spectacular developments in Sinkiang's production of petroleum. As in mining, so with petroleum, production had been the object of joint Sino-Soviet undertakings in the past. After the dissolution of these mixed companies, and though entirely under Chinese control, Soviet specialists are believed to be still employed in both fields.

Exploitation of the Tushantsze oilfields, west of Urumchi, began before 1949 but results were rather modest. In 1955 a new deposit, 'thousands of square kilometres' in extent, was located in the north-west, in the foothills of the Altai range. Soon a new town, Karamai—meaning 'black oil'—emerged as the centre of the new oil region and from a tent-settlement it has already grown into a city of over 30,000 population. Within a year after the discovery, fifteen of the twenty wells drilled brought in oil. In September 1956 the official Chinese News Agency estimated that the Karamai fields contained reserves several times more important than those around Yumen. Later on a third field was located between Karamai and Urmou—to the north-west and in the immediate neighbourhood of the Soviet border—and it is thought that the two deposits may be linked together. Though surveying still continues and the greatest secrecy surrounds the petroleum industry, some responsible foreign observers spoke of the exceptional and even 'sensational' potentialities of Sinkiang's newly discovered oilfields.[141]

In September 1958 when Vice-President Chu Teh visited Sinkiang, he spoke of a yearly production of 20 million tons of petroleum in the Autonomous Region. For what date he foresaw that level of production, he did not specify. It is known, however, that a large refinery is already in operation at Tushantsze—now connected by China's first pipeline to the Karamai fields—and plans are being prepared for a branch-line of the Trans-Sinkiang railway to reach the refinery and thence to spread out over the oilfields, a region destined to become an industrial zone and perhaps even the seat of one of China's large steel combines.

Listening to Sinkiang officials, one is given to understand that all this is but the beginning. Roads are being built, schools and colleges multiply, local technicians are being trained, the immigrants come and, above all, the railway forges ahead across deserts and mountains, coming to integrate Sinkiang into China's feverish rhythm.[142]

'In Inner Mongolia the Mongols have become a small minority. What will happen when you will find yourself in the same position?' I asked a well-known Uighur journalist in Urumchi. 'We and the other nationalities could not exploit all the wealth of our land,' he replied. 'We need more men and more technicians to do it. In any case, we prefer progress to the isolation and the stagnation of the past. We have seen what happened in the Soviet Union across the border. Kazakhstan, on the way to becoming one of the Soviet Union's major economic regions, is our neighbour. Our relations with the Chinese are completely changed. We don't want to lag behind. . . .'

That particular journalist, of course, was an enthusiast of the new régime. It is by no means certain that most of his fellow natives of Sinkiang share his views. Yet, undoubtedly, they have seen their lot improve during these past few years. They, too, are given a purpose and a new generation is growing up already formed for the great common enterprise.

I remember one day seeing some of them in Urumchi's great Exhibition Hall with the projection of Sinkiang's future on show.

As usual at such exhibitions in present-day China, specially trained young girls stood in front of the ingenious animated models, ready to offer their explanations to those unable to read the texts and charts. Each time an inquiring Tartar, Uzbek or Uighur man or woman stopped in front of them, coloured bulbs, model railways and artificial waterfalls cascading down giant dams went into action.

Above the models were the indispensable production curves. They were all mounting steeply.[143] In pictures, in endless columns of figures, and with the aid of the animated models, one could see deserts changing into fertile plains, barrages generating electricity, and bridges helping roads over rivers. By means of coloured liquid, petrol could be seen circulating through the pipelines of tiny model refineries. There was the promise of oil, of uranium, of minerals, of coal mines and of all those toy-like little factories. A network of splendid roads covered the plains and little electric locomotives hurried across the scenery made of cardboard. Next to the melons of Hami, the grapes of Turfan, or the carpets and mutton of the other oasis towns, there were the industrial centres with all their promise of machine tools, automobiles and material comfort. Both the new immigrants and the heavy-booted tribesmen looked on with amazement. All they had seen was henceforth their common future.

Did they believe in it? Probably nobody could tell. Yet, in all probability, the irrepressible dynamism of the Chinese will claim new space. In the best case, the racial domination of the past will give place to the domination of a doctrine which may bring unknown prosperity to the majority and to which at least a minority may sincerely adhere.

Should it be so, Chinese and Soviet Central Asia, dead for centuries, and unapproachable for the Western sea-powers, may become industrially—as it is geographically—the centre of the Asian continent. In that case, nowhere are Communist plans heavier with future consequences than in that hitherto neglected region. Such a new power-centre would inevitably alter the political future of South Asia or even that of the Middle East. Moreover, on the two sides of Sinkiang's Central Asian borders live people belonging to the same races. When the levels of their educational and material existence move nearer to equality with each other, the border now dividing them may pose explosive problems. And when posed, they will have to be solved between two of the most powerful Communist states on earth. That, however, is for the distant future. What is already certain is that Chinese Turkestan is coming to life and that it is going to play a role very different from any it has played during its history of countless centuries.

4 Sinews of the Future

THE MODERNIZATION of a huge and backward country like China is a complex process and any attempt to draw up a balance-sheet of its progress must rely on an arbitrary selection of activities. To begin with, China's planners have secured a modest but equalitarian standard of living for the immense majority of the population. At the same time they have begun to shift the country's economic centre of gravity towards the interior. Simultaneously, wherever political conditions permitted, they started to integrate the remote minority areas into China's overall economic plans.

Before going one step further to attempt a rough balance-sheet of the last twelve years' achievements in industry and agriculture, it might be useful first to glance at another, equally decisive, aspect of China's transformation: at the preparation, so to speak, of the sinews of the future.

These sinews may be grouped in three categories: transport, energy and education. All three are prerequisites of progress. In all three fields China has been woefully backward. Without adequate facilities of transport, China could not move the raw materials which her emerging industries need, nor the equipment from factory to industrial site, or the goods produced to the markets where they are consumed. Without abundant sources of energy China could not hope to turn the wheels of all the machines she intends to build. Finally, no plan of modernization could be more than a sheet of paper if it did not see to it in good time that the foremen, the engineers, the specialists and the scientists are trained, or that the schools, the universities and the research laboratories are opened in sufficient numbers to satisfy the demand which would arise later on.

In each of these three fields China has been making impressive efforts and one can already foresee that, within a few years, she will have wiped out much of her backwardness.[144]

Where the heritage was most modest and, as a consequence, where difficulties are likely to be the most lasting, is in transport. With the exception of Manchuria, developed for their own purposes by the Japanese, China had no communications system worth that name. The approximately 22,000 kms. of railways—mostly built by foreign interests for trade and military purposes—appeared on China's map as timid tentacles crawling along the coast and groping no deeper than the coastal crust of that immense country. Huge areas in the north, the south-west and in the west have never seen a locomotive. As for the highway network, it was equally one-sided and grossly inadequate. Over much of the country, the Chinese relied on primitive means for carrying of goods: upon animals, carts, small river craft, or simply on human shoulders. And many a famine was due to this lack of even simple communications rendering impossible the transfer of food from surplus areas to those stricken by natural calamities.

Backbreaking as that mode of transport had been and still is, not less hard is today the labour of the hundreds of thousands who work on the extension of China's totally inadequate transport network. The principles guiding that expansion have, of course, been connected with the country's industrial plans. First, after war and civil strife, the old lines had to be reconstructed and, wherever necessary, completed by doubling the tracks. As for the new lines built or under construction, they have a twofold purpose. Either they doubled the vertical lines deeper inland, or they have provided new trunk-lines across the country to reach distant border-regions. This way, the vast south-western region is being connected to the coastal network, and new trunk lines cross Inner Mongolia—connecting it both with Peking and the interior—as well as with Sinkiang. As a consequence, cities like Kweiyang or Chengtu in the south-west, Lanchow in the centre, or Paotow in Inner Mongolia—all localities without railways before 1949—are becoming new communication centres. A citizen of a developed Western country could hardly be expected to share the pride of Chinese statements that very soon (with the exception of Lhasa in Tibet) all the capitals of China's provinces and autonomous regions will be connected by rail.

China's first railway—a 15-km. line out of Shanghai—was built in 1876. During the following 73 years, up to 1949, no more than 22,000 kms. had been built. By 1958 their length grew to 31,000 kms. and in 1959 and 1960—counting branch lines and narrow gauge railways—about another 10,000 to 12,000 kms. will have been added.[145] During the twelve years since 1949, then, China will have nearly doubled the railways she had built during the preceding 73 years. Yet even so China will have only about 40,000 kms. of railroads against Japan's 26,000 in an area twenty-eight times smaller.

As for highways, although statistics group together roads of various qualities and importance, expansion has been even more rapid. Against 80,000 kms. of roads in 1949, it is claimed that China had 400,000 in 1958, though a large proportion is probably unsurfaced. Most of the new roads have been built with bare hands or with the help of the simplest instruments only. All this building activity, however, involved also large-scale engineering feats, intensive tunnelling and bridge-building, whose quality is highly spoken of by foreign specialists. One of the most spectacular among these is the bridge, the first one, across the Yangtze at Wuhan. It permits, for the first time, direct rail communications between Peking and Canton. Over 1,300 metres long, with a six-lane highway for road traffic above, and with a double-track railway on the lower deck, it is one of the engineering showpieces of new China. Not less difficult were the problems posed by the two highways leading into Tibet. They meet at Lhasa (whence another one now runs to the Indian border to the south) and much of them had to be built at heights of over 5,000 metres and often in temperatures of 20 degrees or more below zero.

Thanks to all these efforts, China is beginning to have a rudimentary but country-wide rail and road network, supplemented by air-lines. Yet she is still far from being able to equip even this modest system with the required number of freight and passenger wagons or with locomotives. Figures concerning rolling stock are not issued but it is believed that by now both wagons and locomotives are manufactured in Manchuria in fast growing numbers.[146]

It is barely surprising if, on several occasions, it was openly admitted that transport was the major bottle-neck of China's economic progress.[147] It is unlikely that the expansion of the communication system could keep pace with the tempo of industrialization or that the production of rolling-stock could satisfy the growing demand. For many years to come, then, transport will continue to cause serious strains and will make China a potential buyer of large quantities of both rolling-stock and of railway equipment in general.

Thanks mainly to China's immense reserves of coal, the country is better placed in the field of energy. Not only is coal the most easily accessible form of power, but it is also an important export commodity. Either directly, through steam engines, or indirectly through thermo-electric power stations, it is still the major source of the industrial energy used. Known reserves being practically unlimited, the real problems are those of extraction and quality. In 1949, China mined 32 million tons of coal. Three years later the quantity was doubled. By 1959 output was 348 million tons and a target of 425 million tons was announced for 1960. Some Western observers consider these claims to be inflated by perhaps 10 to 20 per cent., due to the inclusion of impurities which must be removed by washing. On the other hand, press reports speak of coal-washing plants being commissioned as well as of the opening of large numbers of new collieries all over the country. Even if the official figures contain such a margin of exaggeration, it would seem that China has already left Great Britain far behind and that her coal output is fast approaching that of the United States.

Of the numerous power projects in China's first Five-Year Plan the most important called for the building of fifteen thermal plants each with a capacity of over 50,000 kw. Most of these are located either in the industrial region of Manchuria, or in the north-western and south-western regions. The largest hydro-electric projects to be completed before 1957 called for the expansion of existing works. Altogether these developments led to a considerable growth of the country's very meagre output of electric power. Between 1952 and 1957 it had grown from 7 milliard kwh. to nearly three times that much. By 1958, however, electricity generated jumped to almost twice that total: to 41 milliard kwh. and a further big advance of sixteen milliard kwh. was planned for 1960. Compared to Japan's 85 or to the U.S.A.'s 650 milliard, this is still modest. But plans are afoot which fore-shadow expansion which will soon surpass Japan and will then continue at a rapid rate.

The explanation lies in the dimensions of the hyrdo-electric installations under construction. They need several years to be completed. China's plans in that field, however, are far-reaching. They are intimately connected with the programme which may be called that of taming the country's turbulent rivers.

With the aid of maps, charts and diagrams, I was given a fascinating lecture on this subject by the Chief Engineer of the Ministry of Hydraulic Works and Electrification in Peking. He was an old man, trained in Kuomintang days. His habit of speak-ing of 'before the change of régime' instead of the stereotype 'before Liberation', as many other small slips in his exposé, have made it abundantly clear that only his great experience assured him his high post while he seemed unable to adapt himself to the changed atmosphere and to the new terminology. Yet there was a curious, almost involuntary admiration in his words once the technician in him overcame his nostalgia for the past. His eyes sparkled with enthusiasm as he raised his hand to emphasize the weight of a figure. Each time I asked him what, in that particular field, was done before 1949, he repeated: 'Yes, yes, but now we have means nobody would have dreamt of before. . . .' And with reluctant but obvious admiration, he told me the story.

China's mountainous west rises over 3,000 metres above sea level and, between June and September, has an exceptionally heavy rainfall. In contrast, the alluvial plains of the east have poor rains and their fertility is maintained by flood-borne silt. With a heavy monsoon-rainfall on the plateaus, there is flooding in the east. When the rains fail in the interior, there is drought in the coastal areas. That has been the central theme of China's history for hundreds of years. Yet this very sloping nature of the country's topography, the source of so much suffering in the past, holds great promise for the future. In the past, in Chinese eyes, the worth of a dynasty was measured by the success of its water-control projects. Often they had mobilized millions of peasants and had built dikes, canals and reservoirs. Even more often things were neglected and, as in the case of a famed Emperor, all that was done was to change the name of a river from *Turbulent* to *Peaceful*, accompanied by appropriate ceremonies to chase away the river's evil spirits.

Today, somewhat more realistic and more systematic plans are under execution. Their aim is nothing less than to tame China's major rivers. From 1950 onwards a complex system of dams, reservoirs and canals has been drawn up for the Yangtze, the Huai and for the most terrible of them all, for the Yellow River. Some of the smaller projects, already completed, help to reduce what used to be regularly flooded areas, or to provide current like the one on the Hai river, north of Peking, which now provides the capital's electricity. But the giant works, the barrages and their hydro-electric plants are still in the making and most of them would require another five to ten years to complete. But at several points along the rivers already the landscape teems with hundreds of thousands of people who dig, carry and cart the sand side by side with rare bulldozers providing some help. Just to give an idea of the magnitude of the labour already invested, by the middle of 1959 the earth works completed involved the excavation of nearly a hundred times the amount of earth moved when the Suez Canal was dug.

The largest of the projects under construction is the Sanmen Dam, 100 kms. below the junction of the Wei and Yellow rivers. It will hold more water than America's Grand Coulee and Boulder Dam combined. Alone, it will generate about a million kilowatts of electricity and will be second only to Russia's Kuibyshev Dam. Several other dams half and three-quarters that size are also under construction. And, in the long run, as these projects get gradually completed, power generated by hydro-electric installations will by far surpass the quantity provided by thermal stations.

As for petroleum, it was the one crucial heavy-industrial sector in which the authorities have frankly admitted that results had been below expectations. Between 1952 and 1957 production grew from 450,000 to only 1·5 million tons and most of the increase was the result of expansion either at the Yumen fields or in the shale oil industry started by the Japanese in Manchuria. In fact, of the 1957 output, natural oil accounted for a little over a half, while the remainder came from oil shale. Since 1957, however, the situation has been rapidly changing. Extensive prospecting has been yielding spectacular results and the expanding railway network permits growing activity in hitherto inaccessible regions.

The oil shale industry still contributes nearly half of China's oil. In 1958, China's hitherto biggest oil shale deposits were discovered in Heilungkiang province, in Manchuria. They are estimated at 120,000 million tons against the previous known reserves of 6,000 million tons only. It is near the industrial base of Fularki and lies astride the Harbin-Tsitsihar railway. Next to Sinkiang's own deposits, the greatest development in the shale oil industry will be in southern Kwangtung province. There, reserves seem to be large enough to justify the construction of an oil-city of 80,000 people as well as a refinery with a yearly one-million-ton capacity.

Although there are hopes in the Shanghai region—where oil seepages have been noted—the real discoveries of China's petroleum prospectors have all been made in the interior. The most spectacular, for the time being, are those in Sinkiang.[148] Another was made in Szechuan, east of the city of Chengtu. Then, more recently, large deposits were found in Western Chinghai province, a remote and sparsely populated area near Tibet, now to be connected through a branch line to the Sinkiang railway. According to unofficial information, those of Chinghai may shortly prove to be China's richest oilfields surpassing in importance even those of Sinkiang. In the meantime, however, the old Yumen fields too are expanded and now extend to Kiuchuan, the ancient city of Suchow, to be developed into an iron and steel centre. Shortly an 800-km. pipeline will connect the Yumen fields with Lanchow's new refinery.

Shale oil production apart, then, after only a few years of systematic prospecting, China already has four major oil-bearing areas. Non-officially the country's reserves are by now estimated to be as big as in some of the major oil-producing countries. In 1959 the Minister of Petroleum Industry claimed that in due course China's annual output should not be less than 100 million tons. That would be almost three-times Iran's present production.

Street lighting in most Chinese cities is still drastically reduced to save coal for the power-stations. Nor are there many cars to be seen on the roads. Yet the austerity of today, unlike that in so many economically underdeveloped countries, prepares much greater productive capacity for the future. After the very modest advance during the first Five-Year Plan, in 1959 crude oil output was already 3·7 million tons. The target for 1960 was fixed over 5 million tons. Production is still below demand. Yet the cumulative effect of intensive prospecting, of railway building, of the manufacture of drilling equipment, or of the erection of refineries, will be soon the great acceleration of China's petroleum production.

Thus, the industrial power at the disposal of China's planners is rapidly growing. Though it had been known long before 1949 that China had large reserves of coal, or that her rivers and topography offered large hydro-electric possibilities, it was generally accepted that, like most of East Asia, China too was an oil-poor region. Not only is China for the first time in a position to harness the energy of her rivers, or to extract her coal on a large enough scale even to permit exports, but it is also becoming clear that she may, within the foreseeable future, become one of the world's substantial, if not major producers of oil.

The third decisive field where China is sparing no effort to keep her appointment with her own future, is in education. The transformation of the country's semi-colonial economy into a modern industrial one in less than a generation, demands masses of skilled workers, technicians, industrial research workers and, above all, teachers.

The basic problem which affects the whole educational enterprise, of course, has been mass illiteracy. According to the Chinese Premier, speaking in 1957, over 70 per cent. of the population was still illiterate in that year. Thus the problem involves nothing less than giving a basic education to some 500 million people. An additional difficulty is in the Chinese script with characters for sense instead of sound. For over 3,000 years these ideograms have been the means of unifying the people of China and attachment to them amounts to a deep tradition. There are some 40,000 such ideographic symbols and an educated person was expected to use several thousand of them, an effort that involved long years of study and, inevitably created a deep gulf between the educated and those unable to write. To remedy the situation, the Peking dialect has been made the nation's official language and a kind of 'basic Chinese'—written in a minimum number of simplified characters—is being popularized and is already being used in newspapers and in popular publications. This, however, is intended as a temporary solution only. The more radical one—which will require long years to overcome habit and tradition—aims at the adoption of a modified Roman script in place of the old ideographs. Though here and there the new phonetic transcription is prudently introduced and some secondary schools already teach the new alphabet, for the time being the main effort is rather along the lines of the reduced number of simplified characters. This 'basic Chinese' is the main instrument of the current anti-illiteracy drive. The 'people to people' movement—implying that each literate person ought to pass on his knowledge to at least one illiterate one—has already permitted an increase in the number of the newly literate by some

50 million thus, probably, raising the level of literacy to around 40 per cent.

But it is the rapid extension of primary and secondary education that really heralds the end of illiteracy in China. Extensive school-building and teacher-training raised enrolment in primary schools—51 million in 1952—to 90 million in 1959, and is expected to mount to 110 million by the end of 1960. The number of students in all types of secondary schools—just over 3 million in 1952—had reached 13 million by 1959 and may surpass 14 million by the end of 1960.[149]

The most important developments, however, affect institutes teaching technical skills and the complete reorganization of higher education. At the beginning, for top-level technical skills Peking relied heavily on Soviet experts. But simultaneously it devoted much effort to training Chinese technicians and skilled workers at all levels so that the number of foreign specialists has rapidly declined. This vast training programme included several methods but, in particular, the large-scale training of secondary school pupils in practical technical work. When visiting factories in various parts of China I could see technical school students working as apprentices, often two or three, next to every worker and every machine tool. In fact, the whole system of secondary education has been completely remodelled so as to emphasize technical training, inspired by Soviet ideas of polytechnical education. The sheer numerical impact of these methods apart, they help to eliminate two serious obstacles to economic progress; obstacles which are only too much in evidence in practically all Asian, if not in all underdeveloped countries. In the first place, they have effectively broken the age-old contempt for manual labour. Secondly, in contrast with most underdeveloped countries where a handful of over-qualified engineers are trained when in practice masses of foremen would be more useful, China's new educational set-up is turning out technicians in large numbers who are able and willing to handle machines instead of hankering for 'white-collar' office employment.

As for higher learning and research work, in 1956 already the Scientific Planning Committee had drafted a far-reaching twelve year plan for their advancement. From the new, sprawling university city of Peking to the large university buildings and scientific institutes in practically all the big cities, one can measure the importance attached to higher education. And official figures complete the visual impression. In 1952 the number of students in China's universities and specialized technological colleges (together referred to in official texts as Institutes of Higher Learning), numbered 191,000. By 1958 their numbers grew to 660,000. By the end of 1960 the total is expected to reach 1,200,000.[150] Moreover, unlike the situation in most under-developed countries, those at the faculties of the liberal arts constitute but a small minority of those who study engineering, agronomy, medicine, pedagogy or economics.[151] Equal priority is accorded to research work and to the establishment of scientific research institutes. They are directed by the Academy of Sciences and are closely associated with the interested Ministries. In 1958 China had 848 such Institutes with over 30,000 research workers and technicians working in them. Constant emphasis on the importance of scientific research makes it probable that their number has further increased during the past two years.[152]

Chinese students who had entered universities in the past—as is still the case even in some Western countries—came almost exclusively from the old intellectual and merchant classes, with the peasant and working-class majority barely represented among them. Each time I visited a Chinese university, it was emphasized that this composition was rapidly changing. Official figures speak of an increase (between 1952-58) from 30 to 50 per cent. of students of worker or peasant origin in China's Institutes of Higher Learning. In technical middle-schools the same increase is given as from 57 to 77 per cent. Whether these figures are exaggerated or not, the fact remains that a genuine, and for those who are barred because of their origin, a cruel effort is being made to bring about a more representative composition of the student population. Another development worth noting is the growing proportion of women in China's schools. In Institutes of Higher Learning their proportion has grown from 18 to 23 per cent. between 1949 and 1958; in technical middle-schools from 20 to

31 per cent.; and in primary schools from a quarter to over a third.

Some foreign observers, over-impressed by all the banners in the universities which declare that 'Education must be connected with Productive Labour', fear that China's youth is brought up in narrow technical specialization at the expense of general culture. Others, more ready to admire China's completely new educational programme, see in it a grandiose attempt to bring out the latent ability of a whole people; the opening of science to all instead of only to a foreign-educated minority as in the past. The truth may be somewhere half-way implying the grafting of a new scientific culture on the old stock of literary tradition. Yet, quite evidently, China's educational effort prepares a personnel proportionate to her ambitions. Already it is fast rendering the country independent of foreign scientists and engineers.

To sum up, then, in expanding her network of communications, in developing her sources of energy, as well as in forming the personnel required by a modern industrial state, China has been making great progress. And these achievements, more than anything else, help to explain her rapid advance on both the agricultural and on the industrial front.

5 Change on the Land

WHILE IT MAY be possible to count generators, machine-tools or industrial plants, no one could ascertain with any accuracy what or how much 700 million Chinese eat. On the Government's own admission, in 1958, a considerable margin of error is possible in crop estimates. Moreover, the published statistics contain ambiguities of definition. It is often difficult to know what is included or what is left out of a given category. One could thus endlessly argue about the real meaning of agricultural statistics, verify and adjust them, accept or reject interpretations by more or less objective foreign specialists, without necessarily coming much nearer to certitude.

There are, however, observable facts which may be more telling even than figures. Before the change of régime, China had known frequent famines. There has been no evidence of any of importance since then. Before the Communists' final victory disorder and provincial barriers had obstructed the moving of surpluses to deficit areas and hoarding and speculation had helped to aggravate local shortages. Today, those artificial barriers to distribution have disappeared and neither hoarding nor speculation is possible. Before 1949 China used to import food, now she exports it together with industrial crops, in payment for imported equipment. Moreover, China's farming was primitive and per-acre yields were often half of even those in Japan. Thus, better organization and tools, pest control, more fertilizers, and the extension of irrigation had a wide scope to fill up the margin of backwardness and so to increase harvests. Quite evidently the Chinese have been making efforts in all these fields. Finally, China had large areas of potentially arable land left untilled. Since 1949 much has been done to reclaim part of them.

On the basis of all this it is evident that agricultural output must have increased considerably during the past twelve years. The number of consumers has grown by 150 million yet the majority of observers agree that most Chinese are today better and more regularly fed than ever before. Though there may have been a change in the composition of the diet to the detriment of high-quality foodstuffs, there can be little doubt that growth, as a whole, was faster than the expansion of population.

China's pre-war peak year in agriculture was 1936, with 139 million tons of grain harvested. When the Communists took over, output from the land, because of years of fighting and disorganization, was below that level by at least 15 per cent. and possibly more. Three years later, when the first Five-Year Plan began, the authorities claimed that agricultural production had regained the pre-war peak level and had even surpassed it in several fields.

The production of cereals—154 million tons in 1952—was claimed to be 185 million tons by the end of the first Plan. That increase, though faster than the growth of population, was not spectacular. In fact, the conclusion appeared to be justified as late as 1957, that even if progress was extraordinary in the industrial field, China's performance in food production did not greatly differ from that of the other economically underdeveloped countries. By that date, however, so it would seem, massive investment of labour in the collection of fertilizers, in pest control, in the improvement of tools, and above all in the herculean effort of canal-building, was beginning to yield its dividends. In 1958 cereal production was claimed to have shot up to 250 million tons, an increase of 35 per cent. from one year to the next. In 1959 a further increase of 20 million tons was claimed, carrying the total to 270 million tons. In 1960, however, in place of an expected increase of another 10 per cent there were natural calamities worse than during any year since 1949. The official press spoke of 'near famine conditions' in some regions. Very probably, then, cereal output in 1960 was not above—and may even have been below—the level reached in 1959. This, of course, could not have failed to affect the production targets of industrial crops or the output of light industries themselves.

On the basis of official figures, then, between 1952 and 1959 the grain crop has grown from 154 to 270 million tons. This represents a two-thirds' increase while population grew by less than 20 per cent. In other words, the average Chinese today is claimed to have a third more food at his disposal than in 1952.

Official figures, again, speak of comparable advance in the output of industrial crops. The quantity of sugar—in the past a luxury in some parts of China—nearly trebled. Raw cotton—a decisive item to sustain the textile industry—1·3 million tons in 1952, grew to 2·4 million tons by 1959 and, with a projected further 10 per cent. increase in 1960, may surpass the United States' output. As for edible vegetable oil—an essential and scarce ingredient of the Chinese diet—983,000 tons in 1952, by 1958 its production increased to 1,250,000 tons.[153]

Progress in all these fields was uneven during the first Five-Year Plan, as it usually is in a primitive agriculture exposed to the caprices of the weather. Some sectors, like animal husbandry, soya beans or tea production, lagged behind.[154] But after the establishment of the Communes and the unprecedented mobilization of labour, China's agriculture appears to have entered a new phase of both accelerated development and of less dependence on climatic conditions. Even if allowance is made for the growing proportion of coarse grains and sweet potatoes in the diet, or for any margin of error or exaggeration in crop reporting, after a yearly 4 per cent. growth of agricultural production during the first Plan, since 1958 that rate seems to have been doubled.

In view of China's low per-acre yields in the past there is nothing incredible about a yearly 8 to 10 per cent. growth of agricultural production, or in a yearly 6 to 8 per cent. increase in the output of foodstuffs. Provided the human and technical means are available to improve yields, it is conceivable that such a high rate of development should be maintained over several years. On the basis of these official claims, then, China's agricultural progress has been much faster than that in any of the economically underdeveloped countries. In most of them food barely kept pace with population growth and increases of 2 to 4 per cent. were rather the exception.

China's agricultural progress, of course, is less than spectacular in comparison with the rise of food production in North America or in Great Britain during the last war. Yet such comparisons are less than fair. In both areas machines, chemical fertilizers and selected seeds were readily available and rich old pastures could be brought under cultivation and they yielded bumper crops.

Realistic comparisons can be made only with other underdeveloped countries where the means of modern cultivation are lacking and which, like China, had to start out practically from scratch. Against such a background, China's real achievements during the past few years ought to be measured not so much by the precise yearly increases already registered—impressive as they already are—but rather by the wide variety of measures which are beginning to transform China's primitive agriculture into a modern one; measures which are bound to produce an even greater acceleration in the coming years.

In agriculture too, China's planners operated with a simultaneous short-range and long-range plan. One was to prepare the ground for the other. While absolute priority of industrialization severely limited investment in agriculture, the first had to rely mainly on human labour. But as heavy industry begins to turn out agricultural machinery, the long-range plan is gradually coming into operation with the beginning of mechanization.

The Soviet Union waited until large quantities of mechanized equipment were available before it undertook the collectivization of the land. In contrast collectivization in China was not a technical but an organizational revolution; it aimed primarily at the more rational exploitation of labour. The first period, the short-range plan, was dominated by three measures. The first was summarized in the much-publicized *Eight-Point Charter* and comprised methods and improvements based on labour mobilization.[155] The second implied all the propaganda and educational effort aiming at the modification of the peasant's thinking, his adaptation to the handling of improved tools and more modern methods and, generally speaking, his preparation for modern farming. Finally, there was the organizational revolution of the Communes intended to provide a large enough frame for the efficient execution of these measures. And all together were to prepare the ground for the coming of mechanization.

Now that the 'basic realization of agricultural mechanization' is foreseen within the next ten years, it is by the measures preparing the execution of this long-range plan that the real achievements of China's agriculture during the past twelve years, can be assessed.

What distinguishes modern farming from the backward agriculture of an underdeveloped country is primarily the application of pest control, improved seeds, and of chemical fertilizers; reliance on modern implements and machines; as well as maximum immunity to climatic vagaries through large-scale irrigation and flood control. Of comparable importance are efficient animal husbandry; the reclamation of potentially fertile land; and, especially in China's case, afforestation.

Pest control and the use of selected seeds have been popularized, with all the might of the propaganda machine. In a country where plant diseases and pests used to destroy up to a quarter of crops and where in some regions superstition still inhibits the peasants destroying even locusts, education has been as important as the aid of industry. However, frenetic campaigns were launched against pests; insecticides have been distributed through the Communes, and even their spraying from the air has become routine practice. Improved seeds have been introduced on a large scale and, seeing all the slogans and posters devoted to their popularization, one is ready to accept the official figures. According to these, the area sown with improved seeds of grain crops has grown between 1952 and 1958 from 5 to 77 per cent. For cotton the expansion is reported as from 50 to 97 per cent. And the rapid change over to selected seeds, as well as to close planting may be major factors in the fast growth of yields.

Chemical fertilizers were almost unknown in Chinese agriculture before 1949. Yet their liberal use has been one of the decisive factors in, for example, Japan's enormous agricultural progress during past decades. While everything was done to increase the collection of organic fertilizers, for several years now China has been importing large quantities of chemical fertilizers from Western Europe. Simultaneously, a domestic industry is also being developed. In 1957, it produced half a million tons of sulphate of ammonia. Although several new plants are being built, hitherto production has expanded but slowly. Yet in 1960 China expects to turn out 2·8 million tons of chemical fertilizers, or double the output in 1959. But even that level, it should be remembered, would provide no more than 5 kg. per acre. In Western Europe's intensive agriculture about twenty-times as much per acre is used. In fact, if China would apply chemical fertilizers on a comparable scale, she would need nearly 50 million tons a year, almost double the actual world output. In any case Chinese production will continue to grow and in 1960 no less than 17 'large' chemical fertilizer plants were under construction, in addition to 140 'small and medium-sized' ones scattered all over the country.

As for the agricultural implements of the Chinese peasant, they are still primitive in the extreme. Their modernization has been one of the main themes of propaganda and no effort was spared to encourage the peasants' initiative in this field. Insistence on innovation and invention has undoubtedly helped both in the mass production of labour-saving devices and in the shaking of peasant inertia and attachment to outdated methods. A wheelbarrow or a rubber-tyred hand cart can mean a revolution over vast regions of China's countryside and it may be difficult to Westerners to appreciate the promise of the campaign launched in 1958 calling for the replacement of shoulder-poles with simple, wheeled vehicles equipped with locally manufactured ball-bearings. Yet, while the traditional figure of the Chinese cultivator with the two baskets hanging from his shoulder-pole may one day be merely a memory, modern industry is taking on a growing share of the equipment and modernization of agriculture. Millions of wheeled and double-shared steel ploughs have been turned out during the past year permitting the planting of closer rows and the reduction of loss of moisture from the soil. Equally, simple vehicles, irrigation pumps and rubber-tired hand-carts are distributed through the Communes by the million.[156] Moreover, as China is tooling up for large-scale tractor and lorry production, the more important instruments of mechanized agriculture—beginning with tractors and combine harvesters—are making their appearance in the countryside.

From 283 in 1952 the number of combine harvesters had grown to 2,000 by 1958. In 1960 China is planning to build another 2,000 and output will rapidly grow in the years to come. The story is similar for tractors. Less than 2,000 in 1952, their number reached 45,330 by 1958—all imported. Now in 1960 alone, 22,000 will be domestically manufactured.[157] Sixty thousand tractors in a country of China's size is very modest indeed when compared to the nearly 5 million in the U.S.A. or to the yearly production of over 200,000 in the U.S.S.R., not to speak of China's own estimates of her need for one and a half million. Yet production on a large scale has begun, imports continue, and in this field too, China will soon be far ahead of other countries embarking on their modernization.

It is not surprising that China's progress has been still faster in those spheres where human labour rather than industrial equipment can be relied on. This is particularly the case with water conservancy projects, involving the mass building of large and small reservoirs as well as canals. Apart from preventing the loss of crops by flood, or countering the effects of drought, they also store water for irrigation and thus render possible the extension of double-cropping. The unprecedented efforts of veritable armies mobilized for these purposes needs no recounting. The results, confirmed by all foreign observers, have been stupendous. In the course of the last decade China has raised her irrigated area from 16 to around 70 million hectares, or from one-sixth of the total cultivated area in 1949 to over two-thirds within twelve years. Though large-scale projects had contributed to these results, the small-scale ones provided most, involving limited investments and enormous quantities of human labour. While probably they have been decisive in increasing yields, they have also permitted the extension by more than a tenth of the area over which more than one crop can be grown each year.[158]

Another field of activity where the massive investment of human labour could produce astonishing results has been afforestation. The presence of trees is one of the most conspicuous changes in China's countryside. Savagely deprived of forests, China's denuded mountains have been the principal sources of many of the country's natural calamities. During the past few years hundreds of miles of shelter belts have been planted and the barren slopes of the mountains along the rivers are beginning to turn green again. Along the dusty roads stretch once again avenues of poplars and acacias, and saplings in ranks four deep stand guard along railway lines. All the millions of trees planted will help to conserve soil and water, conquer flood and drought and, in due course, they will supply much-needed timber for construction. Since 1952 the newly afforested area has grown from 1·5 to nearly 60 million hectares and it is expected that the country's depleted forest area will double within ten years.

The greater all these efforts to improve yields, the more urgent becomes the question how much new land China can hope to bring under the plough. Sooner or later the doctrinaire obstinacy which ignores the ultimate dangers of unchecked population growth is bound to focus attention on the problem of virgin land. Yet if human labour can work miracles in water conservancy or in afforestation, reclamation of wasteland depends on the rate at which heavy industry can supply equipment to do the job. That within her borders China has large expanses of wasteland capable of being cultivated, is generally admitted. What proportion of it could be brought under cultivation at a cost likely to be justified by results, is more open to debate. Some estimates put the extent of cultivable virgin land at over 200 million acres: half of it in the north-west, some 30 million in the north-east, and over 60 million in the rest of China. If all could be reclaimed, the present farmed area would grow by nearly half. More prudent estimates, however, maintain that the uncultivated land which could be opened up without prohibitively high investment costs is not more than 50 million acres, about a fifth of the total area now farmed. It is known that tractors and other heavy equipment, mostly imported from Russia, are already breaking up virgin land in different regions. Some idea of this work can be had in Sinkiang. As for the rest of the country, it is believed that some 10 to 12 million acres have already been reclaimed.

Such dry figures could hardly convey the amount of labour that went into the changing of China's land. Nor could they alone project the uneven but impressive progress China's agriculture has been making during the past twelve years. To force the land to keep ahead of population growth has been and is likely to remain the major challenge the Government has to face. Yet one can discern the outlines of a systematic, long-range plan which is bound to yield even more important results. In higher yields, in irrigation and afforestation, they have already been spectacular. With progressive mechanization and the wider education of the peasants, the gains will become yet greater and even more general. The Chinese cultivator is already less dependent on the weather than he used to be. China's primitive agriculture is being modernized at a rapid rate and there is change all over the countryside. And that is certainly much more than can be said of agriculture in most of the economically underdeveloped countries.

6 'Made in China' in Twelve Years

IN THE IMAGINATION of the non-Western majority of mankind the modern factory represents the magic carpet on which it hopes to escape dependence. For the same reason, in China it is an object of veneration. To have modern factories and to multiply them fast has become the collective expression of national pride. In the words of the first Five-Year Plan the long-range goal is 'to transform China from an agricultural into an industrial nation'. In most Western countries the same process took up to a century. Japan compressed it into some sixty years. The Soviet Union nearly halved that period. China intends to do it still faster. And considering her performance during the past twelve years, she might do it in record time.

To begin with, the modest heavy industrial base developed by the Japanese in Manchuria served as China's industrial springboard. That apart, her own industrial competence had not gone much beyond the manufacture of cotton textiles. Yet since 1949 the bulk of the prodigious effort expended by China's masses has gone into industrialization. And the major part of that effort went not so much into the production of goods for consumption but rather into building the means of even faster industrialization. Like mushrooms after the rain, thousands of modern factories have appeared all over the country. If only twelve years ago China had to import most manufactured goods, today her own products range from blast-furnaces for steel plants and complete sets of hydraulic generating equipment, to precision instruments and antibiotics; or from trucks, merchant vessels and jet aircraft to seventy types of heavy machine-tools, and the products of synthetic and electronics industries. Production per head of the population is still modest. But in some decisive sectors China's output is approaching Japan's or those of the older West-European industrial powers and, at its present rate of expansion, may soon establish her as one of the major industrial powers of the world.

To breathe descriptive life into a long string of visits to industrial plants is a hopeless enterprise. The automatized Changchun works, which turn out over 30,000 trucks a year, are comparable to similar establishments in Detroit or in Western Europe. The giant Anshan steel complex, with its yearly production of over 3 million tons of steel, or the ultra-modern Wuhan and Paotow steel companies now being commissioned are, to the non-specialist, similar to those in Pittsburgh or in the Ruhr. The same is true for all the electrical industries, the tractor plants, the fertilizer factories, the refineries, the barrages or the locomotive building works which one is shown. Yet, still, there are some significant differences. Most of the workers or even the engineers who had built and who are manipulating those machines in China, were peasants only a few years ago; anonymous members of a superstition-ridden, backward agrarian community that changed but little for centuries. All those complicated machine-tools filling enormous factory halls come not from the savings of people who sacrifice only a tiny margin of their comfort for their sake, but are the three-dimensional results of the immense exertions of masses who express through them their self-confidence and their will to change their own future. Moreover, seeing the frenetic speed with which men handle their giant tools, and knowing that most of them labour to turn out even more machines, one has the inevitable sensation of assisting a process that is not merely transforming the way of living of the world's most populous nation but is also contributing with dramatic speed and with incalculable consequences to the changing of the world's existing balance of power.

Whatever doubts may exist concerning the rapidity of China's agricultural progress, no serious observer has yet questioned China's extraordinary industrial growth. According to official figures the value of the output of China's industry between 1952 and the end of 1957 increased by 128 per cent.[159] But as in agriculture so in industry too, there came a great acceleration with the inauguration of the Great Leap. If in agriculture the massive investment of human labour was beginning to pay dividends after 1957, the major cause of acceleration after that date in the industrial sector was due to the coming into operation of important plants in construction during the first Five-Year Plan. Following on the 128 per cent. growth during the first Plan period, there was a 65 per cent. jump in 1958 alone. That was followed by a further advance of 39 per cent. in 1959, while a 29 per cent. increase is foreseen for 1960. Taking 1952 as the base, then, up to the end of 1959 the gross output value of China's industry is claimed to have increased by 319 per cent. Since the beginning of the first Plan, this would represent an average yearly growth of 45 per cent.; or nearly double the yearly average if one takes the first Plan alone.

But in these figures all manufacturing, handicraft, consumer goods and capital equipment are included. The share of handicraft products, a quarter of the total in 1952, has been in rapid decline and by now may account for little more than a tenth. Consumer goods, which made up more than half of total industrial production in 1952, represents by now a little over a third. Clearly, then, the average yearly increase in the output of capital goods—of the products of China's new heavy industries—must have been even higher than the yearly average might lead one to suppose.

The transcription of these claims into the terms of Western statistical terminology, their cross-checking, or the evaluation of probable error or exaggeration in them, has already produced a voluminous literature. It could hardly be summarized. It should be said, however, that the most serious and the less biased among them maintain that, in Western terms, the figures relating to the first Five-Year Plan period may need a scaling down by up to a third. As for the claims after 1957, they have been so startling and, until now supported by, so little reliable data that no balanced judgment can be passed about the degree of their authenticity. Generally, however, the corrective reduction appears to be more necessary in the consumer goods sector; perhaps less severe in the heavy industrial field where the unprecedented rate of advance is generally admitted. Though far from amounting to a complete confirmation of official claims, it is worth mentioning that some of the best qualified opinions—like, for example, those of Hong

Kong banking and trading specialists—tend to confirm an astonishing rate of expansion.

Appreciation of China's industrial progress, however, is on a somewhat safer ground when total figures are abandoned in favour of individual industrial sectors.

Attempting an unorthodox classification, four major divisions can be distinguished. In the first place, there are handicrafts. Its borders are not easy to define. Into it may enter the products of surviving individual craftsmen, those of the rural Communes, or the output of the more recent Communes set up in the cities. The relative value of their combined output represents a fast shrinking segment of the country's total industrial product.

Secondly, there are the products of the small-scale industries set up as a result of the new policy of decentralization. Most of them are under the municipalities or under the management of the Communes. They may range from 'factories' which employ 'indigenous methods' for the production of chemical fertilizers, to small-scale oil refineries or medium-sized iron plants which took the place of the useless 'backyard furnaces' of 1958. In terms of efficiency, when compared to modern methods of industrialization, they may appear wasteful. Yet, as Japan's example had shown with surplus population to be put to work and with urgent ambitions to become industrialized, they make sense both as productive units and as instruments to train backward villagers for industrial pursuits. How many such small factories already exist or how much exactly they produce, no outside observer could possibly ascertain.[160]

Then comes modern industry. It may be classified in two main sectors. In the first are light industries. Most of them produce consumer goods and depend on raw materials of agricultural origin. For obvious political reasons their output may be exaggerated. Their raw material supplies come from the land and thus depend both on climate and on the peasants' ability or willingness to produce. Food processing industries and textile mills are the most important in this category. Even the official figures admit that progress in this field has been uneven. While between 1952 and 1958 the gross output value of heavy industry is claimed to have advanced from 100 to 380, that of light industry was much slower: from 100 to 245. But within this category some items went ahead much slower—as is the case with edible oil which is also an important export article—or progress was erratic under the influence of the previous year's harvest. This was the case, for instance, for cotton yarn and cotton cloth.[161] To what extent this lower rate of the progress of light industry is due to relative parsimony in investments, to weather, or to the impact of collectivization on the peasant, it would be difficult to tell.

Finally, there is the dominant sector of modern heavy industry whose phenomenal progress accounts for most of the steep rise in total industrial output figures. In ideological and political attention, as in investment, this has been all along the privileged sector. It is there that modern imported equipment played the greatest role, and on which the country's own machine-building ability was concentrated. Last but not least, this has been the sector where the virtuosity of Communist organization could make its full impact from miner, railwayman or engineer, to the factory worker.

We have seen how rapid has been the expansion of power generation and how important are the projects under construction. Equally, available figures illustrate the extraordinary growth of coal mining.[162] The backbone of the heavy industrial sector, however, is provided by China's iron and steel industry.

On the eve of the first Plan, steel production was reported to be 1·35 million tons. At the end of it, in 1957, it reached 5·35 million. Output was claimed to have reached 13·35 million tons in 1959, and is expected to rise to 18·4 million by the end of 1960.[163] Considering that the large Wuhan and Paotow works are not yet in full production and that further big and small units are projected, it is clear not only that China is about to surpass in steel production France or Japan, or that she will probably forge ahead of Great Britain and Germany within a few years, but also that in the foreseeable future she may well become the world's third steel-making nation behind the U.S.A. and the U.S.S.R.

It is a matter of interpretation whether these production levels are regarded as impressive or relatively modest. Given China's political system, capable to circumscribe internal consumption, the quantities of steel produced or to be turned out in the coming years, provide a solid basis to China's claim of being a major industrial and military power. Considered from the consumer's viewpoint, however, next to the per head share of a yearly 140 kg. of steel for the Japanese, or the 440 kg. for the citizen of the United Kingdom, the average Chinese has as yet only a modest 25 kg. at his disposal. Yet whatever measure is applied, the extra-ordinary rapidity of expansion has to be recognized.

The advance of all the other heavy industries whose output is linked to the growth of iron and steel production has been pro-portionately fast. Not only is this true in the first place of all the various machine-making industries which turn out heavy equipment, power-generating plants, large hydraulic forging presses, heavy-duty machine-tools, complete sets of mining and drilling equipment, but also of a wide variety of other means of production as well.

In 1957, for example, China manufactured power-generating equipment amounting to 198,000 kw. In 1959 it was 2·15 million kw., and 3·3 million are expected for 1960. The number of metal-cutting machine-tools turned out in 1957 was 28,000. Two years later 70,000 units were finished and it is hoped that this will grow to 90,000 during 1960. In 1960, again, China expects to build 50,000 lorries, 22,000 tractors, 800 locomotives, 150,000 tons of ocean-going vessels (of up to 6,000 tons deadweight), and an unspecified number of jet aircraft—none of which could be built in the country only a few years ago. Nor is progress less spectacular in the chemical industry. Production from dye-stuffs with reactive colours, to synthetic rubber, or to the most complicated pharmaceuticals, is in steady expansion. In the machine-building industry alone, 203 'above-norm' projects are under construction in 1960 (with 55 of them for agricultural machinery, including two new tractor works) and over 60 such large-scale projects are in building in the chemical industry (including large fertilizer plants, as well as acids and synthetic products).

As for cement, a reliable index of general building activity, in

1952 China produced 2·9 million tons. By 1959 it was more than trebled. In 1960 it is expected to reach 16 million tons.

All these, of course, are official figures. Whatever degree of exaggeration they contain is probably less in actual quantity than in the quality of the goods produced. Yet both Japan's and Russia's example is there to warn that the inferiority of first, hurried products helps to accumulate experience and gradually gives way to quality and precision.[164] Moreover, the factories are there, many more are in the making, resources of essential raw materials are plentiful, and markets are practically unlimited. And the combined effect of all these developments is already a marked change in the structure of China's economy. In 1949 industry accounted for less than a third of the national product, and heavy industry within that third had played only a minor role. Today, twelve years later, industry's share has grown to over two-thirds, and within it much more than half is contributed by heavy industry.

Not so long ago a backward agricultural country, China is realizing almost visibly her aim to become an industrial one. It is claimed that she is building already three-quarters of her requirements of industrial equipment. Yet, whatever the precise yearly percentages of her expansion, no one doubts its main trend or questions its extraordinary impetus.

Quite evidently, China has already crossed the frontier of absolute industrial dependence and her own production is fanning out into unexplored fields. There is new specialization; industrial development steadily widens the range of new products; and more and more Chinese industry can rely on its own momentum. There is indeed no reason why a self-generating economy with China's human and material resources should not aim at production levels comparable to those of the two other temperate-zone, transcontinental Powers of the world.

7 The Levellers' Race

PEOPLE AND machines have that much in common that the more numerous they are the faster they can produce many more. In four war-years and without any great strain, the United States increased its productive capacity by more than what China may achieve at a price of great sacrifices with her first three Five-Year Plans. Within five years, almost as easily, Japan hopes to add to her means of production about the equal of what China had at the end of her first Five-Year Plan.[165] Yet the rule applies also to developing economies. Once their take-off has been accomplished, and they are assured of the human and material resources required, and having then entered their phase of self-propelling development, their progress too becomes cumulative and leads to a fast expansion.

Whether China accomplishes that climb slower or faster than other powers before her is a question whose answer may influence the political future not merely of Asia but also of economically underdeveloped countries on other continents.

But to be realistic, the comparisons ought to be made with countries which had to face, or are facing similar problems. Inevitably, then, they will be extra-occidental experiments in modernization. In fact, they number no more than three: Japan, the Soviet Union and India.

Japan's industrialization stretched over some six decades and, being a country singularly poor in raw materials, it has relied on the resources as on the markets of foreign lands forced under Japanese control by conquest. Then, Japan's extraordinary rate of economic growth after the second World War has depended both on large-scale foreign aid and on the availability of foreign markets and raw materials, none of which could be relied on as permanently assured on existing terms.

The really relevant comparisons, then, are with the continental economies of either the Soviet Union or that of India.

But before looking for similarities in China's growth and that of the Soviet Union during its corresponding phase, it may be useful to mention some of the circumstances which, in comparison with Russia's experience, have either helped or hindered China's progress.

The level of China's economy in 1949 was far behind the U.S.S.R.'s on the eve of its first Five-Year Plan. In fact, industrial production in the China of 1949 was more comparable to Russia's towards the end of the nineteenth century than in 1928. Moreover, with an economic development starting out from a so much lower rung, China's population has been steeply increasing, while in the Soviet Union it had actually diminished during its first Five-Year Plan.

These substantial disadvantages, however, may have been compensated by a number of circumstances working in China's favour. Structural changes in China were more gradual and assured the collaboration of a higher proportion of adversely affected classes or individuals. While Soviet leadership had no organic contact with the peasantry, the Chinese leaders' experience grew out of long collaboration with it. Collectivization, therefore, could be carried out with far greater ease in China. While production on the land actually declined in the Soviet Union between 1928-32, in China there was increase both during the three years leading up to the Plan and during the Plan itself.

As for the entrepreneurial class and the experienced commercial and industrial personnel bequeathed by the previous régime, China's more subtle methods brought a large proportion of them into more or less enthusiastic collaboration with the State. The gradual nature of the socialization of agrarian, commercial and industrial structures has certainly caused less dislocation in China than did that of the Soviet Union.

Also, incomparably more favourable has been China's position concerning external aid. While the U.S.S.R. had much difficulty in obtaining modern equipment or qualified specialists, and had to pay exorbitant prices for both, right from the start China has been assured of vast quantities of modern machinery and technical assistance, both available at the required moment and in exchange of products whose lack on the home market, even if it

created shortages, did not lead to the kind of prolonged malnutrition the Russians had endured. Equally important, though less
often remembered, is the fact that while China has been assured
of a regular market for her agrarian exports in exchange for fixed
quantities of capital goods, the Soviet Union had been obliged
to throw on the world market her grain exports at a time when,
as a result of the Great Depression, prices were at their lowest and
had thus imposed on the Russians cruelly unfavourable terms of
trade. Finally, due probably to extensive help in the form of
teachers and technicians, China could increase the number of her
students at universities faster than the Soviet Union at its corresponding period of development.

To begin with, then, compared to Soviet production in 1928,
China had a great quantitative lag to fill. Expressed in per head
shares, of course, that lag had been three times greater than
absolute figures suggest. Yet, because of all the circumstances in
her favour, within a few years China could expect to achieve a
rhythm of development superior to even what the Soviet Union
had experienced. In fact, this is precisely what available figures
confirm.

If one compares growth of production in half a dozen decisive
industries of the U.S.S.R. during its first Five-Year Plan (1928-32)
with those of China during her own first Plan (1953-57), each
will be found to have advanced at a combined average annual
rate of around 19 per cent. While China made much faster progress in the production of iron and steel, in contrast her advance
was slower in the generation of electricity and especially in her
production of chemical fertilizers. As for quantities, in 1957
Chinese output was near the 1932 Soviet level in iron and steel;
ahead in electricity; almost double in coal and cotton cloth; and
well behind Russia in chemical fertilizers. These quantities,
however, were to serve the needs of a population three times
more numerous than that of the Soviet Union.[166]

Then, after 1957, came the Great Leap and the astonishing
production increases, permitting the achievement of the targets of
the second Five-Year Plan in three years. The Communes
gave the State far more complete control over the energies and over

the products of the peasantry than Moscow had over the country-side in 1932. From 1958 onwards a large number of plants and generators started to produce, those which were under building during the first Plan. The new universities were beginning to turn out technicians in large numbers. The newly completed railways offered access to the resources of hitherto isolated areas. Above all, China's absolute dependence on imported capital equipment was lessening with growing machine-building at home. The combined result has been the great acceleration of China's industrial growth. If during their respective first Five-Year Plans the rate of growth in the two countries was comparable, between 1957 and 1960 China gathered speed and her rhythm of progress far surpassed that of the U.S.S.R. after 1932.

In fact, China's production in 1960 no longer corresponds to the 1935 Soviet level (which would be three years after Russia's completion of her first Plan) but rather to that reached by the U.S.S.R. in 1940 when the German invasion interrupted its third Five-Year Plan. More simply, China's industrial production has grown after eight years of planning to a level comparable to the one the Soviet Union had reached after twelve years of planned effort.[167]

China's industrial performance between 1953-60, then, need no longer be compared with the Soviet Union's corresponding eight years between 1928-35, but can already be matched to Russia's progress during the twelve years between 1928-40.

In that frame, the rate of growth of China's iron production was three times faster than Russia's. Of steel, it was over twice as rapid, and of coal one and a half times. The rhythm of growth was only a little faster for cotton cloth and cement. On the other hand, the rate of growth in the generation of electricity and the manufacture of chemical fertilizers was much slower than that of the U.S.S.R.

As for actual quantities, in 1960 China produced three times as much cement as the Soviet Union in 1940; two and a half times that much coal; nearly twice the amount of cast iron and cotton cloth; a quarter more electricity; and about reached the 1940 Soviet level in steel and the manufacture of chemical fertilizers.

On the other hand, the China of 1960 was still far behind the U.S.S.R. of 1940 in the output of crude oil, but was fast catching up in the production of vehicles such as lorries, tractors and locomotives.

Of course, once again, these quantities were to serve the needs of three times more consumers. In that sense, the per head share of Chinese industrial output in 1960 was comparable to the 1940 Soviet level only for cement, and was close to it in the quantities of coal available to each citizen. In all other sectors per capita Chinese production was still far behind.

Prognostics concerning the future would be hazardous in view of all the imponderables. The discovery of unsuspected natural resources, population policy, as much as the international situation, may influence China's future course. All that can be concluded from available facts is that China's industrialization is progressing in an even higher gear than did the Soviet Union's at its corresponding period, a rate of growth which, on that scale, had been considered without precedent.

Instructive as such comparisons are between two countries transforming themselves with the aid of the same ideology and methods, it is of no less interest to confront the results of China with those of India, where both the principles which inspire the change and the methods employed are totally different.

China and India are the world's two most populous countries. Both had a heritage of widespread destitution. There were strong parallels in their pre-plan structure, and both have launched their first Five-Year Plan in the early 1950's. The international significance of the relative progress in their material development is becoming obvious. Moreover, the comparison of their performance is bound to influence not merely the future course of the other economically backward countries, but even the foreign policies of the Great Powers.

India's first Five-Year Plan began in April, 1951, almost two years before China's. At their beginning India's population was 362 million against China's 600. By the time they were completed India's population grew to 390 million and China's stood around 660. Generally speaking, at the outset India's per head share of agricultural output was a little lower than China's, but was higher in most other fields and particularly in heavy industry.

From 1950 through 1957, *the general output of agriculture* rose in India by nearly a fifth, while its growth in China was nearly a third. Yet in China especially the focus has been on staple food, in other words on food grains. During India's first Plan *grain output* increased from 53 to 69 million tons, or by 30 per cent. During China's first Plan grain produced went up from 154 to 185 million tons, or by 20 per cent. only.

But if one goes beyond the end of the first Plans, India expects to harvest 75 million tons of grain in 1960, and China 297 million tons. While India's increase of food grain output during her two Five-Year Plans (1951-61) will have been 22 million tons, China's will have grown by 143 million tons: a growth of 92 per cent. in seven years in China, against India's increase of 42 per cent. in ten years. Thus, in 1960, the amount of grain on the plate of the average Indian is less than half of what is the share of the average Chinese in the same year.[168]

Part of the explanation for the much faster growth of China's grain output is in the far more important extension of irrigated surface in China. Of equal importance is the erratic course of year to year grain output in India in face of the regular yearly increases in China, especially after 1957. During her first Plan India bene-fitted from three unusually good harvests, due to three excellent consecutive monsoon years, while the weather was rather un-favourable in China. In fact, in India weather has remained the decisive factor and still reserves surprises for the future, while in China, irrigation and other measures have somewhat lessened the impact of the vagaries of climate on agricultural output.

Yet if, after an even trot for over five years, China's agriculture left India's behind in a fast gallop, she has outdistanced India with even greater speed in industrial production. The output of some consumer goods has probably expanded faster under the liberal economy of India than in China. But industrial production as a whole, and in heavy industry in particular, grew incomparably quicker in China. In some of the decisive sectors—like steel, coal, cement, fertilizers, or the generation of electricity—India started out with equal or even higher levels than China. Today, after two Five-Year Plans in India and eight years of planning in China, in all these fields China's output is two to seven times higher than India's. If in 1957 India still retained some advantage in *per capita* output of cement and fertilizers, by 1960 even on that basis China was far ahead.[169]

As a whole, during their respective first Plans already, China's national product had been growing almost three times faster than India's. After 1957 the difference became even greater. If by 1960 India's rate of investments was barely a tenth of her national income, in China it was three times higher. Moreover, if these high Chinese investments came entirely from the country's own, current production, India has been relying on very large-scale foreign assistance in the form of loans as well as grants.

Significantly, the calculations of specialists show that China applies her investments with about double the 'efficiency' of India in terms of production resulting from them. Between 1950 and 1957, China seems to have generated every unit of increase in her national income with half the amount of investment needed to achieve the same advance in India.[170]

Thus, notwithstanding continuous foreign capital injections to aid India's effort, the rhythm of her economic development is lagging far behind China's. Some of the basic economic problems still remain without solution. The cultivator is given little incentive to produce more. There is no organizational effort to put the unemployed or under-employed segment of the country's over-abundant manpower to constructive work. And while China is experimenting with some revolutionary solutions with apparently revolutionary results, India's progress seems to be bogged down in routine and lack of enthusiasm.

To catch up with the overall production of Great Britain within ten years—as propaganda exhorts the Chinese to do—may be a modest target for a nation fifteen times more numerous. Yet by concentrating their effort on industries like iron and steel and machine-making, in those sectors at any rate, the Chinese may overtake fairly rapidly some of the advanced industrial states.

That, however, is for the more or less distant future. What is clear already is that China is now probably making more rapid progress in building industrial power than any other major economically underdeveloped country, even allowing for population growth. Her advance is certainly much faster than India's and quicker even than the Soviet Union's at its corresponding period. The potential psychological and political impact of this fact is bound to be considerable in a period when half of mankind's desire for modernization and for rapid economic progress is acquiring a passionate force. And with China's continued advance, that impact is likely to grow like a shadow, until gradually it will extend over three continents.

PART FOUR

The Shadow

QUITE NEAR TO the Imperial Palace, the *Peking Hotel* is a large and ornate building with hundreds of comfortable rooms along its endless corridors. It is within its walls that a foreigner discovers the new China's missionary urge in its organized form. The rooms are full all the year round and rare are those who have to pay their bill. All the guests receive on their breakfast tray the *New China News Agency's* daily bulletin with its own particular view of world events, and in each room Picasso's peace doves, woven into a bright blue background, provide the pattern of the bed covers.

The guests who people the hotel fall into three main categories. The least numerous are those from the West. They may be professors or even industrialists, unsuspected of Communist sympathies, who were invited to examine China's achievements in their own special field and who are expected to relate what they had seen among their influential colleagues. They may be writers or public figures whose favourable disposition makes it likely that they would repay generous hospitality with printed flattery. Or, there are the avowed enthusiasts who can be relied on to piece together selected details into a glowing picture of what to them is the whole and shadeless truth. Finally, there are the rare Americans, treated like heroes for having braved the State Department's passport-curtain in search of the forbidden land.

The second category, somewhat more numerous, is made up of people from the 'fraternal countries'. They may be specialists on mission, voluminous Russian or Eastern European matrons whose zeal in social activities earned them a conducted tour across China, or simply the Sofia dance-troupe or the Hungarian table-tennis team participating in the current tournaments.

But by far the most numerous is the third category. It is composed of people from colonies or from ex-colonial countries in Asia, Africa or Latin America. Most of them have black or brown skin and they receive particular attentions from their hosts.

One meets them in the lifts, in the corridors, or in the salons where they sit around sipping tea. Arabs, Koreans and Burmese with attaché-cases mix with lamas from Tibet or with tribal chiefs from Africa, all in national costume and loaded with coloured magazines or mimeographed committee-papers. Voluble Indian intellectuals are in debate with Indonesian writers and Haitian poets; Nigerian trade unionists exchange ideas with those from Chile; and budding Ceylonese politicians try to follow the halting English of Japanese students. Delegations from Latin America are shepherded towards the fleet of large *Zis* cars waiting to take them to a new factory, and motley groups of Africans are packed into other vehicles waiting to transport them to the Institute of Nationalities. They are all given the same sense of importance and are shown the sort of things which are likely to underline their frustration when they compare them to what is left undone in their own countries. During their tours, as in the dining-room, they are treated with extreme attention and with informal hospitality. They are surrounded by devoted, blue-tunicked Chinese interpreters who speak either Spanish or the required Asian and African languages. The particularly influential among them may be given the news one day that a Minister would receive them next morning. In exceptional cases, Mao Tse-tung himself would sacrifice an hour to meet them in person and to be photographed in their company. All during their stay in China, the Latin Americans, the Asians and the Africans are treated with the consideration due to men of the future. They don't live in luxury but in sober comfort. In place of the provocative and unattainable opulence and eroticism of Western palaces, there is an atmosphere of brotherly simplicity: the hospitality of another poor land which has just progressed far enough to be generous. Sober waitresses in slacks and with their hair done in plaits, take the orders and the interpreters see to it that no one goes dissatisfied. The fraternity of the Communist world is offered in a fashion that won't embarrass even the most timid or the most modest.

The organization of *Peking Hotel*, however, is but an isolated aspect of China's missionary effort. There are the massive pilgrimages for the first day of May and October when, from every corner of the world, fraternal delegates come to admire the rejoicing and the massive displays of the Chinese people. There is the Foreign Languages Publishing House on the outskirts of Peking, printing books, pamphlets and speeches in several languages and sending them all over the world free of charge or for a token price. There is the steady stream of newspapers, periodicals and illustrated magazines taking their message of giant plants and smiling faces into millions of homes on all continents. At Trade Fairs, in dozens of countries, the imposing Chinese pavilion displays gay pictures, optimistic charts and the huge machines the peasants of yesterday had built. The antennae of China's radio stations broadcast for over 150 hours each week China's achievements and opinions in nearly three dozen languages. Moreover, at regular intervals, there are the giant demonstrations in front of the Gate of Heavenly Peace to protest, to warn or to support. From half to two million people assemble on the immense square to protest against American oppression in Japan, Korea, the Lebanon or in Cuba; to encourage the Algerians or the Congolese; or to approve the actions of Turks, Japanese or Venezuelans. The speeches are punctuated by slogans roared in unison and by the brandishing of clenched fists. Thousands of militia men and women raise their rifles with fixed bayonets and shout their approval. And at the end of it, giant balloons rise into the sky, trailing slogans denouncing imperialism and colonialism wherever it still exists.

In deeds as in words, China is on the march. She does not hide her determination to re-establish the power and influence which had been hers for two millennia. Convinced that she has something to offer to the economically backward majority of mankind,

China too succumbs to the contemporary temptation to export her utopia. And far from doing it surreptitiously, her missionary aims are announced with the confidence of a country knowing itself to be on its way to become a world power.

'The way taken by the Chinese people in defeating imperialism and its lackeys and in founding the People's Republic of China is the way that should be taken by the peoples of the various colonial and semi-colonial countries in their fight for national independence and people's democracy,' recommended Liu Shao-chi already in 1949.[171] Two years later a leading member of the Party, Lu Ting-yi, was even more explicit: 'The classic type of revolution in imperialist countries is the October Revolution. The classic type of revolution in colonial and semi-colonial countries is the Chinese revolution.'[172] Almost a decade later, though in a way less likely to provoke the Soviet Union, Liu Shao-chi once again reaffirmed his belief in the appeal of China's example to the underdeveloped countries: '. . . Of course, revolution and construction in China have features peculiar to this country,' he wrote. 'But it is also possible that some of these important special features may reappear in some other countries. In this sense, Chinese experience is to a certain extent of international significance.'[173]

That 'international significance' is due to the appeal of China's revolution to most economically backward countries. It is one of China's major diplomatic instruments. And her fast growing physical might apart, the impact that instrument can make is determined by three main components: the power of China's example, her foreign trade and the direct aid she begins to distribute.

1 A Model for Half of Mankind?

WHILE IN *Peking Hotel*, I have tried hard to get into conversation with visitors from underdeveloped countries. I wanted to find out why they had come and what had impressed them most in what they had been shown. Some were critical. Some others considered themselves as mere tourists. Many more, however, were passionately interested in China's methods and results and did not hide their enthusiasm.

Their majority were earnest young men, idealists, and more or less influenced by their readings of Marxist literature. Nearly all were frustrated by their own experiences at home or because of the general performance of their countries. Whether they came from Latin America, Africa or from Asian countries, their stories were almost identical. There was unemployment while there was widespread and crying need. Both the ideal and the organization were lacking to exploit natural wealth. Tiny privileged classes were living in modern towns, attached to a way of living and thinking that completely cut them off from the misery and the stagnation of the rural areas where the majority lived. They all complained of corruption, of slow progress if any, or of complete dependence on foreign economic forces. In what they had been shown in China they professed to have found the answers to at least some of the problems of their countries. Whether it was a question of colour or of the brotherhood of still visible backwardness, most of them appeared to be more spontaneously attracted to China's rather than to the Soviet Union's example. And one could amost see them returning to their countries as carriers of arguments and of convictions which, in the long run, were bound to exert considerable influence.

A young Brazilian teacher shared with me his enthusiastic discovery that his country's problems were comparable to those of China. With similar methods, he thought, Brazil too could become a great power within a generation. A negro trade-unionist from Guinea seemed to be particularly impressed by

China's ability to train technicians fast and on a large scale, and with persistency he explored how the Chinese students' time was divided between school and workshop. An Indian economist, a young man from the South, was overwhelmed by China's mobilization of her labour. 'Imagine, no unemployment in China,' he repeated. 'If all the idle hands could be put to work in our country . . .'. When I objected that climate, if nothing else, made Indians perhaps less capable of the sustained physical effort the Chinese were putting up with, he bitterly swept aside my objection: 'That may be so. But if the Chinese could advance from ten to thirty, with similar methods we might have gone from ten to twenty. Yet we haven't advanced beyond fifteen. . . .'

All these, of course, were generalizations. Also, most of the residents of *Peking Hotel* were selected on the basis of their receptivity. Yet all the enthusiasm was symptomatic. It only helped to confirm my conviction that by now, the Chinese experiment must be regarded as far more revolutionary in its scope, and far more interesting for the future of the world's poor areas, than the Soviet Union's experience. And at least three main reasons seem to justify that impression.

Unlike the Soviet revolution, China's has a peasant base and the overwhelming majority in all underdeveloped countries is made up of cultivators. The change in leadership and in social organization in China did not come from a shift of power within the urban, commercial minority, but from its transfer from those tiny privileged groups to the peasant majority who, for the first time, were organized and educated for that purpose.

In the second place, no government in any of the under-developed countries, democratic or totalitarian, has as yet found a method to turn to constructive use the energies wasted through large-scale unemployment or under-employment in the country-side. With the organizational innovation of the Communes, not only has unemployment disappeared but under-employment too has been transformed into productive effort. The Commune system, even if a few more years will be needed to assess its balance-sheet, appears workable in China. Adapted to local conditions, its variants may serve the same purposes in other overpopulated, predominantly agrarian countries.

Finally, and as a result of the previous two innovations, China's experiment is revolutionary also in its emphasis on the simultaneous development of modern and small-scale, decentralized industry. In most underdeveloped countries either there is a one-sided and sentimental emphasis on large-scale industries—which may provide symbolic satisfaction but few openings for employment—or on archaic cottage-industries, as in India, which are wasteful, uncompetitive, and fail to prepare the rural masses for modern industrial pursuits. China's experience permits the introduction of relatively modern manufacturing processes into rural surroundings without prohibitive investments. It encourages the utilization of local raw materials. Moreover, it exerts all the sociological influence desirable to prepare the skills and the way of thinking of the peasants for times when large-scale industry reaches their region. This same experiment permitted in China a vast increase in the supply of tools and of simple equipment which, in other underdeveloped countries, are expected from urban industries only. And while small-scale but modern rural industries already contribute to overall industrial progress, they also help to transform the attitudes of a peasantry which have been immobile and imprisoned in traditions for centuries.

Social transformation with the peasant majority as its armed vanguard; rural industries as agents of the mental and material modernization of the countryside; and the massive investment of idle labour as a means to accumulate capital for development—these are, simplified to the extreme, the three major characteristics of the Chinese model.

They are primarily economic in character. Though Communist organization and indoctrination may have been decisive in their realization, they were secondary in importance behind the imperatives which have dictated the main lines of the solutions to given problems.

Yet besides these principal characteristics of the Chinese model, distinguishing it from that of the U.S.S.R., observers from underdeveloped countries may find a number of supplementary features likely to claim their attention.

While in Russia the Communist Revolution established itself through continued mass arrests and executions aimed at the elimination of the condemned upper and middle classes, China has been making great efforts, and with some success, to win them over to collaboration with the new régime. There had been mass executions of landlords and there have been waves of terror. But their aim and duration was limited. At the same time everything was done to facilitate the integration of those capable to comply. Quite often former industrialists and merchants now are directing State-enterprises or occupy other important posts. Though they may be closely supervised by a less qualified but politically more reliable cadre, their lot is still enviable compared with that of their Russian counterparts in their mass-graves. As late as 1956 there were claimed to be 65 people in China with an annual income of over U.S. $400,000, capitalists who had the wisdom to go into partnership with the State in good time. Then, one may come across processions of 'reformed exploiters', demonstrating with flags and banners their change of heart. 'They were unfortunate to be born capitalists,' a Chinese was reported to have remarked on their passage. All these, of course, may be no more than exotic exceptions. Yet their existence is symbolic of an attitude, one that basically differs from the absolute solutions employed in the Soviet Union.

Of course China's present rulers can be extremely cruel when they have no alternative. But, as a rule, they prefer to convince or to shame before they employ force. And this addiction to persuasion may not be lost upon observers from underdeveloped countries especially when they compare Soviet and Chinese experience.

Should one add to all this China's success in avoiding the excessive urbanization which characterized Soviet development; the steady encouragement of peasant initiative and inventiveness; the State's continued ability to command the selfless devotion of large masses; or that unprecedented venality has been replaced by almost puritanic honesty, permitting the world's lowest insurance rates, then, it may be admitted that, in the eyes of a visitor from an underdeveloped country the result is infinitely more subtle than Slavic Communism. For the same reason the Chinese model may seem tempting to many who are dismayed by the inability of their countries to overcome their backwardness, or even to those who are already disillusioned by the Soviet Union.

China is the second backward, agrarian country being transformed by Communism into a great power and within one generation. For the time being no underdeveloped country has found a satisfactory answer to this challenge. Whatever the merits of alternative methods may be, hitherto their results have not been comparable either in quantity or in speed. So long as the answer to that challenge will be lacking, China's example will continue to help to expand her influence in the world. And the impact of that formidable weapon the power of her example, will only be enhanced by the lever provided by China's growing economic weight.

2 The Strategy of Trade

OVERLOOKING THE Pearl River stands Canton's Export Exhibition Hall, one of the city's most modern buildings. Conveniently situated for traders from every continent who would make the short train journey from Hong Kong, it displays all that China wants to sell to the world. Its four floors are covered by a permanent exhibition of the samples of some 15,000 export articles. In glass cases are displayed all the grain, the metals, the herbs, the silk and the handicraft products which have been China's traditional exports. On other floors, there is machinery. First, only pumps, bicycles, radios and sewing machines. But they give way to ingenious mechanical toys, to electronic equipment and to precision instruments, none of which had been manufactured in China in the past. Along yet another floor stand massive machine tools, drilling equipment, and a wide range of heavy

machinery for the equipment of entire plants. Some of them may
be no more than models whose production had scarcely begun.
Yet most of them are manufactured in series and have already
been sold abroad. Twice a year, for the Canton Trade Fair, the
foreign traders arrive. They crowd the Exhibition Hall and,
sipping tea in the monumental arm-chairs of the private rooms,
they sign important contracts. China is growing into one of the
world's great trading nations.

If as yet the Western world has had little opportunity to meet
China in that new role, it is for two main reasons. The less
important one is of the West's own making. With the restrictions
it had imposed on trade with China, the West has deliberately
deprived itself of its due share. But the more important reason
is in China's own decision to integrate her economy with that
of the other centrally-planned economies of the Communist
bloc.

Before the war China's principal trading partners were Japan,
Great Britain and the United States. Trade with the Soviet Union
had amounted to less than one per cent. of the total, and with
Eastern Europe it had been insignificant. But from 1949 onwards
China's foreign trade was completely reoriented. By now, 80 per
cent. of it is with the Communist bloc, and much of the rest with
the countries of Asia and Africa. The West and Japan account,
henceforth, for only a small fraction. Yet if there was a drastic
reorientation of China's foreign trade, there was also a great
change in its composition.

The Chinese authorities are most secretive about their foreign
trade. If statistics are sparse this may be partly because they don't
want to reveal the amount of food and consumer goods sent
abroad while there are shortages at home or, perhaps, because
they would reveal China's terms of trade with the Soviet bloc
which are not always advantageous to Peking. In practice, then,
more often than not, one has to deal with selected figures or,
simply, with estimates.[174]

From less than the equivalent of 2 milliard U.S. dollars in 1950,
China's foreign trade has increased during the past ten years to
over 5 milliard dollars. In other words, China now imports each

year commodities worth nearly 3 milliard dollars, and sells abroad goods for about the same value. If before the war China used to have a large and persistent trade deficit, she has achieved a balance in her international payments since 1950 onwards. In fact, with repayments on past Soviet loans falling due and no new ones being forthcoming, China for the past four years has been regularly exporting more than she has been buying abroad.[175]

The change has been no less spectacular in the composition of China's external trade. In the past she imported mainly consumer goods. Now it is predominantly industrial equipment with only a trickle of goods for direct consumption. Inversely, while for centuries China had been exporting raw materials and agricultural products, now manufactured goods, including machines, make up a growing share.[176]

During the last four years there have also been changes in China's trade with the Soviet bloc itself. The proportion of trade with Eastern Europe—and with Eastern Germany in particular—tended to increase at the expense of exchange with the Soviet Union. Yet long-term trade agreements as much as the other signs of growing economic integration into the bloc as a whole, render unlikely any sudden switching of an *important* proportion of China's foreign trade to the non-Communist world. Henceforth China's major trading partners are the Communist countries. Two significant trends, however, ought to be noted.

The first is connected with the rapid growth of China's external trade. In fact, while it now amounts to over 4 milliard dollars a year with the Communist bloc alone, *in addition* her trade with the non-Communist world has, in 1958 already, surpassed its pre-war volume with those countries. With the continued expansion of Chinese production, and even if her trade with the Communist bloc is maintained at its present level, China may also be able to sell growing quantities of raw materials and manufactured goods on the non-Communist markets.

The second trend concerns changes in the very economic structure of the country. China is making great efforts to cover more of her needs in machinery from domestic production and thus to reduce very expensive imports of capital goods. Recent emphasis on small-scale industries serves the same end. Simultaneously, however, China's machine-building capacity does grow and gradually she will have larger quantities of light machinery and manufactured consumer goods for sale abroad. They could help her to earn precious foreign currency and improve her freedom of manœuvre on foreign markets. The combined influence of all this will tend to broaden China's trade with the non-Communist world. And, given the nature of her exports, her best chances will be not in the industrialized West but rather in underdeveloped countries where her cheap industrial products may find ready buyers.

This does not, of course, exclude Sino-Japanese trade on a larger scale once political conditions again become favourable. This time, however, against coal, iron-ore and other raw materials, China would buy machines rather than consumer goods, as in the past. Nor is it excluded that for political or for purely economic reasons China may one day desire to lessen her economic dependence on the Soviet bloc. With or without such a major change China might increase her trade with Western Europe or, eventually, even with the United States. As the Soviet Union's example proves, for many years to come China will need important quantities of specialized equipment, of rolling stock, or of entire industrial plants in some of the more advanced technological fields, all of which she might prefer to buy in the West. In fact China's trade with Western Europe—and with Western Germany and Great Britain in particular—is slowly but steadily expanding. Yet for the foreseeable future the bulk of China's non-agricultural exports will consist of cheap machinery and this will broaden her trade primarily with the underdeveloped countries. And that is likely to have important economic and political implications bound to affect the power rivalry in the contemporary world.

At present China accounts for about a fifth of the Communist bloc's total trade with the rest of the world. But East Asia taken alone, that proportion is much higher. In some South-east Asian countries China's trade penetration is already on a fairly large scale. It is beginning to hurt Indian and, in particular, Japanese interests. If, as it is likely, Chinese exports towards the non-Communist world continue to expand, they may seriously affect Japan's economy on some of her vital Asian markets. The same competition may slowly extend to Africa and even to Latin America.

Though the basic motivation of such trade drives may be economic, they will not fail to be related to the Communist bloc's general economic strategy. Its centrally planned economies have inherent advantages over liberal ones in their dealings with underdeveloped countries. To countries suffering from the oscillation of raw material prices, or of being unable to sell their commodities regularly and thus undertake their planned industrialization, the Communist countries can offer long-term contracts: to buy their essential exports in exchange for much desired equipment. And, as a rule, they can do so by offering tempting prices even if thereby they impose additional sacrifices on their citizens. Indeed there is already sufficient evidence that the Chinese too will yield to the temptation and exploit these specific advantages of their economic structure for their own political ends. Though in this field China's means are as yet relatively modest, they are growing more important each day. Moreover, when concentrated on selected countries or regions, they can already yield important political dividends.

The value of China's trade with the non-Communist world amounted to $1·5 milliard in 1958 and has probably grown since.[177] From countries outside the Communist bloc, China imported mainly chemical fertilizers, rubber, cotton, wool, dyestuffs, chemicals as well as machinery of all kinds. In exchange she sent her traditional agricultural products—like soya beans, grain, vegetable oils, fruits, pork, tea, dairy products, coal and silk—together with growing quantities of manufactured goods like cotton textiles, fountain pens, enamelware, bicycles, sewing machines, as well as iron and steel, machine tools, or complete equipment for textile mills and other plants. Due to the opening of new mines, it is expected that iron-ore and coal will soon be available for export in far larger quantities. Probably less than a quarter of this trade with non-Communist countries is with the industrial West. Three-quarters is with the Afro-Asian world. And if China's trade with Western Europe scarcely had any political implications, that with Japan and the Afro-Asian countries had obvious political undertones.[178]

In South-east Asia, China is using her external trade to promote closer relations and has been quick to take advantage of special deficiencies and surpluses in the area. Her chief targets have been the neutrals, though pro-Western countries were not neglected either. Addressing itself to South-east Asia, Chinese propaganda does not tire to repeat that only co-operation with China and with the Communist bloc can help solve their economic difficulties or bring about their industrialization. Such and similar exhortations leave little doubt that to encourage neutralism, to undermine economic ties with the West, or to enmesh the economies of the South-east Asian countries with that of the Communist bloc, is very much in the forefront of the pre-occupations of those who direct China's external trade. Then, in South-east Asia, in particular, important Chinese minorities are of great help to Peking's export drive. While the overseas Chinese constitute only about 5 per cent. of the region's population, their unique position in the commerce and the finance of their countries of residence, can significantly further China's aims.[179]

Though only part of China's external trade is on a barter basis, it is shrewdly employed and yields important economic and political results. Ceylon may be a good example. Her interest in trading with China stemmed from the economic necessity of selling rubber and obtaining rice in exchange. In 1952, after fruitless efforts to dispose of her rubber profitably in the West, Ceylon received a five-year barter offer from China. 'We could have got rice at £80 or £90 per ton,' Ceylon's Minister of Trade and Industry explained, 'but we could not afford to pay that price. The price of Chinese rice for the first year of the agreement was £54 per ton. Rather than to go to China were we to starve? Were we to reject the Chinese offer of 1·75 rupees per lb. for rubber, take the world price of 1·10 rupees and throw 300,000 labourers out of employment?'[180] Indeed the agreement has been renewed since. Now each year Ceylon is sending to China more than half her rubber output and obtains rice and industrial equipment in exchange. Both as a buyer and as a supplier of Ceylon, China is playing a growing role. And despite some problems, the Ceylonese express satisfaction with the barter deal as providing them with an assured rice supply and a stable market for their major export.

Though not always leading to the same degree of mutual satisfaction, there have been similar arrangements between China and other South-east Asian countries. Price manipulation, or the re-export of, for example, Burmese rice to other countries in the region, have repeatedly caused irritation. Yet, dependent as the prosperity of those countries is on the export of a handful of primary products, and constantly in search of stable markets and prices, they naturally find it tempting when China offers to buy their commodities at premium prices and offers in exchange manufactured goods or industrial equipment. Not even the government of Pakistan—though strongly anti-Communist and member of the pro-Western S.E.A.T.O. alliance—could afford to ignore such offers. 'In the recent past, there were times when China's entry into our cotton market sustained the prices and saved them falling to an uneconomic level,' commented in 1957 an influential Pakistani economic publication; and it urged closer economic ties through the exchange of the country's jute and cotton for Chinese manufactures.[181]

How skilfully such practices can be made to serve political ends was spectacularly demonstrated, and in a far removed region, through China's trade deal with Cuba. Following the Soviet Union's example, in July 1960 China signed a trade agreement with that country. She undertook to take a yearly half a million tons of sugar over five years, as well as tobacco, nickel, copper, manganese, fruit and various other products. Politically the deal was a service to Cuba and, no doubt, it will also help to diversify her production. In return China agreed to supply tea and pork, as well as steel, machinery, and electronic and telecommunications equipment. Besides procuring diplomatic recognition by a Western hemisphere country, the display of Chinese industrial products in Latin America will not fail to produce the desired psychological effect. In actual practice, China is taking from Cuba goods which she does not really need, in exchange for articles she cannot really spare. The occasion, however, was far too tempting. And acting in concert with the U.S.S.R., the political yield is bound to be considerable.[182]

The underdeveloped countries' understandable desire for stable external trade is only accentuated by racial sentiment, by latent anti-colonial feelings, or by a vaguely defined concept of Asian or Afro-Asian solidarity. They all tend to help China's economic initiatives in Asia or Africa and, later on, in Latin America too. Whatever misgivings there may exist, they are probably outweighed by the desire to accelerate national development. In fact, it is likely that countries further removed from China's borders—and thus less apprehensive of her growing power—will be even less inhibited than are her neighbours to trade with her. To many of them China may even appear as a welcome extension of the Soviet counter-weight in their dealings with Western countries.

But when considering China's utilization of trade for political ends, her dealings with Japan constitute a special chapter. Apart from Hong Kong, China's most important non-Communist trading partner in recent years had been Japan. Remembering pre-war days when nearly a fifth of their country's foreign trade was with China, Japanese public opinion as much as her industrialists attached great hopes to renewed trade with their giant neighbour. Though the embargo imposed by the Americans severely limited the scope of Sino-Japanese exchanges, still, trade between the two countries grew tenfold between 1952 and 1956. Yet even when it reached $150 million in 1956, it was no more than 2 per cent. of Japan's external trade and remained far below expectations. Then, in May 1958, in the very moment when agreements were ready for a further extension of exchanges, China suddenly decreed the complete rupture of her trade relations with Japan. The pretext was a totally insignificant incident. A drunken Japanese had torn down a Chinese flag at an exhibition and in retaliation Peking decided to bring strong economic pressure on Japan. The issue was promptly broadened into a demand for the protection of the Chinese flag on Japanese soil. As Japan had not yet recognized China, this had obvious bearing on Tokyo's relations with Taiwan, still a more important trading partner for her than China has ever been since 1949.

Yet a succession of other political measures have soon made it clear that Peking's decision had even more far-reaching aims. China obviously intended to exert pressure on the Japanese electorate in the country's forthcoming elections. Designed to favour the Socialists, and openly declared to be aimed at Mr. Kishi and at his compliance with American demands, China's transparent intervention in Japan's internal politics misfired. It had probably contributed to Mr. Kishi's ensuing electoral victory.

By the end of 1960, however, Sino-Japanese trade had not yet resumed. Some Japanese industries, traditionally dependent on raw materials from China, have suffered gravely. A number of others have lost important orders. Public opinion as a whole has been made even more acutely aware of Japan's economic vulnerability as long as she is not allowed to have her normal share of trade with the Communist countries. Moreover, in the meantime China has been making unmistakable efforts to squeeze Japan out of some of her Asian markets. She has been selling, and at lower prices, exact imitations of Japanese toys, cameras and other articles, including cotton cloth rendered even more competitive for being perfumed. And forgetting the past, the Japanese were quick to accuse China of 'dumping'. Of course it may be argued that China's boycott indirectly contributed to the passions which, in 1960, sent Japanese demonstrators into the streets to prevent the American President's coming. Equally, it could be maintained that China's action strengthened the pressure which forced Mr. Kishi's resignation. At the same time, however, China's manner of acting must also have reminded many Japanese of how vulnerable their new bargaining position had become in face of their fast changing neighbour.

If, between 1952 and 1956, due to the American embargo, Japan could not sell China the heavy equipment China needed, on her part China failed to offer Japan the essential raw materials— the coal and iron-ore—which Japan needed and used to obtain from China in large quantities before the war. The question inevitably arises whether, in view of her rapid industrialization, China will ever again be in a position to supply those commodities in important quantities? or, whether she is desirous at all to lessen her economic integration in the Communist bloc and let Japan's industry supply at least part of her requirements in heavy equipment? In fact, China's action clearly poses the fundamental problem facing Japan: whether it is possible to have the large-scale trade with China which the Japanese trade-promotion societies hope for, without the integration of Japan's industry into China's economic plans to a degree incompatible with Japan's economic and political independence?

Here, of course, the stakes are much higher than in other parts of the world. What is involved is a political issue decisive both for China's and Japan's future and, indirectly, for that of the whole of East Asia. China's relations with Japan and the methods she is employing towards her, then, are not necessarily typical of China's utilization of her trade for political ends.

Yet even if China's dealings with Japan are considered an exceptional case, there can be little doubt that political considerations—as in the case of most other countries, Communist or not—play an important role in her general strategy of foreign trade. That role will be even more powerful as her trade expands. And as that expansion is likely to be fastest in the underdeveloped countries, it is there that the political impact will be the strongest. In that sense, it will reinforce the influence the Soviet Union already exerts in those regions. Together, they will act even more effectively to bring nearer the ultimate objective: the West's political and economic isolation. And nothing could show more clearly China's determination to participate in the process with all her force, than the fact that she too is already distributing foreign aid on a growing scale.

3 Gifts to Gain Friends

CHINA'S OWN FOREIGN aid programme is probably the most striking illustration of her ambition now unfolding on the world scene. What is surprising is not that China too wishes to participate in the contemporary rivalry to make friends and allies with the aid of gifts, but rather that she is doing so so soon. The Chinese people are still overstraining themselves to pay for everything they buy from their Communist allies and from other countries. China is believed to have received from the Communist countries no more than half a milliard dollars worth of *loans*. Yet the Chinese themselves have already distributed over a milliard dollars worth of *gifts*.

China's activities in this field began as early as 1953 and developed in three distinct stages. First she offered grants to three Communist countries along her borders: to North Korea, to North Viet-Nam, and to Outer Mongolia. Since 1956 came grants to Asian neutrals, like Cambodia, Nepal or Ceylon. Finally, aid-programmes were gradually extended to neutrals further away, as to Egypt, the Yemen or, more recently, to Cuba.[183]

By far the greatest part of Chinese grants were given to the three small Asian Communist countries. In North Korea and North Viet-Nam they amount up to date to about $400 million each and were intended to help post-war reconstruction. In both countries Chinese aid already surpasses the Soviet Union's and besides the construction of industrial plants, it involves large quantities of equipment, raw materials, technical assistance, goods which China herself has to buy from the Soviet bloc, as well as, probably, military supplies. In both cases China's political influence has become paramount and both North Korea and North Viet-Nam play a docile supporting role seconding her economic and political decisions. And the new relationship unmistakably recalls the 'tributary' system which had existed in the periods of China's imperial greatness.

The narrowing of the gap between Soviet and Chinese

influence is still in process in Outer Mongolia. That territory—seven times the size of France though with only a million inhabitants—became independent of China after 1921 and had fast been transformed into a virtual Soviet protectorate. China recognized the Mongolian People's Republic in 1945 but had little direct contact with it. Since 1949, relations have gradually become closer and the new Trans-Mongolian railway—built with Soviet help—provides China with direct access by rail for the first time. China offered Mongolia a grant of about $40 million as well as a smaller long-term loan, to finance the building of factories and power plants and, significantly, a fairly large number of Chinese workers were sent to participate in their construction. In May 1960 when Mr. Chou En-lai visited Ulan Bator, the capital, Mr. Tsedenbal, the Mongolian Premier, was reported to have remarked that while in the past the Mongolian people had only one reliable friend, the Soviet Union, since 1949 a 'staunch friendship' has developed with China. Then, enumerating all the realizations with China's assistance, he hoped for 'more huge aid' from her to help Mongolia's next Five-Year Plan.[184]

Outside the Communist bloc, China offered grants to Cambodia, Nepal, Ceylon and to Egypt. Cambodia—with a $22·4 million grant in the form of factories, commodities and technical assistance—has hitherto been the most favoured. China is openly supporting her neutralism, considering the country a friendly bridgehead in the very heart of a neighbouring region covered by hostile governments more or less directly associated to the anti-Communist S.E.A.T.O. alliance. With nearly $16 million, Ceylon is second, though there regular barter trade provides an even broader basis for economic collaboration. Nepal, a Trans-Himalayan friendly outpost on the Indian peninsula, received grants of close to $21 million and, notwithstanding China's recent differences with India, or, for that matter, the direct dispute over the proprietorship of Mount Everest, economic collaboration seems to be developing in a satisfactory way. All three countries receive complete factories (paper, plywood, textile or cement) or, as in the case of Cambodia, also radio stations and other equipment. The $4·7 million grant to Egypt was of a different nature and was extended to that country after the Suez expedition, both to aid reconstruction and as an expression of political solidarity.

But next to these outright grants, since 1956 China has been extending long-term loans—usually at the standard Communist condition of repayment in ten years and at 2·5 per cent. interest— to a number of Afro-Asian countries. Hitherto Ceylon, Indonesia, Burma, the Yemen and Cuba have been the principal beneficiaries. Here, as in the case of grants, it is always emphasized that 'no conditions whatsoever' are attached. Their sum varies between 6 and 20 million dollars and they usually are intended to cover the cost of a textile factory or some other plant. A curious exception is that of the Yemen where besides a textile factory, China is also building a strategic road with the aid of Chinese labour and technicians sent to that country. It is not without interest that the post-Suez grant to Egypt as well as part of the aid extended to the Yemen was in Swiss francs.

Thus the three neighbouring Communist countries apart, Chinese grants and long-term loans are as yet on a relatively modest scale. But they tend to expand both in volume and in their geographical distribution. Similar offers to several newly-independent African countries are reported to be under negotiation. That such aid will be used with the same shrewd timing as China's ordinary barter-trade, has already been demonstrated on more than one occasion. The grant to Ceylon, in September 1957 was intended to compensate the Ceylonese when, on expiration of the five-year rice-rubber barter deal, China wished to reduce the relatively high price she had been paying for rubber. As for the latest grants to Nepal, they came after the Sino-Indian frontier incidents which were likely to influence Nepalese public opinion too.

While these aid programmes are steadily expanding, China also receives a growing number of foreign students and technicians. In 1959-60 nearly 1,000 students from twenty-four countries were reported to be attending her institutes of higher learning. Though no figures are available, it seems that far greater numbers of foreign technicians are receiving training in China.

Obviously, these aid programmes help to expand China's influence abroad. Notwithstanding pressing domestic problems, they are supplied with growing funds and are allocated precious equipment.

Already skilfully projecting her experience as an example for all underdeveloped countries, and utilizing the traditional trading skills of the Chinese people to turn expanding foreign trade to good political advantage, Peking sees in direct aid an important additional instrument of its diplomacy. And there can be little doubt that all this powerfully reinforces China's position in her relations with the rest of the world.

4 China and the West: or the End of a White Peril

CHINA'S TRANSFORMATION within a few years from a sup-plicatory, semi-colonial country into one whose influence is now felt on all continents, is fast becoming the central theme of con-temporary world politics.

For the first time China is successfully translating the potential strength of her masses into a proportionate factor in international relations. From Manchuria to Kashmir, she has been reasserting her old, imperial borders. In Korea, in Viet-Nam, and perhaps in Mongolia too, she is on her way to reconstitute her past system of tributaries. For the first time she had her say in the affairs of Europe. With verbal and material support from Cambodia to Ceylon, from the Yemen to North Africa, and from Guinea to Cuba, she is serving early notice that she regards neither Africa nor Latin America as exclusively within Western spheres of interest. And while readjustments within the Sino-Soviet alliance will soon permit her to deal with the U.S.S.R. as an equal, and while her policies towards her neighbours bring continental leadership in Asia within her reach, China is rapidly emerging as a world power without whose collaboration none of the decisive global problems of our age can be solved.

Within this framework, the transformation of China's relations with the West have not been less spectacular. The ebb of Western supremacy in China had begun with Germany's departure from the scene in 1918. The renunciation of Tsarist Russia's privileges by the Soviet Union, constituted the next stage. The remaining privileges held by Western Powers were liquidated before the end of the second World War. 'By the time the Communists came to power, the old edifice of imperialist oppression in China had been practically destroyed,' wrote Ping-chia Kuo, the Chinese historian. 'The Communists had little difficulty in liquidating whatever remained in the form of foreign business interests and holdings and foreign missionary establishments.'[185] The real target of the new and bitter nationalism of the Chinese, then, is no longer to remove foreign privileges but rather to replace inherited inferiority and vulnerability by a new sense of security and by a new position of strength able to extend China's control and influence.

This basic aim in mind, since 1940 China's foreign policy has passed through four distinct phases.

The first was dominated by the consolidation of China's new alignment with the Soviet Union and by her hostile posture towards the United States.[186] A general stiffening of attitudes was the immediate result. America armed Japan, South Korea and Taiwan and gave encouragement to all anti-Chinese movements. China, on her part, backed with equal persistency all anti-American action in Asia and beyond. The resulting second phase was characterized by continuous tension and led to China's expansion into specific areas across her borders. It is a matter of interpretation whether this was essentially defensive in nature in fear of American aggression or, more simply, sprang from the desire to extend China's control and influence wherever this could be done without risk of major war. Yet having fulfilled these aims in Korea and in Viet-Nam, and with the tension threatening to get out of control, from the Bandung Conference onwards Chinese tactics began to change.

After the spring of 1955, China preferred to emphasize her desire for peaceful co-existence and to canalize the Asian sympathies thus gathered for the support of her claims against the United States. Under the influence of China's spectacular economic progress, and the resulting reinforcement of her position within the Communist bloc, however, once again China's more accommodating mood gave way to the aggressive assertion of her external ambitions. Yet while pressure was brought on both India and Japan, China continued to cultivate her good relations with a number of smaller Asian neutrals, and even extended them deep into Africa.

Throughout these changes, relations with the West meant primarily relations with the United States. Western European influence in Eastern Asia emerged from the war reduced to modest proportions. If this unfavourable posture could have been corrected by suitable Western European initiatives, they were deliberately avoided in deference to America, or were rendered impossible by support to the S.E.A.T.O. alliance whose only Asian members were violently anti-Chinese governments. A number of smaller Western European countries recognized China and have benefited from trade with her. As for Great Britain, although she recognized the Peking régime, she continued to deal with Taiwan and simultaneously refused to support China's admission to the United Nations. For the time being, then, China's relations with Western Europe are mainly commercial. Though growing in importance, that trade could hardly expand significantly without the aid of suitable political relations or, what is even less in view, without China's willingness considerably to lessen her economic integration in the Communist bloc. Thus, for the foreseeable future, contact between China and the West will continue to be overshadowed by the evolution of Sino-American relations.

The hatred that colours the Chinese Communists' view of America springs from Marxist theory, had been reinforced by wartime experience and seemed to be confirmed by the corruption, the cruelty and the decadence of the régime which the United States continued to support in China after the war.

Their fear and hatred appeared to them strikingly confirmed when after Japan's defeat, the Americans provided Chiang Kai-shek with an air-lift and thus frustrated Communist hopes of taking over the areas abandoned by the Japanese. It is from that American intervention in the civil war that dates the Chinese Communists' almost maniacal hatred of a United States associated in their minds with all the counter-revolutionary forces in Asia. To them, the only conceivable policy towards the Americans was one of uncompromising resistance with the elimination of U.S. power from the Asian continent as its ultimate aim.

Officially, the American attitude towards China has been based since 1949 on the assumption that juridically she does not exist and, in fact, her régime is only temporary. As late as November 1959 the State Department restated that attitude by quoting the late Secretary of State John Foster Dulles: '. . . We can confidently assume that international Communism's rule of strict conformity is, in China as elsewhere, a passing and not a perpetual phase. We owe it to ourselves, our allies and the Chinese people to do all we can to contribute to that passing.'[187] Until then, in the eyes of the United States, China is represented by the Government of Taiwan.

To comprehend such and similar statements, it is advisable to take into consideration not merely the political motives but also the emotional attitudes behind them. Not so long ago most Americans believed that they and the Chinese were devoted friends. For a century American missionaries have made China their chosen field of endeavour, and the charitable instincts of most Americans had been mobilized in aid of hungry Chinese children. Throughout the thirties American sympathy for the Chinese people in their struggle against Japan grew, while Chiang Kai-shek and his American-educated wife—both of them Christian converts—had been surrounded by publicity on a scale meted out to Hollywood stars. Then, in 1941, Pearl Harbour brought America into the war on China's side. For nearly twenty years the Chinese people, and Chiang Kai-shek in particular, had been, as it were, the American people's protégés and, in 1949, it suddenly became clear that the Chinese had rejected both Chiang and the Americans. Ever since America has been trying to explain away the shocking news.

The first myth this effort produced was that only the betrayal of some Americans could have provoked those changes in China. The second myth pretended that Communism was imposed on the Chinese from outside and that they could not have ceased to love America. To a somewhat deeper analysis of the events in their economic, social or political context, the average American newspaper reader has not yet been invited. Behind these simple emotions, however, there were some less naïve considerations: genuine dislike and fear of Communism, the lavishly financed activities of political pressure groups, and the strategic shock of having been deprived of a dependable ally on a decisive but more or less hostile continent.

The complete sterility of the official American attitude towards China, however, has been slightly mitigated by inevitable confrontation with reality. Growing awareness that all American policy in Asia is compromised by lack of relations with China, fears concerning the future political evolution of Japan and Taiwan, as well as commercial considerations have been instrumental in pressing for change.[188]

Tension between the two countries had been steadily rising and became particularly explosive during the Korean War and in connection with Peking's reluctance to release illegally detained American airmen. In the winter of 1954-55, when Congress authorized President Eisenhower to act as he deemed it necessary for the defence of Taiwan and the Pescadores, Peking seemed to have realized that her intransigence was reaching the limits of safety and that Asia's neutrals were beginning to hesitate in their support. The Chinese desire to change course found expression at the Bandung Conference and led to the limited diplomatic contact in the form of meetings between Chinese and American ambassadorial representatives first in Geneva and then in Warsaw. During these intermittent encounters—which are officially not yet interrupted—the Americans were pressing China to declare that she would not use force to liberate Taiwan, while the Chinese called for a broader political conference between the Foreign

Ministers of China and the U.S.A. to discuss all issues open between the two countries.

For over three years these contacts yielded absolutely no results, each side maintaining its inflexible position. In their wider context, however, these conversations took place against a background of growing Western enthusiasm for the so-called 'two-China-policy' as a solution to the Taiwan problem. In the mind of its sponsors, this policy would permit the creation of two sovereign entities, and the admission of both Taiwan and China to the United Nations. Taiwan's immediate security would be guaranteed against invasion, the tension of the Taiwan Straits would disappear, and the final status of the island may be determined by a plebiscite later on. The Chinese have repeatedly stated that they would not hear of this solution. It would not merely demonstrate before Asian public opinion that the United States could impose its will on her, but would amount to China's implied admission of the existence of a rival government with claims to speak for its inhabitants.

Why, then, did Peking carry on with the negotiations for three years, well knowing that she would inflexibly turn down the American plan? The only explanation is in China's conviction that she will 'liberate' Taiwan without the use of force, by applying the very methods which had led to Chiang's own downfall in China, namely, by isolating him through popular defection. The negotiations with the Americans were destined to shake the confidence of the island's people in the Chiang régime's political future. The longer they went on, the wider must have spread the doubts. When, finally, the Ambassadorial contacts were broken off, the Americans rushed rockets and missiles to Taiwan and Chiang Kai-shek began to fortify his garrisons on the offshore islands. It was upon this that Peking thought it timely to shake again Taiwan's morale. On August 23, 1958, the Chinese began the shelling of Quemoy to demonstrate the vulnerability of the territory under Chiang's control. There were air-battles and within a few days the new crisis in Sino-American relations over the future of Taiwan threatened with global war. In actual fact, however, it was merely the beginning of one of those masterly diplomatic actions which ought to help to measure both China's diplomatic skill and the solidity of Sino-Soviet collaboration when common interests are involved.

It will be remembered that early in September the Americans warned China of retaliatory action in case of an attempted invasion of territory under Chiang's control. China's response was to reopen the Warsaw meetings between the Ambassadors. On September 8, 1958, Mr. Khrushchev notified the American President that he supported China's action. Eleven days later he specified that in case of atomic attack from Taiwan on China, the U.S.S.R. would riposte by the same means. At that stage the usual fissures appeared in the Western front. Public opinion on both sides of the Atlantic moved against involvement. Finally, at his press conference on September 30, Mr. Dulles envisaged in exchange for a 'dependable cease-fire', the reduction of forces on the offshore islands as well as a promise that Chiang Kai-shek would openly abandon his plans for the reconquest of China. The crisis was over. But the diplomatic situation was completely changed.

The provisional cease-fire was followed by renewed bombardment of the offshore islands while Mr. Dulles and Chiang were formulating their pledge not to use force for the reconquest of China, and to express continued American support to Taiwan. Thus, after three years of effort to induce Peking to renounce the use of force to liberate Taiwan, finally the symmetrical commitment was made by Chiang and the State Department, though without any concession on Peking's part. The 'two-China-policy' was accepted by America and Taiwan, but not by China. And with that diplomatic victory, China could resume her effort to weaken the morale of the islands' population. She began bombing them on alternate days, while China's radio stations beamed towards Taiwan the comforting words: 'We are all Chinese. . . . The Americans are bound to go. They have to go. . . .'[189]

The masterly timing of Sino-Soviet action in inflating and then dismantling the tension, highlights China's determination to exploit to the full the inflexibility of American policy towards China. Evidently, China is not particularly concerned by the prolongation of the stalemate in her relations with the United States. Time is working for her. She can wait.

The question of the offshore islands is outstandingly suitable to the general Communist purpose of dividing the West and isolating the United States. The doubts about involvement over Quemoy felt by some Americans are mild when compared to the feeling of America's allies. Almost the same applies to a number of political régimes which the Americans support in Asia mainly because they are willing tools against China. In fact, it is probable that the same lack of concern characterizes Peking's attitude regarding her admission to the United Nations, or her recognition by some Western Powers, all eminently suitable to weaken Western unity and to procure Afro-Asian sympathies, without at the same time causing China any serious harm.

In the meantime China is looking forward to the day when the Taiwan problem will be resolved between Chinese. Chiang Kai-shek is an old man. The anti-American riots on Taiwan, in May 1957 may have been a rehearsal only. Above all, while diverting American attention by diplomatic battles which have no real importance to her central purpose, China is concentrating on building up her internal strength and external contacts for the day when, rather than complying with Western conditions for the recognition of her existence, she will be in a position to pose the terms at which she would agree to be recognized. By then, those terms may contain her own solutions to the dead-locked problems existing between her and the West.

Western preoccupation with the rhetoric of China's new, self-confident and even arrogant nationalism, tends to divert attention from the tactical flexibility and dogged consistency with which China advances from one controlled tension to the other in pursuit of her long-range aims. For many more years Western analysts will be busy sticking their labels of orthodoxy or deviationism to the fall-out from Peking's verbal fire-works. There will also be justified fear lest her control of the tensions she had created should falter and war might result. Her continued exclusion from international councils will certainly not lessen such dangers. Such ostracism, rather than obstructing China's progress, is henceforth more likely both to retard the solution of problems concerning the security of all mankind, and to accelerate still further the menacing isolation of the West.

Western and especially American hostility towards China, however, could hardly be expected to change fundamentally before some uncomfortable though basic facts are faced.

In the perspective of history, the white man's presence and political power in Asia had been artificial and therefore transitory. Moreover, China being the neighbour of most Asian countries, and comprising half the continent's population, she is bound to become Asia's political centre of gravity: when these obvious facts are digested, the West may seek a new and more realistic posture in the new Asia. Until then, China's answer to the West's obstruction will be the continuous build-up of her internal strength for the coming struggle for supremacy. And during that period her diplomatic attention will be more usefully employed in the Afro-Asian world and especially on Asia's political fronts.

5 China and Asia: or the Iceberg of a Continent

WITH THE VICTORY of Communism in China, what was formerly a vacuum, inviting intrigue and adventure, was filled by a new force whose presence, interests and ambitions have begun to condition all Asia.

At the beginning, the external projection of that new power derived its main force from its alliance with the Soviet Union. One can now discern with some certainty the main outlines of the political strategy for Asia which Stalin and Mao must have worked out during their first meeting, in the spring of 1950.

Their common aim was to destroy American prestige on the continent, to drive away her physical power and, by doing so, to win over America's principal Asian bastion, China and Russia's common antagonist, Japan. Direct action in Korea and against

Taiwan were to be the main weapons. A diversionary move towards the south was to give help to the Viet-Minh. Simultaneously, revolutionary movements were to be encouraged and aided all over South-east Asia. If completely successful, the results would have been advantageous to both partners, particularly by removing the potential threat of Japan. Should, however, China run into difficulties, and Stalin's calculations probably included that possibility, he may have considered that Chinese involvement with the Americans would both weaken his giant neighbour and provide him with opportunities to act as a mediator.

As it happened, the historic American decision to fight in Korea rapidly frustrated the great design. Action against Taiwan took a correspondingly modified form. As for the revolutionary movements in South-east Asia, in most cases local nationalist forces triumphed over them. Finally, the plan yielded positive results in Viet-Nam only, where Western failure had driven nationalism and Communism into alliance.

This, the first phases of Chinese policy towards post-war Asia, drew to its end towards 1954. At the Geneva Conference, Chou En-lai emerged in his new role as Asia's flexible arbiter in face of, what appeared to be to most Asians, Dullesian rigidity. The turning point, of course, was not so clearly fixed in time. During the armistice negotiations both in Korea and in Indo-China, the Chinese had occasion to appreciate the usefulness of the backing of Asia's neutrals. China's military performance procured her great prestige before Asian public opinion and enhanced her authority on the continent. Finally, in face of the American-sponsored South-east Asian military alliance, China could mobilize with relative ease a coalition of Asian countries willing to consider the cessation of Western interference in Asian affairs as their urgent foreign political aim. The impact of these converging developments has probably convinced China that her attempt to win continental hegemony might be more successful if it relied on persuasion rather than on force. The platform to launch the new policy was provided by the Bandung Conference.

Little as is known about the inner workings of Peking's political councils, one cannot help feeling that this new phase in

Chinese policy towards Asia was very much the making of Mr. Chou En-lai. A man of subtle intellect, a Talleyrandian master of the diplomatic arts, and probably the one among China's leaders most aware of foreign opinion, he orchestrated the new campaign with outstanding virtuosity. From Geneva to Bandung, and from the reception of most Asian leaders in Peking, through repeated tours of South-east Asia, he established the Five Principles of neighbourly relations as China's new diplomatic emblem and, like an apostle of peaceful co-existence, he triumphantly harvested the sympathies of the continent. The West, without any constructive Asian policy, found itself increasingly on the defensive. The number of its Asian allies melted rapidly to a handful of personalities who were living contradictions of the principles the West professed to stand for.

Asian neutralism was powerfully encouraged, even in Japan. Everything was done to remove irritants from China's relations with the rest of the continent. Even the overseas Chinese were advised to take up the nationality of their countries of residence. Trade and aid were enlisted to support the new line. China became an Asian brother nation rather than a Communist Power. And the swelling sympathies all over the continent seemed indeed a more powerful diplomatic weapon than all the Asian revolutionary movements put together could have been.

But the honeymoon lasted barely five years. From the beginning of 1958 conciliation gradually gave way to truculence. Though continuing to be Premier, in February 1958, Chou En-lai ceased to be Foreign Minister as well. Whether this was mere coincidence or whether it was the real turning point, it would be difficult to tell, China's foreign policy began to change and neither its new objectives nor the causes of the new departure could be clearly defined.

In May 1958 the wooing of Japan came to a sudden halt with the 'flag incident' and the subsequent breaking off of trade relations. Soon after the crisis in the Taiwan Straits developed and continued to strain Asian opinion for several months. By the beginning of the following year there was fighting in Tibet and soon after relations with India were poisoned by the revelation of a long string of frontier incidents. Relations with Indonesia became stormy over Peking's violent reaction to measures designed to limit the influence of Chinese traders in that country. Even in the Middle East Peking's smiles were gradually replaced by hostile salvoes at President Nasser. In the meantime, towards Asia as towards the rest of the world, China's tone grew less compromising and even threatening. Much of the edifice built under the sign of peaceful co-existence fell in ruins. A great deal of Asian sympathy, so assiduously built up during the previous five years, has been thrown away.

Why did China change her tactics again? and why, in place of being liked, did she rather prefer to be feared?

In times of revolutionary change, a country's foreign policy is least likely to break completely with the past. There, geography, if nothing else, imposes a degree of continuity. Thus, in a sense, China has been going through the usual evolution which has followed the consolidation of new dynasties. Former frontiers at their maximum extent had been re-established. The old tributaries had been brought, or are being led into, China's new orbit. Dependence on Russia is slowly giving way to equality and that, it is hoped, may lead to supremacy later on. Thus, to satisfy the historical urge to become the Middle Kingdom again, the continental hegemony of China had to be reasserted in a fashion leaving no room for pretensions at equality, for rival methods of national emancipation or, above all, for the presence of a non-Asian military power challenging China's very existence.

In her internal development, by 1958 China was realizing with self-confidence that she could forge ahead with more revolutionary methods and with greater speed than she had expected in the past. That mood must have had its influence over her external strategy too. Moreover, Peking's leaders may have come to the conclusion that their diplomatic successes among Asia's neutrals have after all little furthered their ultimate objective, to remove the power of the United States from the Asian continent. The American bases remained and they had been equipped with even more dangerous arms.

Over Tibet, China's hands were forced by the spreading

revolt of the Khamba tribes. Perhaps there were provocations from some Indians. In any case the reception given to the Dalai Lama and the political exploitation tolerated around his activities, may have been construed as in contradiction with the Five Principles implying non-interference. Perhaps even Indian neutrality ceased to serve Peking's new purpose and it may have seemed more urgent to tilt towards China the allegiance of the small Kingdoms south of the Himalayas. As for Japan, notwithstanding growing neutralist sentiment, her alliance with the United States did not weaken. And the military threat represented by the anti-Communist Asian régimes sponsored by the U.S.A. was not really offset by the sympathies of their Asian neighbours.

The Chinese may have felt that for all these reasons the time had come for a new course, to force America's military presence out of Asia. This need not damage China's good relations with selected neutrals whose help may be further encouraged by economic aid. As for those who remain adamant—whether Japan, India or Indonesia—the new policy may even help to bring them under more hostile governments which, however, could be subverted more easily by propaganda and would leave in their wake far stronger revolutionary movements.

With her renewed drive for world-wide political polarization, China may indeed help in a number of Asian countries to bring into power governments sufficiently to the right to provide new opportunities for the reorganization and the rapid growth of their revolutionary movements. India, Burma, Malaya, as well as Indonesia, have frustrated Communist parties whose freedom of action at the moment, is severely limited. Under increasingly reactionary governments, they may once again become important. And they may gain that new strength at a moment when both China's greatly increased power would become manifest, and when disappointment would become generalized with the West's continued inability to help significantly their countries' economic progress.

If such or similar arguments were behind China's new course in Asia, then, both its stakes and its dangers were high. Moreover, its success was to depend on Soviet willingness to provide it with the indispensable nuclear shield. Indeed that co-operation was forthcoming, and it helped to achieve the diplomatic victory in the autumn of 1958, in the Taiwan Straits. Yet by the beginning of 1959 something evidently went wrong.

Mr. Khrushchev did not hide his irritation with China's actions along the Indian border. After China broke off her trade relations with Japan, Russia proposed the expansion of her exchange with that country. A little later the Soviet leader even had to undertake a journey across South-east Asia to try to repair some of the damage done to the Communist cause in that region by China's new belligerence. In fact, it was from the beginning of 1959, the time of the Sino-Indian frontier incidents that the doctrinal arguments between China and the Soviet Union began to mount towards their virulent crescendo of 1960.

Did things go wrong over China's treatment of India? was, perhaps, the full extent of the new Chinese line insufficiently defined to the Russians? isn't it possible that Soviet support was promised for action serving common aims, particularly the weakening of American power in Asia, but not for moves likely to alienate neutrals; in one word, that China has gone beyond what the U.S.S.R. had promised to caution?

The Bucharest ideological show-down, followed by signs—especially after the Communist 'Summit' in Moscow, in November 1960—that China was once again modifying her Asian policy, would seem to indicate that the 'misunderstanding' has been cleared up. There may be a new, concerted Sino-Soviet policy in Asia, more adjusted to the extent of Soviet willingness to take risks. Maybe there is only a transitory compromise to await the results of Mr. Khrushchev's attempts at reconciliation with Mr. Kennedy. Or, what is more likely, China is simply yielding *some* of the intransigence of her new Asian conception, in expectation of either her own atomic armament or of the definite failure of the Soviet policy of détente with the West.

Whichever hypothesis is nearest to reality, it is unlikely that the Chinese have lost faith in *all* the arguments which had induced their change of policy. China has powerful cards in her hands even without complete Soviet backing behind her actions in Asia. She may put less emphasis on military pressure and more on the economic, political and pan-Asian arguments at her disposal. Also, China must know that her growing influence and power in Asia leaves the West with scarcely any other positive policy on that continent but to offer support to neutralist régimes. That support, in the form of external guarantees in place of military bases in protected countries, would eminently suit China's purpose whether it is considered a final solution or merely a transitory phase before the neutrals begin to gravitate in her own orbit.[190]

Moreover, China's latest approach to inter-Asian relations may also be built on the basic assumption that her growing economic power, combined with her masses and with her geographic situation, make her role in Asia already comparable to that of an iceberg. Though only a part of it is yet noticeable on the surface, its immense mass already lies below every important problem concerning the future of that continent. Its real weight and influence may still be a matter of discussion, yet all plans may be wrecked which try to ignore the still submerged reality of her continental hegemony.[191]

If indeed such are the assumptions behind China's current diplomatic strategy in Asia, then, we are witnessing the beginning of her bid for influence over the potential power-house of future world domination. That potential power-house is made up of the three major countries of East Asia. And to control its levers involves China's relationship with Japan and India.

6 The Triangle of Decision

LET'S IMAGINE FOR a moment that from one of those outposts which will soon be deposited on the moon, someone, observing our earth, would try to locate the decisive changes in process, likely to transform its existing equilibrium of power.

From that distance, of course, he would see the essential only. He would note that neither in North America nor on its Latin twin are any transformations visible important enough to change, within a few years, the role of those continents in the world. Over the immense surface of Africa he would see new blots of colour, each representing a new state, without, however, any real modification in the productive capacity, the material equipment, or the power of their dispersed populations. In search of the decisive, then, his attention would inevitably turn to the dominant Eurasian land-mass.

In its heart, behind the rapid material progress and the imposing uniformity of the Soviet Union, he might discern the uncertainties of an approaching choice: between the temptation to continue the quest for the leadership of the underprivileged majority of mankind, and the equally tempting decision to harvest at last the fruits of decades of exertions and opt for a society of high mass-consumption.

To the left, in the West of the European peninsula, he would recognize the historic mosaic of nations. He would note the fragile tentacles groping across venerable borders in search of wider unity as well as Western Europe's remarkable economic vitality. Yet, trying to answer why that economic growth is un-accompanied by any corresponding extension of European influence, his telescope would point at a number of causes, ranging from economic contradictions in Western European relations with the rest of the world, to the paralysing influence of colonial rear-guard actions.

Then, in contrast with the hesitant pace of change all over these regions, at the other extremity of the Eurasian land-mass, he would come upon some unusual happenings. In fact, the masses moving around, the scale and speed of their activities, and the areas and the resources involved, would soon convince him that *it is there* that a new power centre is in the making. Examining its dimensions, he may even conclude that the new power centre emerging there, may not merely tilt the balance of the Eurasian axis but, within the foreseeable future, might alter the entire power-equilibrium of our world.

Inspired by the simplified strategic maps of newspapers, one might imagine a triangle with its angles at Tokyo, Peking and New Delhi. Without minimizing the importance of changes in Europe, America or Africa, one might call it *the triangle of decision*. Within it unfold the destinies of Japan, China and India, together with the smaller South-east Asian countries traditionally under their influence.

India alone is inhabited by nearly twice as many people as the whole of Africa. China, by more than the combined population of Europe and the Soviet Union. Japan, India and China together contain already 1,200 million people, or 40 per cent. of the world's present population. A bare fifteen years from now they will represent five of every ten inhabitants of our globe. And if the demographers' forecasts are to be·believed, before the end of this century the Indians, the Chinese, the Japanese, and the populations of South-east Asia, will, between them, account for well over half the world's population.

Demographic quantity, however, is not the sole index of the supreme importance of that triangle of decision. Within it three major civilizations adapt themselves to the imperatives of industrial society. It is there that the most impressive rates of material development hitherto known are being achieved. It is there, again, that unprecedented efforts are being made to transform illiterate peasants into qualified members of modern societies. Finally, it is within that triangle that are shaped those models of development which, because of their scale and originality, are bound to influence the thinking and the decisions of hundreds of millions of people on several continents.

What are, then, the likely developments within that triangle during the next few years? how will the evolution of the three major countries within that area influence each other and the 200 million others living in their shadow in South-east Asia? and, finally, how will the transformation of that region as a whole influence the future of the West and of the rest of the world?

China constitutes the 'heartland' of the East Asian triangle, henceforth barely vulnerable to the sea-power that had shaped the world's balance of power for the past four centuries. Her territorial and racial homogeneity is in striking contrast with the geographical or ethnic heterogeneity of most of her neighbours. In population, in natural resources, in the size of her internal market, as much as in the skill of her people, China alone in the region can aspire to build heavy industries on a scale, or even surpassing those, now possessed by two Great Powers only. For all these reasons the political, economic and psychological impact of China on East Asia is already considerable. In the next few years it is likely to become even greater. Yet how that growing impact will shape the future East Asia, will depend primarily on China's relations with Japan and India.

Being at very different stages of their development, China's impact on them is likely to take very different forms.

Perhaps the most remarkable contribution to civilization by the Japanese is their art of camouflaging the ugliness of poverty. Thanks to their remarkably evenly spread aesthetic sense, they can render poverty less repulsive and therefore more tolerable. Agreeable as this is to the eye, it can mislead many visitors. After nearly a century of industrialization Japan is still a poor country. Her living standards are somewhere half-way between that of China and of north-west Europe. A recent White Paper revealed that at least one in every ten families have to live on a monthly income of 8,000 yen (about £8), or far below subsistence level. The reasons are simple. Ninety-five million Japanese crowd four islands which together are little more than half the size of France. The islands are very poor in raw materials and only a fifth of their surface can be cultivated. Already a fifth of Japan's food has to be imported and her population still grows by about a million each year.

Japan was the first non-Western country to accomplish its industrial take-off. To compensate for her lack of raw-materials, she went in search of them across the seas. And the areas she conquered also served as markets for her manufactured goods. Like Great Britain before her, and for similar reasons, Japan was bound to import her raw materials and send manufactured goods abroad. But while British expansion was at the expense of distant continents, Japan colonized the countries of her Asian neighbours.

After 1945 Japan lost her colonies and thus her protected markets. But thanks to the industry of her people, to American aid, to industrial modernization, and to the absence of large-scale defence expenditure, Japan fast recovered and, in fact, has never been more prosperous. Her industries and her national income during these past few years have grown nearly as fast as China's and she now exports more than ever before.

Yet, notwithstanding all these achievements, the Japanese live in fear of the future. And the causes of their anxiety are both psychological and economic.

The first defeat and occupation in Japan's long history have abruptly broken the nation's mental continuity. Half-pleased by the sudden release from a disciplined existence, and half-terrified by the dangers implied by drift, the Japanese of today are like the crew of a boat who have suddenly lost faith in the reliability of their trusted compass. The post-war enthusiasm for everything foreign has gone too far and by now, visibly, the pendulum is swinging back. The nation is searching for its new course and no sudden change can be ruled out. Meanwhile, the liberal wind and the American influences have scarcely penetrated to the villages where the majority live. The traditional hierarchical structures of Japanese society remained intact. The basic and hard realities of Japanese existence have not changed. And the spiritual vacuum left behind by the collapse of the pre-war mental world of the Japanese is there to be filled by any formula able to offer a new ideal and, simultaneously, to provide economic security as well.

For economic insecurity is, probably, the major component in the fear of the future of the Japanese. Its roots run deep into the changes imposed on the Japanese by their defeat.

One of its main causes is in the artificial shift of Japan's post-war trade away from Asia. Before the war over half of Japan's imports came from Asia (including her possessions on the continent), and nearly two-thirds of her exports went there. Loss of her empire and restrictions on trade with China, imposed by the Americans, have drastically changed what was a natural trade pattern. Today, in contrast, Japan's trade is dispersed over the United States, South-east Asia, and other far-away areas scattered all over the globe. Raw materials which used to come from neighbouring Asia now have to be carried across oceans; and often hard currency is needed to pay for them. So Japan has to rely on an increasingly vulnerable network of trade while both her population and her appetite for better living are growing. Political complications in the Far East, sharper competition in South-east Asia, or a prolonged recession in the United States— and the whole delicate structure may be upset. The result would be even more Japanese unemployed, even less chance to get a job, still lower living standards, and in all probability, the collapse of still fragile post-war political institutions.

But two further factors contribute to that anxiety. Within eighty years—and while her population trebled—Japan transformed herself from a society in which four out of every five of the population lived and worked on the land into one where, today, only two in every five remain there. This feat of rapid industrialization was certainly an inspiration for the rest of Asia. And it is only natural that Japan's self-confidence was flattered by the conviction that her method of modernization made her an example to the Asian continent. But now another system seems to offer even quicker results and appears to be even more adapted to conditions prevailing in Asia and beyond.

Then, there is the question of scientific personnel. China, as Russia before her, is building up a considerable framework for scientific education and already turns out scientists and technicians on an impressive scale. Japan achieved her industrial supremacy in Asia by what may be called 'imitative' methods. But to retain her lead she ought by now to move towards 'inventive' methods. In other words, instead of mere industrial quantity, Japan should now be planning to export more and more technological quality. But to achieve this there should already have been large-scale investment in education and research. Instead there is already a shortage of highly qualified technicians and Japanese industry increasingly relies on imported patents.[192] The Government of Japan is now spending on scientific research only a third of the amount that was expended on it before the war.

All this is, for the time being, camouflaged by the growing volume of Japan's exports as well as by continuing American aid.[193] In the background, however, there is the increasing fear of what the future will bring. That, together with Peking's propaganda, is responsible for Japan's growing 'China complex'. There is a vague but widespread impression that something decisive is happening in Asia and that Japan, an Asian power, is prevented from sharing in it. The anxious feeling grows that Japan may find herself cut off from both the motive ideas and the results of that great transformation. And beyond it all looms the danger that one day China may squeeze Japan out of her essential Asian markets.

Most Japanese look upon China's transformation with feelings ranging from incredulity to dazed admiration. They are surprised to discover that the China they once regarded as little more than a potential colony, may soon overtake them in production. The 1958 trade drive in South-east Asia came as a great shock and a foretaste of things to come. Meanwhile, Sino-Japanese trade-promotion societies promise prosperity *and* security once China's coal and ores can be bartered for Japanese equipment. If they welcome the rapid growth of Japan's heavy industries as a source of new employment, they also fear that it will further increase the country's economic vulnerability. For the same reason, they argue, Japan will be only the more in need of the Chinese market with its unlimited capacity to absorb industrial equipment. That China will have sufficient surpluses of raw materials for barter notwithstanding her own fast rate of industrialization is usually taken for granted. Be it as it may, respected Japanese industrialists, as well as politicians, make their pilgrimages to Peking. And they usually come back with vague but spectacular promises for the future.

In the meantime, Japan is facing some crucial years for simple demographic, if for no other, reasons. The energetic post-war measures of birth-control have checked the population explosion. It is foreseeable already that around 1985 Japan's population will reach its high-water mark—with about 104 million—before it will begin its decline. Very soon, however, there will be significant changes in the age structure of the population. Its immediate result will be that during the next few years the number of those reaching working age will be superior to the expected number of births.

Japan's land is already grossly overpopulated. Under-employment is extensive and the productivity of small-holdings is rather low. The industrial sector is of a dual nature: next to very large, modern and efficient industries, there are vast numbers of medium and small-scale enterprises on an artisanal level, whose production is uneconomic, whose existence is precarious, and where under-employment is endemic. Of the twelve million newcomers who will swell the labour force in the next ten years, fast growing modern industry won't be able to absorb even half. The majority will have to join the already under-employed or the unemployed in the agricultural or in the small enterprise sectors. The political impact is bound to be considerable. It is likely to accentuate the already widespread fear of the future. And, inevitably, it will render even more acute the political passions which urge Japan towards great decisions.

Simultaneously, the undercurrents of neutralism are steadily widening. The traumatic experience of Hiroshima and Nagasaki, the continued American occupation of Okinawa, the hysterical fear of involvement in an unwanted nuclear war, together with the inevitable irritations of a long occupation, are all there ready to be exploited by anyone who wishes to mobilize latent anti-American, anti-white and pan-Asian sentiments.[194] Any jolt in the international trade structure can demonstrate the extreme economic vulnerability of post-war Japan. Meanwhile, across the water is China, the embodiment of the ideological certainty Japan seeks, and a country with whom the ties of economics, culture and thought have a history of many centuries.

Will Japan persist in her vulnerable existence on the margins of the continent whose leader she once wished to be? will she once again seek a solution of her problems in external expansion? will she yield to the growing demand for a neutral posture between the West and the Asian continent? would a political shift to the left be the pre-condition of such a precarious neutrality, or would the Japanese accept it with greater self-confidence under the guidance of their traditional ruling classes? or will Japan, one day, strike a bargain with China and, compensating for her strategic and numerical inferiority by her temporary industrial advance, attempt to dominate jointly what the white man used to rule in Asia?

There is no ready answer to such questions. All that is probable is that of all the factors likely to influence Japan's course, China's impact will be the most decisive.

As for India, until the transformation of Tibet into a military platform, she has been a neighbour of China on the maps only. Snowy peaks and empty regions kept them apart, with little trade and barely more cultural intercourse. But today the two countries have live frontiers. Moreover, after China, India is next on the list of the large, economically backward countries attempting their take-off. She tries to do with her own methods what—on a comparable scale—hitherto only Communist organization could accomplish. Should she be able to achieve a rhythm of material progress acceptable to her people, without the Communists' forced march, she will have demonstrated to all the under-developed countries the existence of an alternative method. That, in a nutshell, is the significance of India's experiment. But will India succeed?

In spite of all the dams, the bridges, the locomotives, and the industrial plants built in the course of two Five-Year Plans, the Indian masses have no real sense of participation in the efforts made by their country. They have not yet been shaken out of their apathy. Notwithstanding all the incontestable achievements since 1947, they have failed to create that dynamism or that sense of sharing in a common adventure which—in a country with India's problems—seems to be the pre-condition of any real progress.

Figures available as much as personal observations confirm that impression.[195] The progress, though remarkable in some fields, has been, as a whole, incomparably slower than in China. And the main reason is probably in the fact that while a number of secondary problems have claimed attention, most of the country's *basic* problems remain untackled. It is this failure to deal with basic problems that makes so many Indians feel that the progress of the past twelve years has done little to change their own conditions of life or their children's prospects for the future.

According to serious estimates more than a third of India's immense agricultural population is either under-employed or has no work at all. Two Five-Year Plans have not made the least difference, so far, to this mass-unemployment in the countryside. On the contrary, thanks to the taming of murderous diseases the yearly population increase, less than 5 million in 1952, is now approaching 9 million each year. India just cannot save enough to provide a livelihood for all those tens of millions of unemployed. Nor can foreign aid supply the needed equipment. Existing and archaic 'cottage industries' offer no serious solution. On the other hand, taken as a whole, the idle hours of the partially or totally unemployed represent an immense untapped capital. Suitably invested in constructive projects, it could bring bigger changes to the subcontinent than all the machines India may hope to buy or to build. China's example shows that this can be done. That example applied in a less rigorous way, would not necessarily destroy the essentials of democracy.

Then, in carrying out her industrialization plans, India has relied too much on the creation of large units. They employ relatively few workers and they absorb large amounts of capital and precious foreign exchange on which they are slow to return a dividend in the shape of finished products. In any case, the large plants alone cannot be bought and built fast enough to keep up with the rapid modernization programme that India needs.

The pace of India's progress is bound to remain disappointingly slow if she has to wait until all the latest types of tools and utensils can be supplied by her own modern factories. Small-scale, decentralized, modern industries—relying more on labour than on big machines—would be better suited to satisfy the demand for simple goods. As China's example shows again, they would give work to more men and would leave big plants free to support the momentum of further industrialization.

The third basic problem concerns the occupation of seven out of every ten Indians. It is the failure to tackle the problem of agriculture that is the most immediate threat to India's further progress. Decades of malnutrition, exploitation and indebtedness, coupled with continuing impoverishment of the soil hungry for water and chemicals, make the output of the Indian cultivator pitifully low even compared to his least efficient Asian neighbours. Yet in 1956 a World Bank mission estimated that India's agricultural output could increase three to fivefold. To achieve that increase the Indian peasant would have to collect more natural fertilizers and he would have to dig many more irrigation canals. He would have to be taught improved methods of cultivation and to be provided with cheap credit facilities and cooperatives to free him of the usurer's iron grip. He ought to work much harder to improve his land and, to do so, he ought to feel that a really honest land reform would allow him to reap benefits proportionate with his efforts.

To arrive there, a series of bold and overdue reforms would be needed. Without them, and despite some isolated successes, the much-publicized 'village community schemes' were condemned to fail. The extent of that tragic failure has been reflected by the recent report of the agricultural experts of the Ford Foundation. They warned that, given the rapid increase in population, between now and 1965 India's output of food grains ought to rise by over 9 per cent. each year (about the rate of present increase in China, according to official figures), to meet only essential needs. If food production continues to rise only at its present rate of 2 to 3 per cent. a year, the gap between supply and subsistence demand will be about 25 per cent. within five years. 'No conceivable programme of imports or rationing can meet a crisis of this magnitude,' was the report's alarming conclusion.[196]

The major obstacles to India's agricultural progress, however, are human rather than natural. The existing economic and social structure of Indian agriculture rather than to stimulate the cultivator's initiative, tends to discourage it. The majority of legislators in India's central parliament or in her provincial assemblies are either landowners and money-lenders themselves, or are spokes-men of their interests. They could hardly be expected to legislate the abolition of their own economic and social privileges. That, in its turn, explains much of the widespread disillusionment with the parliamentary régime. The frustrated apathy of the Indian masses is their verdict on a system which has failed to tackle their country's basic problems and seems even to expose them to large-scale famine.

Parliamentary democracy survived in South-east Asia so long as a dominant party could continue to fill the role of the unchal-lengeable imperial authority. Its prestige was usually derived from the part it had played in national liberation. Its leaders were often national heroes. But once disillusionment with unkept promises set in, once an opposition had grown sufficiently strong to chal-lenge the ruling party's monopoly of power, the days of parlia-mentary democracy were numbered. A jolt, like the collapse of raw material prices, and the dictators stepped in. This is what happened during the past few years in one after the other of the South-east Asian countries. This is, in fact, what is likely to happen in most of the decolonized countries. India's immediate neigh-bours were no exception. In India, too, the Congress Party's monopoly of power is now increasingly challenged. Only Mr. Nehru's continued presence at its head counterbalances its fast growing unpopularity. Yet the principal support of Indian democracy is ageing and the problem of his successor dominates the political scene. In this situation, even in India, the trend to-wards authoritarian government may be hastened by some unexpected shock. A large-scale famine would certainly be one. Should such a shock occur simultaneously with Mr. Nehru's disappearance from public life, the survival of parliamentary government in India would soon be at stake.

Paradoxically enough, it is the democratic system—and the planning through persuasion rather than through force—which is invoked to justify India's sluggish rate of economic growth compared to that of China. But notwithstanding that slower rate of progress, already during her second Plan, India had to fall back on large-scale foreign aid to realize even much reduced targets.

As for the third Plan, about to begin, though it still promises incomparably slower economic progress than in China, no less than one-third of its total cost is expected to be contributed by foreign assistance. Should it not be forthcoming in the desired volume—7 milliard dollars in five years—the Plan's targets would have to be scaled down and rising unemployment and frustrated hopes might drive Indians towards more efficient expedients. But even if foreign aid is forthcoming on anything like the expected scale, many of the planners' assumptions may turn out to have been much too optimistic. Imports of food might divert larger funds from industrialization than foreseen. Defence costs, already abnormally high owing to unsettled disputes with Pakistan, will further grow to the extent that the borders with China need further reinforcement. Thus, increased regimentation and more austerity may be necessary even if foreign aid contributes an important proportion of the third Plan's cost. It seems indeed more and more doubtful whether the take-off of a society of India's size and problems is compatible at all with a north-Atlantic type of parliamentary system and with the democratic liberties usually associated with it.

That India encounters so much greater difficulties than China in her attempt at modernization has a wide variety of reasons. They range from climate, and the biological heritage of endemic famine, to centrifugal ethnic and linguistic forces, and to stagnant illiteracy and ignorance. Yet there has been no really serious attempt to help the purely economic, with a genuine educational and social take-off as well, and the causes of that failure are in the economic and social structure of Indian society itself.

Mr. Nehru, Indian by birth but his formation deeply marked by British liberal ideas, has tended to act, as it were, as the first Indian Viceroy of independent India. He has been more concerned to stabilize than to prepare internal forces for fast enough change. His task would not have been easy. Yet in face of the existing coalition of the forces of conservation, nobody else has commanded, or is likely to command in the foreseeable future, any comparable degree of authority or the trust of the masses. Whatever external prestige his statesmanship could gain for

India, it does not compensate for unsolved basic problems at home. Their solution, however, becomes each day more urgent. It calls for nothing less than a revolution in India's economic and social structure. Even with large-scale foreign aid, that transformation will have to be directed by new men with new ideas. This would require the organized pressures of a disciplined mass movement. Its leaders would have to be sufficiently dynamic and would have to inspire enough confidence to be able to change the traditional way of life of 400 million Indians dispersed in their half-million villages.

There is no sign that any such dynamic new force is emerging in India. Yet the country's basic economic problems have to be tackled soon if an explosion is to be averted. India can and should feed herself. The country can and should within a few years, reach the self-sustaining stage of economic development where it ought to finance its needs through the export of both its raw material surpluses and its industrial products. Population pressure, the decay of the Congress Party, together with the proportionate dangers of territorial fragmentation, call for swift action. As in Japan, then, though for very different reasons, some fateful decisions will have to be taken within a few years.

Frustration with the leisurely pace of progress, implied by the parliamentary system, is preparing the Indian masses for more authoritarian methods in the hope that they might yield faster results. At present, however, the country's commercial and industrial classes—with more or less open reliance on the Army— are best placed to apply those methods. But without Mr. Nehru's liberal influence, they would be even less likely to carry out overdue economic and agrarian reforms and, in all probability, would limit the scope of economic planning in favour of wider liberty for the free enterprise system. But would not the origins and the interests of such a régime fatally condemn it to repeat the Kuomintang's performance in China? and inversely, noting the prestige and the independence of action China had gained, would informed Indian opinion comply with the fast growing external influences over their government, implicit in increasing dependence on foreign loans and private investments?

On the other hand, if government by the traditional ruling class, or by the Army, fails to satisfy hopes, may not, then, ideologies offering different and more efficient methods seduce the masses? yet once the need for such a new approach is admitted —whether in the utilization of idle labour, the recasting of agricultural structures, or in the mobilization of the enthusiasm of the masses—would not its sponsors inevitably be driven to imitate China's example in the solution of comparable problems? In that case, again, would not India's Communists—already widely supported in some regions—be able to exploit discontent as well as ethnic and linguistic rivalries, and offer themselves as best qualified to carry out those organizational tasks? And, finally, should such developments lead to internal strife or to the eventual fragmentation of India, would China refrain from lending her support to friendly elements among the border regions' ethnic minorities, or in India as a whole?

Once again, there is no ready answer to such questions. What is probable is that among all the external factors which will influence India's course, China's impact will be decisive.

It is thus impossible to foresee in what direction events will go within that triangle of decision. Their interdependence, however, is obvious. Yet, in case of the least favourable constellation of developments for the West, it is conceivable that China, Japan, India and South-east Asia—with or without the Soviet Union— may emerge one day as a group with sufficiently homogeneous economic and political interests to bring about a major change in the world's existing balance of power.

Japan as well as India will move under the influence of their own political, economic and psychological imperatives. South-east Asia, vulnerable as it is, will endure rather than shape the evolution. Understandably, China will do her utmost to encourage developments in a way most favourable to her interests. Her power to do so will grow each day. As for the West's chances effectively to counter the temptation of the alternative world organization sponsored by the Communists, it could scarcely improve significantly without fundamental modifications in the West's economic concepts.

As long as each time the West's economy coughs the whole non-Communist world risks catching pneumonia, the seduction of the economic stability offered by the Communists will not cease to grow. If the enormous lead still held by the West in 1945 has been narrowing so fast, that has primarily been the reason. Much of the room so vacated has been filled in by hesitation, neutrality or by nothing more than a vacuum. Yet Western influence is receding and the regions of neutrality and hesitation are expanding at a time when mankind is approaching the biggest crisis in its history. In the minds of hundreds of millions of people the importance of politics or of ideology are eclipsed by the preoccupation of procuring their daily food. Between the West's shrinking world organization and the expanding one of the Communist bloc, the hesitants, lacking the instruments of their own emancipation, will inexorably begin to gravitate towards the side able to offer a method which can provide them with elementary dignity and with food for survival. Racial arrogance, rivalry, as much as the structures of Western economies, have hitherto prevented the emergence of a coherent Western philosophy about the world's economically backward areas. The Communist Powers have one. Whatever its shortcomings, it is reinforced by the power of example.

In possession of such a philosophy, the West's offer may once again become competitive. If it includes the method and the organization for the ordered emancipation and the systematic take-off into industrialization of the world's economically backward masses, then, the West will cease fighting rearguard actions in its retreat towards isolation. Until then, the rival power centre will continue to extend its influence. Within that influence, however, China's shadow will not cease to grow. Neither the attempt to ignore her existence, nor efforts to hinder her progress, will prevent her from becoming, by the last quarter of this century, the decisive factor in human affairs. And, ideology being unable to transcend power politics, by that time, China may even emerge as the new, third, and major power centre of the world.

EPILOGUE

AND SO ON . . . The ardour and the endurance continue. Laughing faces, hygienic nurseries and rising production curves will exhale optimism. The dissenters, the hesitant, or those unable to stand the pace will disappear on the way. The haters of injustice will applaud the effort of a nation claiming its rightful place under the sun. Millions of words will be spoken and be printed to repeat that China is groaning under terror. Those able to simplify the infinitely complex will go on welcoming the millennium. Honest men will continue to call the world's attention to the less attractive by-products of a nation's titanic endeavour to catch up with the more fortunate segments of mankind. The less honest will persist in seeing those by-products only, and nothing else. Words like liberation and slavery will be hurled against each other again and again. Dogma and idealism, intolerance and compassion, will remain intertwined. The existence of people, families and of whole communities will be upset, changed and recast again.

Yet mothers will continue to sing to put their babies to sleep; people will laugh at acrobats in circuses; and the Chinese opera will be sold out as before. Men and women will continue to hate or to be generous, to marry, to celebrate old and new holidays with food and drink, or to weep at funerals. The Chinese, like all other people before them, are shaping their future in the joy of enthusiasm and the tears of suffering. Meanwhile, their skill, their discipline, their devotion and their heroism should be acknowledged, their sacrifice admired, and their progress recorded. From the two equally distorted pictures of the terrifying and the admirable China, slowly, the three-dimensional real China will emerge, as if a stereoscope were being focused. It will be neither frightening nor angelic. It will be human.

It seems to me unnecessary to end this account with personal judgments. 'The meddling of values in world history,' in the words of Jacob Burckhardt, 'is as if in the sea of time one wave wanted to shout insults against all other waves.' I prefer to end on two personal recollections; on two chance-encounters in the China of ten years after the greatest turn in her long history.

The first was in a prison, in Central Asia, with a young man from Shanghai, serving the first of a twelve year sentence for 'sabotage' in Sinkiang's oil-fields.

A heavy snowfall upset the prearranged programme and left me with an unexpected free afternoon in Urumchi. I asked my Uighur interpreter whether he could arrange for me to visit the local prison. He came back from the telephone saying that the director of the prison thought that there was nothing interesting to inspect in his establishment. I told the interpreter that the Prime Minister himself authorized me to visit any prison in the country. A few minutes later he came back saying that soon a car would come to pick us up.

An hour later a man of the Security Department arrived. He was a massive, melon-faced brute who tried hard to conceal his personality behind an irritating, high-pitched giggle. In his car we travelled for about two hours across the most desolate, frozen scenery I had ever seen. It was a perfect introduction to China's remotest gaol.

Once inside the high wall, we were ushered into the director's office. It was a small and nude room, with a shaft of light falling from the small window to the stone floor as its only decoration. In blue tunic and blue cap, the director was sitting behind a pile of *People's Dailies*. He was correct but not friendly. On his right stood the prison warden, his face pock-marked and with a broken boxer's nose. We sat down in our coats and fur hats, and the thick mugs of tea served to warm our hands.

The director's answers to my questions were stiff and succinct.

His prison was the only one in Sinkiang and it held 325 inmates. They were common criminals and 'reactionaries'. To my question what the crimes of reactionaries were, his answer was crisp: 'They organized resistance against the authorities, as during the agrarian reform, they even killed cadres; or they had been working for the Kuomintang.' When I enquired if there were reactionaries condemned for lighter crimes, the warden shook his head in visible disapproval of my insistence. 'They are condemned for conspiracy or reactionary organization,' the director said in his cold and hard voice. 'But what is the definition of reactionary organization?' I asked. The irritation of the warden now became obvious, and the Security Department man in the background emitted a short, condescending giggle before he went on sipping his tea with the noise of a motor-cycle racing across the room. 'Everybody knows what reactionary organization is . . .' the director replied unperturbed.

He supplied some more information and figures. After that I wondered if I could see prisoners with my interpreter only. 'That's impossible, we shall come with you,' he ruled and we got up. We walked across the snow of the court-yard and entered a nearby large building. It was not less friendly than other prisons. There was an armed guard in the tower above the main gate but there were no bars on the windows. In that part of Sinkiang, in any case, it would have been a hopeless enterprise to try an escape. We walked along a corridor and I stopped in front of one of the doors. The room we entered was big and about half of the twenty prisoners in it were working on sewing machines. The other half were busy cutting blue cloth along long tables. I asked if there was anyone there sentenced to death. The answer was that all those condemned to death had seen their sentence commuted to life imprisonment and that there were six cases of that kind.

I was led to a woman of about forty-five, who abandoned her scissors and faced us passively. She explained in a colourless voice that her husband, now dead, was the feudal lord of a district and when she had inherited the land she denounced people to Chiang Kai-shek's police. She had a pale and wicked face, making her story quite credible. Did she kill? I asked her. She looked at the director, at the Security Department man, at the warden and, finally, she turned towards me: 'No, I did not kill with my hands. But I gave lists of names to the police and that was as much as killing.' Then, with barely concealed hatred, she turned and continued her work. The others were either thieves, ordinary criminals, or 'reactionaries', offering almost identical stories. A man described as a 'reactionary bandit' turned out to have violated young girls. He was most amused by the misunderstanding. We moved on. I entered other rooms and heard about the same stories. Evidently, such a visit, in the presence of all the officials, could hardly yield any interesting results. We were in the corridor again and the warden suggested that I should visit the dormitories. They were heated, he insisted with pride. The walls of the corridor were plastered with production charts, red flags and with the hand-painted sheets of individual resolutions, similar to those I had seen in offices and factories all over China. The director was explaining that every morning and evening the prisoners had to study; it was 'Socialist education', he added. Next to sewing, the prisoners were also making bricks, and, just across the courtyard, a new carpet factory was under construction.

In that moment, there was sudden wild noise made by drums and cymbals. I asked if I could see what was happening but the director dismissed it as of no interest. Some prisoners were preparing for a theatrical performance, he explained. I insisted. We walked down the corridor towards the music and I opened the door.

The room was obscure and, if possible, still colder than the rest of the building. Two men and two girls were moving in line, lifting their legs like show-girls on the stage. Each wore tall, red paper helmets and their shabby padded clothes were decorated with garlands made of coloured paper. One of the girls was drumming and the younger of the two men was wildly beating together the brass plates. It was after a few seconds only that they noticed that we had entered. They stopped. There was sudden silence and they looked at us with the consternation of children caught unawares. As my eyes got used to the dimness, I looked amazed at the spectacle before I could distinguish their features. The girls looked vulgar and the director explained that they were petty thieves. The middle-aged man, still visibly gay, was described as a 'reactionary captain'. The younger man was slender and strikingly handsome. There was something in his features that made him an alien figure among the prisoners I had seen. They stood there panting after their romp and one could see their breath as if it were cigarette smoke. The carnival atmosphere was in macabre contrast with the dirty, thick walls and with the dead silence after our eruption on the scene.

'So the two men are politicals,' I asked the director. He presented the 'reactionary captain' first. He was a captain in the Kuomintang police and, masquerading as a plain-clothed policeman, he had committed crimes against the People long after 1949. 'I was caught in 1955 only. I have one more year to serve,' he said willingly. As for the girls, they admitted freely that they were caught stealing. Their story was credible. They looked like it. Then, I turned to the young man.

Somewhat timidly he explained that he was twenty-one and that he had eleven more years to spend in prison. 'I was a reactionary,' he said answering my question.

'Where did you commit your crime?'

'In the oil-fields in the north.'

To my question what exactly he did, his reply was that he spread rumours. But following a questioning look at the warden, in a soft and respectful voice, he added: '. . . and I committed sabotage.'

I enquired what kind of sabotage it was. 'I organized a reactionary group and incited workers,' he listed like a good pupil.

'Where do you come from?'

'Shanghai . . .' he replied on a guilty tone, looking down at the stone floor. 'Shanghai, of course . . .' the melon-faced commissar repeated with his high-pitched giggle.

'What was your father?' I continued.

After some hesitation the boy answered: 'He had no profession . . .'—and his voice was hardly audible. What was his father doing now, I asked, but it was the director who answered: 'He now works on the land. He is a peasant near Shanghai. . . .' The young man dutifully repeated: 'He is a peasant . . .'

'Do your parents know where you are?' I addressed him again.

'I don't know . . .', was his cautious answer.

'Don't you write to them?'

He looked at the director again as if in search of guidance. 'I do . . . but not too often . . .'—he spelled it out at last.

'They don't answer?'

The boy looked down, uncomfortable. The director gave a disapproving cough. There was a moment of dead silence. The 'reactionary captain' profited to take the copper plates from his comrade's hands. 'It takes a long time. . .', the young man said finally while the captain placed the cymbals in a corner of the room.

'Did you live in a comfortable house in Shanghai?' I asked.

He nodded approvingly and then, once his eyes met the warden's, he quickly completed it: 'Not during the last years. . . .'

'Can you give some details of the sabotage you have committed?' I changed the subject.

'He organized a reactionary group and spread rumours', the hard voice of the director forestalled his answer. And the warden took it up on a still harsher tone: 'He wanted to become a bandit in the mountains.' Leaning against the wall, the boy looked pale and he was biting his lips. The 'reactionary captain' gently took off the young man's paper helmet and held it for him.

'How did you get from Shanghai to the oil-fields here?' I asked.

'I left school and there was a call for volunteers,' he explained on a more self-confident tone. 'I wanted to help to build up the interior of the country.'

'You wanted to come?' I repeated.

'Of course,' he replied much louder.

'How long were you there when you were caught?'

'Less than a year.'

'Was the work hard?' I enquired.

'Work in the oil-field is not hard for those with the right attitude,' the director answered in his place.

'Did you have a trial?'

'Yes.'

'Did you have the right to defend yourself?'

His fine face looked helpless. He swallowed hard and peered at the director. Then, with the relief of the right answer found, he replied: 'Yes, of course, but I did not want to use it.'

Surprised, I exclaimed: 'Why?' In a soft, barely audible voice again, he said: 'I was guilty. . . .' A moment of silence descended. The melon face of the Security Department man split into a grin in my direction, implying, no doubt, that the time had come to leave.

'Would you have preferred to work near your parents?' I asked.

'No. I preferred to come to build the interior.'

'But you didn't do it. . . .' I remarked with a smile.

'He got into bad company,' the Security man interjected and followed it up with his high-pitched giggle.

The director was beginning to move to break up the conversation. I asked for one more question. 'You will be thirty-two when you'll leave this building,' I turned to the young man again. 'What will you do then?'

A fleeting smile lit up his face and he answered almost eagerly: 'That depends on the State, on what the State will want me to do.' And quickly he added: 'That depends in what way I could be useful to the country. . . .'

We shook hands. 'I am going to Shanghai,' I said. 'Do you think that I could tell your parents that I have met you?'

He looked at me in a reflective mood. For a moment his face softened in an adolescent shape and then, quickly, he steadied himself: 'They won't be there. . . . I don't think that you could see them . . .' and, almost instinctively, with the perfect manners of the well-to-do Shanghai bourgeois' son, he muttered with a slight bow: 'But thank you very much. . . .'

We moved towards the door. 'The years will pass quickly and you will be still a young man when you restart your life,' I remarked while we shook hands again. He seemed less tense and even smiled. And as I looked back at him from the corridor, I was not at all sure whether he knew what price he was paying for being allowed to fit in.

That was in Sinkiang. The other encounter took place in Peking. It was no more than a brief exchange of words. It happened in a terribly crowded tram-car yet, paradoxically, it was my only conversation in China with someone all alone.

On a Sunday afternoon, after a walk in the gardens of the Temple of Heaven, I decided to take the tram to return to my hotel. The streets were full with Sunday promenaders and when the tram stopped I had a hard time to push my way into its interior. As the doors closed, we stood like sardines, each body held steady by the combined pressure of all the others. The general noise was dominated by the hoarse voice of the woman ticket-collector. In an interminable flow of words she informed customers of the price of the ride and of the name of the next stop, all mixed up with comradely exhortations to let her penetrate the human wall in pursuit of her professional duties. Most of the passengers seemed to be provincial visitors, massive, hard-featured peasants, some of them in fur hats. I could feel their breath on my neck and their strength on my ribs as they were trying to extricate and to lift their hands holding the coins. After a stop, as the ticket-collector charged again, there was a slight movement and, like in a kaleidoscope, one was forced on, surrounded by new faces. What attracted my attention first to the man facing me was, I think, his spectacles. Their thin gold rim seemed strangely delicate after several weeks in China. My nose almost touched it. The face was slim and sad, with nervously fine features. It was the kind of head one associated with ivory carvings. I kept on peering at him each time our heads parted a little, as the tram rattled on. Then, my turn came to pay and when I raised my arm I had slightly hit his glasses.

'Excuse me . . .' I said automatically. He nodded with a kindly smile, implying that he did not mind. I was looking at him with curiosity, almost inviting him to talk.

'Tourist?' he asked.

'Journalist . . .' I answered, speaking almost into his ear. The ticket-collector just shouting at the top of her voice, I thought the moment opportune to carry on. 'Official?' I asked.

'Professor at the University . . .' he replied pressed over my shoulder. Then, with the noise continuing, I remarked: 'You speak good English. . . .'

The tram was taking a turn, wildly swinging its human cargo. 'Learnt it in America . . .' he muttered as his face was almost touching my head.

The car stopped, a few passengers got off and new ones clambered in. We were pushed on together. When the girl began her exhortations again, I was driven still closer to him and profited of the occasion: 'Your family came back too?' The tram bumped on and as his head thrust near my face, he said almost in a whisper: 'They are in Hong Kong . . .' and looked towards his neighbour as if to check whether his voice could be heard that far.

I waited for the next favourable position: 'Are you glad you came back?' I said in a subdued voice as my forehead touched his glasses. I could see his fine face turn reflective. Then, in the next bend, I could hear his faint voice over my face: 'It's hard, very hard. . . .'

We kept silent for a little while, each of us watching our neighbours. They appeared unaware that we were exchanging words. The ticket-collector was continuing her verbal bombardment. 'Wouldn't you like to be with your family?' I murmured as my lips were near his ear. He waited with his face expressionless. The next time when he had to lean towards me, he said: 'My place is here . . .' and his face being so near I could see its muscles nervously hardening. Behind me a giant was trying to reach his pocket and his elbow pushed me forward. 'You said it was hard, very hard . . .' I said softly, on a questioning tone.

A stop was approaching and a new movement was driving us still closer together. 'Yes, very hard . . .'—I heard in my ear his curiously grave whisper, 'but they are doing what had to be done. . . .'

I had the impression that his sentence was not finished, but we were separated in the jostling. We drifted apart and I was surrounded by new faces. We were approaching the Imperial Palace. I had to find my way to the door. At the next stop I got off.

From the street I looked back, hoping that I could wave him goodbye. I recognized his greying hair as he stood there pressed together in the crowd of passengers. But I could see his back only; a figure in the blue tunic, like all the others.

NOTES

1. According to the April 5, 1955, editorial of the *People's Daily* (*Jen-min Jih-pao*), Peking, planning work began in the spring of 1955. The first full outline of the Plan, however, was published on July 8, 1955, only. It appeared in the same journal under the signature of Li Fu-chun, Chairman of the State Planning Commission. The basic document was published in the following month.

2. These two celebrated campaigns took place between October, 1951, and June 1952. The 'five anti' were aimed at bribery, tax-evasion, fraud, theft of state property, and leakage of econmic secrets. The 'three anti' mobilized against corruption, waste and 'bureaucratism'. All these evils have been associated primarily with free enterprise and the middle class and involved heavy penalties.

3. 'Capital construction' is a budgetary term and refers to the government's fixed capital expenditures, whether for economic, social, military or administrative purposes. It also includes expenditures for the repair and replacement of capital assets. But it does not include non-budgetary investments as, for instance, those by co-operatives for their own improvement projects.

4. Between 1931 and 1936 estimated, yearly capital investments in China varied between 50 and 400 million dollars (1936 value) with up to half of it provided by foreign investments.

5. These percentages were given in Po I-po's speech in Peking, on September 18, 1956. Foreign estimates claim that they are exaggerations. Different methods of accounting are also responsible for varying evaluations. William W. Hollister in *China's Gross National Product and Social Accounts, 1950-1957* (1958) estimates gross domestic investments at 14·9 per cent. in 1952; 17·8 per cent. in 1954; and 20 per cent. in 1957.

6. At the official exchange rate 2·367 yuans equal one $U.S.

7. Most of these figures, particularly when relating to a distant past, ought to be considered as mere approximates. Yet even after proper allowance is made for varying definitions in each country, for the inadequacies of data collection, or for the differences in statistical methods, they do provide a useful background for comparison.

8. Virtually, all Soviet aid to China has been in the form of loans. See Chapter 4, Part II.

9. In *The Conditions of Economic Progress*, Colin Clark estimated that the net income produced per head of working population in China (1933-35) was 138 International Units, while in India (1944-45) it was 246. For Japan (1940) the figure was 600. On the other hand, the *Economic Survey of Asia and the Far East, 1950* (U.N.O.) put China's per head share of national income at U.S.$27 (in 1949) against 57 in India (in 1948-49), and 100 in Japan (in 1949).

10. According to T. H. Shen; *Agricultural Resources of China* (1951), in 1939 an agricultural worker averaged 0·58 Chinese dollars per labour day (without board), while 1·16 dollars were paid for a draft animal.

11. Less than 0.6 per cent. of the population. See Chou En-lai's article 'A Great Decade' in the *People's Daily*, October 6, 1959.

12. See Liao Chi-lih's article 'Accelerating Agricultural Development—A condition for Accelerating the Development of Heavy Industry', in *Planned Economy* (*Chi-hua ching-chi*), August 4, 1957. (The figures relate to 1953-56.)

13. See Deputy Premier Teng Tzu-hui's report in *People's Daily* of February 22, 1957.

14. Into landlords, rich peasants, middle peasants, poor peasants and farm labourers; a classification that provides the basis for land policies ever since.

15. The Chinese historian Ping-chia Kuo, himself one of Chiang's officials until the Kuomintang's defeat, and now professor in the United States, writing of the terror waves accompanying the land reform and later against 'counter-revolutionaries', said: '. . . the campaign . . . during which scores of thousands were put to death as enemies of the state, while many others were sentenced to forced labour. . . . Unlike other reigns of terror in history, this movement did not get out of control. As soon as the intended purpose was achieved, Peking wound up the drive.' (Ping-chia Kuo: *China, New age and New Outlook*, London, 1960.)

16. In *New China's Economic Achievements, 1949-1952* (Peking). Though questioned by most foreign analysts, this figure of 700 million *mu* is regularly used in all official publications. Yet the figure of 300 million peasants (including their families) needs revision in the light of the 1953 census results which have revealed a far larger peasant population than had been accepted in 1952. But even on the basis of these figures, each person sharing in the land reform received on an average a little over 2 *mu*, or a third of an acre only. Considering that middle-peasants also obtained land, the average share of the new owners must have been even more modest. (One *mu* equals 0·1647 acres or 0·06 hectares.)

17. From *On the People's Democratic Dictatorship*, written for July 1, 1949, in commemoration of the twenty-eighth anniversary of the Chinese Communist Party.

18. Chinese terminology distinguishes between 'primary producers' co-operatives' and 'developed type of agricultural producers' co-operatives' or collectives. In the first, the income of the members depends on the contribution they make to the common pool, including labour and land which is still considered his own. In the second, land, farm tools and draft animals are collectively owned and members are paid according to the number of their workdays.

19. In *People's Daily*, November 13, 1955.

20. Editorial in *People's Daily*, May 24, 1956.

21. In *Ta Kung Pao*, December 21, 1955.

22. New China News Agency (NCNA) bulletin (Peking), Chen Yun's statement, March 10, 1957.

23. See Choh-Ming Li, *Economic Development of Communist China* (1959).

24. 582 million for continental China.

25. According to official figures, between 1953 and 1957, the birthrate varied between 37 and 34; while the death rate steadily declined from 17 to 11. Natural increases, thus mounted from 2 to 2·3 per cent. Pre-war death rates were estimated between 30 to 35 per cent. and, therefore, growth rates between one-half and 1 per cent. only.

26. The overall national increase conceals considerable disparity between rural and urban population growth. According to some estimates the latter is considerably higher than in the villages. Health insurance and other social benefits in towns may be partly responsible for this difference. In any case it has direct bearing on the planners' job in projecting employment opportunities in urban areas or, alternatively, in prescribing the transfer of population to the countryside.

27. In the summer of 1955. The Speech was published under the title *Measures relative to the Development of the National Economy and the Second Five-Year Plan* (Peking, 1955).

28. Throughout the campaign, in order of importance, propaganda was directed along four lines: contraception, late marriage, abortion and sterilization of either partner.

29. I am quoting these extracts from Dr. Ma's speech from its English language translation as reproduced in Professor S. Chandrasekhar's article 'China's Population Problems' in the June 4 and 11, 1959, issues of the *Far Eastern Economic Review* (Hong Kong).

30. Su Chung, 'Facts About China's Population'; *Peking Review*, July 1, 1958.

31. 'Superior intellectuals', apparently, were doctors, technicians, writers and professors. 'Ordinary intellectuals'—numbering 3,800,000—ranged from laboratory workers to technical specialists.

32. This period is analysed in detail in *The Serpent and the Tortoise* by Edgar Faure (Macmillan 1958).

33. On June 18, 1957; NCNA, Peking.

34. The two most important of the auxiliary parties are the *Democratic League* (with strong following in the Universities and business circles), and the so-called *Revolutionary Kuomintang* (composed mainly of former Kuomintang generals and officials). Two vice-chairmen of the *Democratic League*, ministers until July, 1957, lost their posts.

35. How the whole economy follows the fluctuations in agricultural output with a time-lag of one year, is clearly analysed in *Economic Development of Communist China* by Choh-Ming Li.

36. In 1956, the affected area was 15·3 million hectares while in 1957 only 14·7 million.

37. It was estimated that, from 1957 onwards, of 5 million persons coming to working age each year (1.3 in the cities and 3·7 in the villages) only about one million could be absorbed in state enterprises (industrial and commercial). See Cheng Kang-ling's article 'Summarizing the Experience of Labour-Force and Wage Planning for 1956', in *Planned Economy*, August, 1957.

38. To help reduce China's increasingly difficult balance of payment difficulties, the U.S.S.R. later agreed to the postponement of deliveries (see Chapter 4, Part II). Though, especially in the West, it was interpreted mainly in political terms, the same difficulties largely explain China's great export drive on Afro-Asian markets from 1954 onwards, as well as its intensification after 1956.

39. Issued on September 14, 1957 (Article 6). Quoted from Choh-Ming Li's article 'Economic Development' in *The China Quarterly*, No. 1 (London).

40. *Planned Economy* (Peking), October, 1957. Published by the State Economic and Planning Commission.

41. In its March 8, 1960, issue the *People's Daily* revealed that in 1957, able-bodied peasants put in an average of 249 days work; in 1959 this increased to 300 days. The respective figures for women were 166 and 250 days.

42. *Report on the Work of the Central Committee of the Communist Party of China to the Second Session of the Eighth National Congress*, delivered in Peking, May 5, 1958.

43. One *mu* equals 0·06 hectares or 0·1647 acres.

44. The *tatsepao* are posters on which criticism and self-criticism are written in large characters. Since the Great Leap, tens of millions of them have been posted all over the country.

45. 'Red and expert' schools are training establishments for Party cadres and for indoctrinated technical specialists.

46. *Resolution on the Establishment of People's Communes in the Rural Areas*, Central Committee of the Chinese Communist Party, Peking, August 29, 1958.

47. Typical of the constantly repeated emphasis on the indispensability of tapping the potential labour reservoir represented by housewives is an article in *New Construction* (No. 10) on October 3, 1958. A great mass of women are still unable to render 'productive' service because they are tied down by work for the family. In a village suburb of Peking, the author says, there were 1,000 women doing household work, each in her family. After their entry into Communes, it was found that one woman could do all the work for four families, so that 750 were free for 'productive' labour. Out of 64,000 families in Hsu Shui county in Hopei province, for instance, 69,000 women were released as new collective workers.

48. 'Greet the Upsurge in Forming Peoples Communes', in the September 1, 1958, issue of *Red Flag*.
49. Editorial in *Peking Review*, August 19, 1958.
50. See article 'Shansi' New Form of Labour Organisation' by Wang Mu-yen, *Peking Review*, August 26, 1958.
51. The *Weixing* (Sputnik) People's Commune in Suiping County, Honan Province, born in April 1958 of the merger of 27 collectives. Its regulations were widely publicized as an example to follow.
52. '. . . everything I saw suggested that this particular Leap Forward was spontaneous and unforeseen by the State Planning Commission . . .', wrote Mr. R. H. S. Crossman, British Labour Member of Parliament, who arrived in China when the Commune movement was being launched (Article in *The New Statesman and Nation*, London, September 27, 1958). Elucidating his view later on (a view supported by a number of other, reputable observers), he wrote: '. . . I am inclined to . . . conclude that the movement . . . did indeed come not from a remote official stratosphere but from that hard puritan élite of peasant Communists who have emerged in their tens of thousands through the countryside. If I am right, this episode confirms that Chinese Communism still remains a dynamic mass movement and that its leaders still respond to pressure from below . . .' (same journal, January 10, 1959).
53. Out of the total basic development investments of 1958 (not including investments by the Communes for their own purposes), only 10 per cent. were devoted to agriculture, forestry and water conservation. In the original plan for 1959 the share of the three together decreased to 7 per cent.
54. The tradition of scattering family graveyards over cultivated land had been condemned by the Party and with the launching of the Communes a radical drive was initiated to uproot and to regroup them. According to some reports cadres have encountered physical resistance in some regions. This is hardly surprising in view of the Chinese family's deep regard for its tombs. In certain parts of the country I could see the tombs untouched while in others they have effectively disappeared from the fields.
55. *Sixth Plenary Session of the Eighth Central Committee of the Communist Party of China*, Peking, 1958. (Resulting from the meeting held at Wuhan from November 28 to December 10, 1958.)
56. September 23, 1958.
57. Notwithstanding the wastage it involved, the 'native blast furnace' movement had been too lightly dismissed in the West as an aberration. It was the first systematic attempt to familiarize peasants with industrial notions. In that sense it was a spectacular prelude to more sustained efforts to encourage 'industrialization' in the Communes. Incidentally, it also stimulated the peasants' 'raw material consciousness' and, so it would seem, led to the discovery of unsuspected coal and iron-ore deposits.

All this said, it is worth reporting that, in its later phases, the campaign was treated with some irony by the population. The only joke about a governmental decision I have heard during my stay in China was by an official who smilingly remarked that the winter was exceptionally mild because of all the heat the 'native furnaces' have radiated. Then, when I asked the director of the Anshan steel-combine whether his works were treating 'native pig iron', he contemptuously dismissed the idea by saying that 'we wouldn't waste our time with that sort of thing'.

58. 'The People Shoulder Arms', September 23, 1958.

59. 'The Myth of Diminishing Returns' by Wang Hsiang-shu, October 28, 1958.

60. One *jin* equals half a kilogramme (1·1023 pounds).

61. 'New Stage in Agricultural Production' by Tsao Kuo-hsing, *Peking Review* December 16, 1958. In March 1959 one of the highest officials of the Ministry of Agriculture assured me that with science working miracles in raising yields in China, it was seriously envisaged to reduce the cultivated surface and to devote an important proportion of it to parks, gardens and lakes for 'purely aesthetic reasons'.

62. 'Family Life—The New Way' by Yang Kan-ling, *Peking Review*, November 18, 1958.

63. Shortly after the rural Communes were formed preparations were being made in cities too. Early in 1959, when I was in Canton, workshops and artisans were being regrouped so as to have entire trades in the same street or in the same district. The fear of urban Communes was reported to lead to wholesale selling of private property, especially sewing machines and furniture in several big cities.

64. The same furious vehemence against the late American Secretary of State was evident also in private conversations. In fact, in Chinese minds his name had been so efficiently associated with evil that his speeches attacking China's Communes were reproduced verbatim in the press, implying, no doubt, that his opposition could be relied on to inspire approval among Chinese readers.

65. These 'five guarantees'—a kind of rudimentary social insurance in the Commune, included a regular supply of food, clothing, fuel, education for the young, and proper burial for the dead.

66. *Kwangsi Jih-pao*, March 27, 1959.

67. 'On the Principle of Walking on Two Legs', *Red Flag*, No. 6, 1959.

68. 'The Simultaneous Use of Modern and Indigenous Production Methods' by Yu Kuang-yuan, *Frontline* (*Qianxian*), No. 8, 1959.

69. According to Chou En-lai's speech on August 26, flood, drought and pests affected close on one-third of the total cultivated area in 1959, i.e. a quarter more than the previous year.

70. *Peking Review*, editorial, August 25, 1959.

71. Steel dropped from 18 to 12 million tons; coal from 380 to 335 million tons; cotton from 5·2 to 2·3 million tons; and grain from 525 to 275 million tons.

72. *Report on the 1959 Economic Plan*; delivered on August 26, 1959.

73. According to the original claim of a 103 per cent. growth in food-crops, the increase was given as 70 per cent. in wheat; 73 in rice; 76 in coarse grains; and 320 per cent. in sweet potatoes. The composition of the revised figures was not published. While the actual increase in cereals may have been modest, it is not impossible that sweet potatoes accounted for a decisive portion of the 35 per cent. growth finally claimed.

74. Following this mission, that of Lowell Thomas in 1949, a 'top-secret' military briefing document was available in Kalimpong. As for Taktser Rimpoche, the brother of the Dalai Lama, it would seem that he participated in important negotiations aimed at sounding the intentions of the Chinese, before he escaped to America. It is worth mentioning that the Chinese Army, already in Chamdo since October 1950 did not march on Lhasa before September 1951, i.e. until after Taktser Rimpoche's flight. This may be mere coincidence. It is not impossible, however, that Peking, understandably suspicious of Western motives, believed in the possibility of intervention and wished to forestall it.

75. On the occasion of the signing of the Sino-Indian Trade Agreement which included the declaration of 'The Five Principles of Peaceful Co-existence' and the recognition by India of 'the Tibet region of China'.

76. On May 6, 1959.

77. Guy Wint in *The Observer* (London), November 22, 1959.

78. Milder attitudes were noticeable after Mr. Khrushchev's visit to Peking in September 1959 and, again, after the coming of a top-ranking delegation of the Indian Communist Party. They came understandably worried about their chances in the elections which were shortly to be held in the State of Kerala where, once evicted from power by a Presidential order, they hoped to regain it through a new electoral triumph. Much later, following Mr. Chou En-lai's visit to New Delhi in April 1960 Mr. Nehru—speaking to Parliament on April 29—revealed that the Chinese Premier did not know about a second road being built by his countrymen in the Ladakh area of Kashmir, occupied by the Chinese Army. 'I must confess,' he said, 'I was a bit surprised to find that he did not know much about it.'

79. Though General Ne-Win reached a relatively favourable settlement with China in January, 1960—on the basis of the exchange of territories—this was widely regarded as calculated Chinese 'magnanimity' to be able to present the Burmese settlement to India as an example to follow.

80. The first map of Ladakh was prepared by Moorcraft in 1822 at a time when few Indians, and even fewer Chinese were familiar with the science of geodetic surveying. It is across this partly swampy area of the

Aksai Chin region that around 1956-57, following an old caravan route, a military road was built by the Chinese. It led to Yarkand in Sinkiang. But on Moorcraft's original map already there was indicated a more direct route from Lhasa to Yarkand (via Gurtok) which lies farther south, i.e. even farther away from the border India considers as correct. It was, apparently, in 1959 only that the Chinese begun to improve this second, shorter road of which, according to Mr. Nehru, the Chinese Premier appeared to be uninformed. This road leads through lower passes than the first one and proceeds within a few kms. from the place where the bloody incidents of October 21, 1959, between Indian and Chinese patrols took place. Moreover, possession of this low-lying part of Ladakh would provide China with a favourable springboard towards the strategic, north-eastern salient of Kashmir presently under the occupation of Pakistan, a member of both S.E.A.T.O. and C.E.N.T.O.

81. *Red Flag*, August 28, 1959.

82. *Red Flag*, September 11, 1959.

83. Altogether 11,693 'counter-revolutionaries' and common criminals were released and the sentences of 389 others facing death or life-imprisonment were lightened. In addition a group of 33 war criminals were also amnestied. (N.C.N.A. Bulletin, December 8, 1959). Simultaneously, 26,000 'rightists' had been relieved of that designation; meaning, presumably, that they could return to their normal activities from the villages where they had been sent to be reformed through labour (N.C.N.A. Bulletin, January 3, 1960).

84. 'The Victory of Marxism-Leninism in China', reproduced in *Peking Review*, October 1, 1959.

85. The *China Democratic National Construction Association* and the *All-China Federation of Industry and Commerce*. Their joint congress was held between February 19 and 21, 1960.

86. This report and its influence only further underlines how puzzling Sino-Soviet relations can be for foreign observers. While Western journals were spreading the impression that ideological differences might lead to an open break, the advice of Soviet experts on questions affecting China's whole future, were acted upon with due respect. In fact the Soviet specialists called for more heavy industry in Sinkiang, the very region which, according to some Western interpretations, is the most likely future bone of contention between the two countries. Moreover, the report also advised China to rely less on technical assistance from Communist countries and more on her own efforts, once again invalidating current Western belief that the Soviet Union's interest is to prolong that dependence. Whatever the explanations, the need is obvious to reconsider our ideas concerning the incidence of ideological debates between the two countries on the day to day working of their alliance.

87. 'Report on the Draft 1960 National Economic Plan', text of the report

delivered by Li Fu-chun before the National People's Congress on March 30, 1960. (Reproduced in *Peking Review*, April 5, 1960.)

88. N.C.N.A. Bulletin, Peking, July 22, 1960.

89. Membership of the Chinese Communist Party has closely followed its political fortunes. After the break with the Kuomintang in 1927, it fell to around 10,000. Up to 300,000 in 1934, after the Long March it melted to only a fraction of it. Less than 50,000 at the outbreak of the Sino-Japanese war, it grew to over a million in 1945 when the predominance of peasant stock began to be modified with the coming of the intellectuals. In 1949 membership was around 4·5 million; 6·5 million in 1953; and nearly 11 million by 1956. A new recruiting drive brought in more workers and by the end of 1959 the figure of 13·96 million was reached (according to Liuhan-tao's article in the *People's Daily* on September 28, 1959). Members of peasant origin still account for over 60 per cent. of the total; workers for some 15 per cent.; intellectuals for just over five; and women for barely one in ten.

90. See Part I, Chapter 7.

91. 'The Victory of Marxism-Leninism in China' written for *World Marxist Review*, October 1, 1959.

92. To avoid giving the impression of naïveté, I would like to make it clear that it is not my intention to reopen here the discussion on forced labour in China. I am aware of the published proofs of its existence—as in a number of non-Communist countries—on a large scale. Notwithstanding this tragic fact, and in an attempt to analyse the original and positive features in present-day China's thinking, preoccupation with 'reform through labour', so it seems to me, ought not to be dismissed as without significance.

93. For a concise and illuminating discussion of the 'Organisational Principles of the Chinese Communists' see H. F. Schurmann's article in *The China Quarterly* (London), No. 2.

94. See, among others, Edgar Snow's observations in his *Journey to the Beginning* (London, 1960).

95. Speaking to Georgi Dimitrov and Edvard Kardelj in 1948, Stalin confirmed that he had invited the Chinese Communists and told them that uprising had no prospect in their country and asked them to collaborate with Chiang Kai-shek. 'The Chinese comrades agreed here . . .', he told them, 'but went back to China and acted otherwise . . . now, as we see, they are beating the Chiang Kai-shek army . . . we admit we were wrong. . . .' Quoted in *Tito* by Vladimir Dedijer (New York, 1953).

96. All through these closing years of the Chinese civil war Stalin seemed to hesitate like someone who regrets that China will cease to live under a weak government. In 1943 Mao declared that 'Since . . . 1935 the Chinese Communists have received no assistance and no advice from the Comintern.' Before Chiang's final collapse, when his troops lost Nanking,

the capital, and retreated to Canton, Stalin instructed the Soviet Ambassador to follow them even though, by then, most other Powers ordered theirs to remain and await the arrival of the Communists. The only notable exception to this reserve was when, in 1945, after the surrender of the Japanese armies in Manchuria to the Russians, most of their arms were turned over to the Chinese Communists. Yet even after that date there are instances of Stalin's desire not to alienate Chiang Kai-shek and his régime.

97. Three mixed companies were established (the accord being signed on March 21, 1950): a civil aviation company connecting Peking with Siberian terminals; and two others for the prospecting, production and refining of oil, and for the mining of non-ferrous metals in Sinkiang.

98. The departure of the last troops was announced on May 24.

99. According to Chinese sources, the shares were handed back on January 1, 1955.

100. The Trans-Mongolian (opened on January 4, 1956) and the longer line across Sinkiang which is still under construction.

101. Grants or gifts of relatively modest value (for instance in the form of tractor stations) came mainly from the countries of Eastern Europe.

102. The $300-million loan, with an interest rate of one per cent., was to be drawn in five years and to be repaid in ten annual instalments between 1954-63. The terms of the second were not published; merely the indication that it was a 'long-term' loan.

103. Most of these aid-projects are in the field of heavy industry, including steel plants and metallurgical industries; machine-tool and engineering plants; the equipment of mines; automobile, tractor and aeronautical industries; petroleum installations and refineries; scientific research institutes; as well as a wide variety of other factories ranging from chemical and plastic industries to electrical equipment. According to reliable information, the last bunch of 78 projects includes two further steel-plants of the Wuhan size (about 3·5 million tons output each).

104. In October, 1959 Chou En-lai disclosed that 'other socialist countries'—i.e. those of Eastern Europe—also 'helped China build 68 construction projects during the first Five-Year Plan period, (and) later signed new agreements with China to help build another 40-odd projects. . . .' All these, presumably, are on a barter basis and involve enterprises of more modest dimensions than those Russia helps to build. ('A Great Decade' by Chou En-lai, *People's Daily*, October 6, 1959.)

As for the value of the Soviet contribution, Khrushchev stated in 1956 that up to that time, the U.S.S.R. had committed itself to supply $1·4 milliard worth of equipment and supplies for 156 key-projects. Mikoyan's pledge in 1956 involved supplies and services evaluated at about $625 million more and raised the total to over $2 milliard. The 1958-59 engagements, for the further 47 plus 78 projects, were reported to represent a further

Soviet contribution worth another $1·25 milliard to be sold to China up
to 1967.

105. According to some reports, by mid-1957, China received from the
Soviet Union 600 kinds of blueprints for factories and enterprises, 1,700
patents and licences for the production of machines, as well as diverse
forms of other technical data. According to the same sources, 90 per cent.
of the new products manufactured by China's machine-building industry
between 1953-57, was based on designs provided by the U.S.S.R.

106. *A Great Decade* by Chou En-lai. This figure might probably be doubled
if Russian military advisers and instructors were added. Also it may be
remembered that within the U.N.O.'s 'expanded technical assistance
programme' only about 3,000 specialists are employed *in the whole
world.*

107. See *Communist Economic Strategy: The Rise of Mainland China* by A. Doak
Barnett (National Planning Association, Washington, 1959).

108. On several occasions, however, Russia has agreed to delays in Chinese
barter deliveries. Discussions on payment problems are initiated only
after China is more than $75 million behind in her deliveries.

109. Rational as this attitude may be, paradoxically, it is contradicted by the
very fact that China herself, out of her much more limited resources
distributes grants to several underdeveloped countries. See Part IV,
Chapter 3.

110. After a trial period, the definite Conscription Law came into force on
July 30, 1955. All males between 18 and 40 being liable for service (with
specified exemptions), this could yield over 4 million conscripts a year. In
practice only a fraction were called up (from 500,000 to 800,000) and, after
service, were transferred to the reserve. The period of service is 3 years in
the Army, 4 in the Air-force, and 5 years in the Navy. Present strength
of the armed forces is estimated at below 3 million, to which the Communes' militia has to be added. Next to the Army (about 2·5 million)
the Air-force contains over 250,000 men, while the Navy, still the junior
arm, has probably less than 200,000 effectives.

111. Decree of February 8, 1956 (which introduced also decorations).

112. Mr. Dulles' statement containing the threat of U.S. atomic retaliation,
was made on March 8, 1955. The operations in the Taiwan Strait were
wound up soon after. Chou En-lai's speech, calling for negotiations with
the U.S.A., was made at Bandung on April 23, 1955.

113. The successful launching of an inter-continental rocket was announced
by Tass on August 26, 1957. The first earth-satellite was placed in orbit
on October 4. Mao Tse-tung arrived in Moscow on November 2, 1957.

114. 'Take Giant Strides, Holding High the Red Flag of the Party's General
Line and the Military Thinking of Mao Tse-tung', published in *Red Flag,*
October 1, 1959.

115. While Marshal Malinovsky's menace to retaliate against bases from which

planes take off to violate the Soviet Union's air-space was clearly extended also to cover that of China, Khrushchev—addressing a Moscow meeting of labour delegations on May 28, 1960—conspicuously refrained from promising direct support to China's aim to 'liberate' Taiwan by force. He merely said that '. . . the time is coming when the great Chinese people will liberate Taiwan from the Chiang clique and his American patrons . . .'.

116. 'Agrarianism and Social Upheaval in China', by Shu-ching Lee in *American Journal of Sociology*, May, 1951.

117. *Studies on the Population of China, 1368-1953* by Ho Ping-ti (London 1960).

118. *Journey to the Beginning* by Edgar Snow (London, 1960).

119. According to the *People's Daily* (March 8, 1960), out of China's 300 million female population, there were 200 million 'young and middle-aged, able-bodied women', 90 per cent. of whom by then worked in agriculture. In 1959 alone 30 million of them worked on water conservancy projects. In office and factory their numbers increased from 3·2 to over 8 million since the beginning of the Great Leap.

120. The number of those covered by 'labour insurance' (but not including 'collective agreements') grew from 1·4 million in 1950 to 13·8 million in 1958 (*Ten Great Years*, Peking, 1960, compiled by the State Statistical Bureau).

121. At the official rate one U.S. dollar equals 2·367 yuan.

122. Between 1952 and 1957 urban population increased from 71·6 to 92 million.

123. In 1957 the average housing space per head in 175 cities was $3·5\,m^2$, varying from 4·9 in the smaller towns to just over 3 in the big ones. (See 'Municipal Construction', etc., by Tsao Yen-hsing in *Planned Economy*, December 4, 1957.) Between 1949 and 1956 per head housing space had actually declined by 25 to 35 per cent. in Peking, Wuhan and Shanghai, according to an article in the *People's Daily* of November 27, 1957.

124. Tungsten, manganese, antimony, tin, aluminium, copper, molybdenum and lead are the most important. It is claimed that China has the world's largest reserves of molybdenum and tin, and second largest (after the U.S.S.R.) of tungsten. Recently, nickel too has been located though in small quantities only.

125. For details see next two chapters.

126. By definition, the coastal areas are composed of seven provinces: Liaoning, Hopei, Shantung, Kiangsu, Chekiang, Fukien and Kwangtung—including the three special cities of Peking, Tientsin and Shanghai. (See 'The Relationship between Coastal and Inland Industries' by Sha Ying, in *People's Daily*, November 24, 1956.)

127. The construction of the Paotow works started in 1956 and that of Wuhan

in 1957, both coming within the scope of the 156 Soviet aid-projects negotiated up to 1954.

128. These index figures are based on output value in billions of yuan, given by Choh-Ming Li in his *Economic Development of Communist China*. The increase in coastal areas was from 19·7 to 39·83 milliard yuan; and in inland regions from 7·3 to 18·83. A decisive item in coastal growth must have been the enormous expansion of the Anshan steel-plant in Liaoning province in Manchuria.

129. See 'Municipal Construction', etc., by Tsao Yen-hsing in *Planned Economy* December 4, 1957.

130. In the 1953 Census Sinkiang's population was 4,873,608. By the end of 1957, according to *Ten Great Years* (Peking, 1960), it grew to 5,640,000.

131. According to the 1953 Census, the Chinese make up 93·94 per cent. of the total population and the minorities numbered 35,320,360, amounting to 6·06 per cent.

132. China has four autonomous regions (Sinkiang, Inner Mongolia, the Ningsia Hui and the Kwangsi Chuang Regions); 29 autonomous departments; and one autonomous district.

133. Between 1951 and 1958 the number of 'national minority students' in primary schools increased from 943,000 to 4,240,000; in middle-schools, from 40,000 to 395,000; and in Institutes of Higher Learning, from 2,000 to 22,000. The number of newspapers published in minority languages grew from 29,330 in 1952 to 39,800 in 1958; while the number of books published in minority languages, only 6,610 in 1952, reached 23,880 by 1958 (*Ten Great Years*).

134. Addressing a press conference in Mussoorie in India, on June 20, 1959, the Dalai Lama declared that, up to that date and since 1956, the Chinese had killed more than 65,000 Tibetans. His statement, however, that 5 million Chinese settlers had been brought into Tibet and 4 million more were coming, was somewhat surprising. Considering the still enormous difficulties of transport, or that Tibet's total population in 1953 was only 1,275,000—though perhaps a projection of things to come in the distant future—those figures are not calculated to lend authenticity to the exiled God King's statistical information. (See for text of press conference *The Observer*, London, June 21, 1959.)

135. Of Sinkiang's 5,144,700 population in 1954, 3·7 million were Uighurs and 550,000 Chinese. The next largest minorities were the Kazakhs (numbering 510,000); the Hui (145,000); the Kirghiz (71,000); the Mongol (60,000) followed by a few thousands each of (White) Russians, Sipo, Tadjik, Uzbek, Tartar and other ethnic groups.

136. In the early 1930's a mere tenth only of Sinkiang's external trade was with China and four-fifths with the Soviet Union. Both communications and the nearness of Soviet markets favoured Russia's economic penetration.

137. In *The International Development of China* (Chungking, 1941).

138. Regarding the 1958 rectification campaign see *New York Times*, despatch from Hong Kong, January 18, 1958.

139. Revealed by Saifuddin, Vice-Chairman of the Regional Government and the Uighur member of the Sinkiang Central Committee of the Party, before the Eighth C.C.P. Congress in 1956. (See New China News Agency bulletin, Peking, September 25, 1956.)

140. *People's Daily*, Peking, October 1, 1955.

141. It was reported that, near Urumchi, a deposit of 200 million tons of oil shale had been found, with a 6 to 20 per cent. oil content. Its industrial exploitation will be undertaken only after the new railway has reached the capital.

142. News of radium found in Sinkiang has stimulated rumours about important atom installations in the south-west of the Region. According to some reports the scientist Pontecorvo had been seen visiting that area. This news, of course, is unverifiable. It may be of some interest in this connection that in the course of our conversation, the Secretary-General of the Sinkiang Government, who energetically denied the presence of Soviet technicians in Sinkiang, admitted that they were still working in the south-west. When asked in what field of activity they were used, he refused to specify it. 'Not in the petroleum industry . . .', was the only precision he offered.

143. Sinkiang statistics being a scarce commodity, it may be of interest to quote some of the figures copied from those charts. Between 1952 and 1958 the length of roads grew from 6,745 km. to 18,601 km. The number of schools, from 1,870 to 10,499; and their students from 306,000 to 965,000. Taking industrial production in 1958 for 100, the following increases were projected for 1959: iron and steel 253 per cent.; coal 200; electricity generated 243; crude oil 203; chemical fertilizers 250; insecticides 158; cement 256; cotton cloth 167; and sugar 943 per cent.

144. Unless otherwise specified, all figures in the following chapters are based on official statistics, and are given here in round figures. Those relating to 1949-58 are taken from *Ten Great Years* (Peking, 1960). Production figures for 1959 are quoted from the *Press Communiqué on the Growth of China's National Economy in 1959* (issued by the New China News Agency, Peking, on January 22, 1960); and target figures for 1960 are reproduced from the text of the report delivered on March 30, 1960, by Li Fu-chun, Vice-Premier and Chairman of the State Planning Commission (Reproduced by *Peking Review*, April 5, 1960, under the title 'Report on the Draft 1960 National Economic Plan').

145. According to the Deputy Minister of Railways' statement in April, 1960, 8,800 kms. of new railways will be built during 1960 (*The Times*, London, April 14, 1960). It has also been reported that surveying work is now completed for a railway line, across particularly difficult terrain, to lead from Sining, in Chinghai province, to Lhasa in Tibet.

146. In 1960, according to Li Fu-chun's speech, there will be an increase 'of 800 locomotives, 32,000 goods wagons and 1,000 passenger cars'. Though this is not specified, it is likely that all will be manufactured in China.

147. Significantly, while between 1952 and 1957 the railway network grew by 30 per cent., the quantity of goods carried by railways nearly trebled.

148. See previous chapter for details.

149. In 1959 secondary school students were divided between specialized secondary schools, senior secondary schools, junior secondary schools, and agricultural and other technical schools, with the junior and vocational types holding the vast majority. In 1958, in these 'technical middle schools' alone 1·5 million students were enrolled and their numbers are fast expanding.

150. Misleading as comparisons of non-identical categories may be, the number of full-time students at British Universities in 1959 was 101,201.

151. It is interesting to note that of the 70,000 graduates from Institutes of Higher Learning in 1958, about a quarter were engineers; 8 per cent. medical doctors; 5 per cent. agronomists; nearly 5 per cent. pedagogues; 5 per cent. economists; and only 6 per cent. altogether were graduates from the faculties of liberal arts.

152. Of the 848 scientific research institutes listed in 1958, 415 were concerned with industry and communications; 170 with basic science; 134 with agriculture, forestry and fisheries; and 101 with medical science and public health.

153. Output increases between 1952 and 1958 are given for soya beans as 110 per cent.; groundnuts 121 per cent.; rapeseed 118 per cent.; and cured tobacco 172 per cent.

154. While animal husbandry has probably benefited by some increase in foodstuffs, the use of artificial insemination, and a reduced incidence of disease, it has probably also suffered due to slaughter accompanying collectivization. For the same reason official figures ought to be taken with caution. If progress between 1952 and 1957 is described as hesitant, rapid increases are claimed after that date. Thus the number of 'big draught animals'—76 million in 1952—grew to 85 million by 1958. And the 90 million pigs in 1952 are claimed to have doubled by 1959. It should also be remembered that only one per cent. of China's farm area is pasture, against 47 in the U.S.A. or 15 to 50 per cent. in European countries.

155. The *Eight-Point Charter*, driven home by the full weight of the rural propaganda apparatus, contains eight basic prescriptions: deep ploughing and soil amelioration; the rational application of fertilizers; water conservancy; popularization of good strains of seed; close planting; plant protection; field management; and tool reform.

156. The production of 10 million rubber-tyred hand carts is foreseen in 1960 alone.

157. Calculated on the basis of standard 15 h.p. models.

158. In 1958 China's cultivated area was 1,617 million *mu* (one *mu* equals 0·06 hectare). Irrigated area in 1952 was 320 million *mu*. By 1958 it grew to 1,000 million *mu*. In 1959 another 70 million were added, and a further 60 million are projected for 1960. The total irrigated surface, by the end of 1960, then ought to be around 1,130 million *mu*.

159. Including mining and electric power generation.

160. In his *Report on the Draft 1960 National Economic Plan*, when enumerating the 'capital construction projects' of 1959, Li Fu-chun spoke, for example, of 1,341 'above norm' projects (i.e. projects whose cost ranges from 5 to 10 million yuan), as well as of 75,000 'below norm' ones. Moreover, he also specified that these 75,000 do not include projects by local authorities or by Communes.

161. Output of edible oil, for example, stood at 983,000 tons in 1952; 1,009,000 tons in 1953, followed by a slight decline in 1955. It reached 1·1 million tons in 1957, and 1·25 in 1958. The output of cotton yarn, 3·62 million bales in 1952, grew to 4·6 million in 1954 and declined sharply twice after, in 1955 and 1957. Then, it reached 6·1 million bales in 1958. Cotton cloth production followed a parallel zigzag line.

162. See Part III, Chapter 4.

163. The Anshan, Wuhan and Paotow complexes provide the bulk. But a number of smaller steel plants were also restored and expanded at Taiyuan, Maanshan, Lungyen, Peking, Tientsin and Shanghai. Numerous smaller units have been erected all over the country. (Since the 1958 revision of production figures, steel made by 'indigenous methods' is not included in official statistics. However, about a third of the 1959 total came from 'medium-sized and small converters'.)

164. It would hardly compensate the sterility of Western policy towards China if the systematic self-delusion that had for so long underrated Russia's industrial achievements, would now be practised on China. A group of retired Japanese army and navy commanders who were permitted to visit Chinese jet aircraft factories, came back with the observation that they contained original technical improvements over the Soviet models. Or to take another example, the Sheffield information officer of the United Steel Companies Ltd., when announcing that some members of the research staff had begun to study Chinese, declared: '. . . In ten years Communist China could become one of our most serious competitors in steel. I understand, for instance, that the Chinese now have automatic blast furnaces which are bigger and better than any in the United States. Some of the Chinese open-hearth steel furnaces can process 600 tons at a time, whereas our biggest take around 450 tons. . . .' (*The Times*, London, July 18, 1960.)

165. See *New Long-Range Economic Plan of Japan (FY1958–FY1962)*, Economic Planning Agency, Japanese Government, Tokyo, 1958.

166.	Soviet Union			China		
	1928	1932	1928: 100	1953	1957	1953: 100
Cast iron (million tons)	3·3	6·2	188	2·2	5·9	271
Steel (,, ,,)	4·3	5·9	137	1·8	5·3	302
Coal (,, ,,)	35·5	64·4	181	70	130	185
Electricity (000 million kwh) ..	5·0	13·5	270	9·2	19·3	210
Chemical fertilisers (000 tons) ..	135	921	682	226	631	279
Cotton cloth (000 million m.) ..	2·67	2·69	101	4·7	5·1	108

Sources: Sovietskaia Sotzialistitcheskaia Economica, Moscow, 1957; Ten Great Years, Peking, 1960.

167.	Soviet Union			China			
	1928	1940	1928: 100	1953	1959	1960*	1953: 100
Cast iron (mill. tons)	3·3	14·9	451	2·2	20·5	27·5	1250
Steel (million tons)	4·3	18·3	425	1·8	13·3	18·4	1022
Coal (million tons)	35·5	166	467	70	348	425	607
Electricity (000 million kwh).. ..	5·0	48·3	966	9·2	41·5	58·0	630
Chemical fertilisers (000 tons) ..	135	3,000	2222	226	—	2800	1238
Cotton cloth (000 million m.) ..	2·67	3·95	148	4·7	7·5	7·6	161
Cement (million) tons	1·8	5·7	316	3·9	12·3	16·0	410
Crude Oil (million tons)	11·6	31·1	268	0·6	3·7	5·2	866
Tractors	1,800	66,200	—	—	—	22,000	—
Lorries	700	136,000	—	—	—	ca. 50,000	—
Locomotives ..	479	914	—	10	—	800	—

* 1960 figures for China are production targets. According to mid-year reports it was claimed that nearly all would be reached.

Sources: U.S.S.R.-1940: from English translation of Statistical Abstract for U S.S.R. 1956. (London, 1957.) For China 1959-60: Li Fu-chun's report.

168. Based on production targets for 1960 in China, and on 1960 Indian targets as published in *Third Five-Year Plan, a Draft Outline* (Planning Commission, Government of India, June, 1960). For the per head grain shares here mentioned for 1960, it is assumed that both countries targets will be achieved, and India's population is reckoned at 420 and China's at 700 million. (It should be mentioned that natural calamities in China, in 1960, were particularly extensive.)

169.

	India			China		
	1950	1957	1960	1950	1957	1960
Grain (million tons)	53	62	75	123	185	297*
Steel („ „)	1·01	1·35	3·50	0·61	5·35	18·4
Cement („ „)	2·68	5·58	8·80	1·41	6·86	16·0
Coal („ „)	32·5	43·5	55·0	42·9	130·0	425·0
Chemical fertilisers (000 tons)	47·3	383·0	400·0	27·0	523·0	2,800
Electric power (000 million kwh)	5,112	10,836	12,000	4,550	19,340	50,000

* Both for India and China target figures for 1960. According to the latest revelations natural calamities during 1960 in China have been worse than in any year since the present Government came to power. Chinese cereal output for 1960, then, will certainly be below official targets and perhaps not above the production level of the previous year. Thus the advantage in China's favour is bound to be less spectacular.

170. See 'India and China: Contrasts in Development' by Wilfred Malenbaum, in *The American Economic Review*, June 1959.
171. In his inaugural speech at the Trade Union Conference of Asian and Australasian Countries, in 1949.
172. In an article entitled 'World Significance of the Chinese Revolution', N.C.N.A., Peking, June 25, 1951.
173. In his article 'The Victory of Marxism-Leninism in China', reproduced in *Peking Review*, October 1, 1959.
174. Chou En-lai's Report on China's 1959 Economic Plan (August 26, 1959) confirms the Chinese public's preoccupation with this question. 'Some people suspect that the strain on the supply of certain commodities was due to excessive exports,' he said, and proceeded to refute it. 'There is no increase, or very little increase, compared with last year, in the exports of grain and various non-staple foods which are needed at home. Up to August 15 this year, for instance, our exports of rice totalled only 792,000 tons while our pork exports were equivalent to only 1,400,000 pigs, this

constituted less than one per cent. of last year's output of rice and a similar proportion of the total number of live pigs at the end of last year. To speed up socialist construction, it is absolutely necessary to exchange agricultural produce for materials needed by our country. . . .'

175. According to official figures the volume of China's external trade, taken as 100 in 1950, grew to 310 by 1958. The proportion of capital goods in her *imports* remained fairly constant (87 per cent. in 1950 and 94 per cent. in 1958), while imports of consumer goods, 13 per cent. in 1950, steadily declined to reach only 6 per cent. in 1958. In her *exports* agricultural products declined between 1950-58 from 58 to 36 per cent., while the proportion of industrial and mining products grew from 9 to 27 per cent. (*Ten Great Years*, Peking, 1960.)

176. The first complete factory exported by China outside the Communist bloc was a 20,000 spindle cotton spinning and weaving mill, sent to Burma in 1955. Several more—including plywood, cement and paper factories, complete radio transmitters, etc.—have since been supplied to other countries.

177. According to the estimate of the U.S. Department of Commerce. In this connection it is interesting to note that India's *total* external trade in 1959-60 amounted to about $1,350 million, thus to less than what China sells to the non-Communist countries only.

178. During the first Five-Year Plan, according to Chinese figures, 16 per cent. of China's *total* foreign trade was with Afro-Asian non-Communist countries, and only 9 per cent. with Europe and North-America. According to U.S. Department of Commerce figures, in 1956 China's trade with all O.E.E.C. countries (i.e. Western Europe without Spain, but with Turkey) amounted to $362 million; and with the non-Communist countries of Asia, the Middle East and Africa, to $716 million. Since that date, however, there has been a considerable increase, particularly in South-east Asia.

179. Peking's own estimate of the number of overseas Chinese (including students abroad), was 11,743,000 in 1953 (*People's Daily*, November 1, 1954). Their remittances have long been an important source of foreign exchange for China and are estimated at a yearly 110 to 140 million dollars. As for the commercial influence of the Chinese minorities, it is particularly strong in Thailand, Malaya, South Viet-Nam and Indonesia. During the great 1958 export drive instances were reported when Chinese traders in those countries were urged to boycott Japanese goods in favour of Chinese ones. According to other reports, China even extended credits to overseas Chinese traders to enable them to acquire key enterprises capable to further Chinese commercial aims.

180. See J. Cardew, 'Ceylon's Trade with China' in *New Commonwealth*, April 13, 1953.

181. 'Sino-Pak Relations', in *Economic Observer*, Karachi, January 1957.

182. In the first of the five years of the agreement, China will pay a fifth of her imports in convertible sterling. From the second year all will be covered by barter, and partly by Chinese credits. Half a million tons of sugar is more than twice China's maximum annual rate of imports in past years, and about half her estimated consumption. As for the electronic and other equipment or steel, it is doubtful whether China already covers her own urgent needs in these fields.

183. Hungary received a $7·5-million grant after her revolt in November 1956 and a $25-million long-term loan in May 1957. Earlier, in December 1954 Albania received a long-term Chinese loan but its terms were not disclosed.

184. *The Times* (London), May 30, 1960.

185. Ping-chia Kuo, *China, New Age and New Outlook* (London, 1960).

186. On July 1, 1949, three months before the final triumph, Mao Tse-tung declared: 'The forty years' experience of Sun Yat-sen and the twenty-eight years' experience of the Communist Party have made us firmly believe that, in order to win victory and to consolidate victory, we must lean to one side. . . . One either leans to the side of imperialism or to the side of socialism. Neutrality is camouflage, and a third road does not exist. . . .'

187. *The Republic of China* (State Department, Policy pamphlet, Washington, 1959).

188. Contrary to what is generally believed, China has never been a very important trading partner for the United States. Between 1935 and 1941, China's share of U.S. imports never reached 2 per cent.; American exports to China ranged between 2·1 and 3·4 per cent. of the U.S. total. Both Japan and the Philippines were more important. Recently, however, the increase of China's trade with Western Germany and Great Britain has been causing greater American interest in the new China market.

189. 'If need be we shall wait a hundred years, but we shall liberate Taiwan. We are patient . . .', Mr. Chou En-lai told me in Peking on March 11, 1959. When I asked him whether he could confirm the rumours that direct contacts between Peking and Taiwan existed, he answered: 'Yes, they do exist. But this is completely natural. Taiwan is Chinese territory. A solution can be found to the problem and, finally, we shall reunite all our territory. But we need time. . . .' Then, after a short pause, the Premier added: 'Actually, we are shelling them and, in a sense gunfire is also a form of contact. . . . Perhaps it is the most efficient form of contact. On that, I am sure, Chiang Kai-shek agrees with us. . . .'

190. The influence of pan-Asian propaganda at China's disposal may be underestimated in the West. China's pride in frustrating the American army in Korea was widely shared in Asia, even in countries which had no reason to welcome a strong Chinese neighbour. More recently, notwithstanding richly financed efforts to exploit China's methods in

Tibet, they did not yield the expected results even in Buddhist countries. On the occasion of Chou En-lai's passage in Buddhist Burma in 1960, monks were conspicuous in the crowd welcoming him in Rangoon. Nor did the Tibet events prevent Ceylon, another Buddhist country, electing with an increased majority, a Government with outspokenly neutralist views and determined to maintain the friendliest relations with China. Nor is it likely that once the edge of the frontier dispute is blunted through negotiations, that Indian opinion would remain hostile.

191. 'The Asian continent is henceforth not to be considered a subject for future colonization by any Power. With existing colonies or dependencies we have not interfered and shall not interfere. But with the governments who have declared their independence and maintained it and whose independence we have acknowledged, we could not view any interposition for the purpose of oppressing them or controlling in any other manner their destiny, in any other light than as the manifestation of an unfriendly disposition towards the People's Republic of China.' This is not a Peking statement but the text of the Monroe Doctrine of 1823 with the words *Asian* substituted for *American* and the *People's Republic of China* for *United States*. What else is required is that the need for the protection the U.S.A. had provided to the newly independent Ibero-American states, should be replaced in Asian minds by the desire that China should help to maintain Asian solidarity and self-determination. Will Western policy and Chinese propaganda succeed in creating that desire?

192. See *Demand and Supply for University Graduates, Japan* by Research Section, Ministry of Education, Government of Japan, August 1958, Tokyo.

193. In various indirect forms U.S. aid to Japan (though in decline since the Korean War ended) still amounts to about $500 million a year and covers about a sixth of the cost of the country's imports.

194. It is not without significance that the anniversary celebrations of Hiroshima's destruction never had any official support. The fifteenth, on August 6, 1960—and the first after the anti-American riots in Tokyo—was given such official recognition by the presence of the Crown Prince himself.

195. See Part III, Chapter 7.

196. *Report on India's Food Crisis and Steps to Meet It*, by The Agricultural Production Team sponsored by The Ford Foundation (Government of India, New Delhi, April, 1959). If that gap really develops, there will be growing inflation in food prices and the result would be not merely widespread famine but probably also political unrest with incalculable consequences. It is against this background that the United States Government promised to supply India with 17 million tons of cereals during the next four years. That aid ought to neutralize some of the danger of

famine and its political sequels. No doubt, it will save human lives. Its main function, however, ought to be to provide the Indian Government with time to take the necessary measures permitting the country to grow instead of to beg the food its population needs. Tragic as it is, similar help in the past failed to achieve that aim and rather tended to assure the authorities that the overdue reforms could be further postponed.

INDEX

Index